Ernesto 'Che' Guevara

THE AFRICAN DREAM

THE DIARIES OF THE
REVOLUTIONARY WAR IN THE CONGO

Translated from the Spanish by
Patrick Camiller

With an Introduction by Richard Gott
and a Foreword by Aleida Guevara March

GROVE PRESS
New York

First published with the title *Pasajes de la guerra revolucionaria: Congo* in 1999 by
Sperling & Kupfer Editori S.p.A., Milan

First published in Great Britain, by arrangement with Sperling & Kupfer, in 2000 by
The Harvill Press, London

Published simultaneously in Canada
Printed in the United States of America

FIRST AMERICAN EDITION

Library of Congress Cataloging-in-Publication Data

Guevara, Ernesto, 1928–1967.
    [Pasajes de la guerra revolucionaria. English]
    The African dream : the diaries of the revolutionary war in the Congo / Ernesto
"Che" Guevara ; translated from the Spanish by Patrick Camiller ; with an introduction
by Richard Gott and a foreword by Aleida Guevara March.
        p. cm.
    Originally published as: Pasajes de la guerra revolucionaria : Congo. Milan, Italy :
Sperling and Kupfer Editori, 1999. Originally published in English: London : Harvill,
2000.
    Includes bibliographical references.
    ISBN 0-8021-3834-9
    1. Congo (Democratic Republic)—History—Civil War, 1960–1965—Participation,
Cuban. 2. Guevara, Ernesto, 1928–1967. 3. Cubans—Congo (Democratic Republic)—
History—20th century. 4. Guerrillas—Congo (Democratic Republic)—History—20th
century. I. Title.

DT658.22 .G8413 2001
967.5103'1—dc21   2001040160

MAP BY REGINALD PIGGOTT

Grove Press
841 Broadway
New York, NY 10003

01 02 03 04   10 9 8 7 6 5 4 3 2 1

We are grateful for the effort and application that our Commander in Chief gave in carefully checking this document.

CHE'S PERSONAL ARCHIVE

Contents

INTRODUCTION

This book is the missing link in the life and work of "Che" Guevara, one of the great, iconic revolutionaries of the twentieth century. His personal account of the experiences of the expeditionary force of 100 Cuban guerrilla fighters, who were under his command in the eastern Congo for seven months between April and November 1965, remained under lock and key in Havana for more than 30 years, invisible to all but the most trusted supporters of the Cuban government. It is not difficult to see why.

Ruthlessly honest, and unsparing of the weaknesses of friends and allies, Guevara's vivid tale casts a baleful light on a forgotten but significant episode on the Cold War battlefield of newly independent Africa in the 1960s. Neither the would-be revolutionaries of the Congo nor the guerrilla fighters imported from Cuba emerge from his story with much credit, although the odds were stacked heavily against them.

In an earlier work, *Scenes from the Revolutionary War*, published in 1961, Guevara had given a glowing version of Fidel Castro's guerrilla battles in Cuba during the 1950s, in which he himself had played an important role. Later, in his posthumously published *Bolivian Diaries*, written each night in the Bolivian wilderness in 1967, his relentless optimism gave an epic quality to the unequal struggle of a band of brothers that eventually ended in tragedy.

The book on the expedition to the Congo is quite different. Here Guevara presents an unvarnished account of what, for both the Cubans and the Congolese, was an unmitigated disaster. Some of its details began to leak out in the 1990s, when a handful of the surviving Cuban participants began to feel that it was time to tell the story, as one book title puts it, of "The Year When We Were Nowhere". Guevara's deputy commander, Captain Víctor Dreke, here code-named Moja, and Pablo Rivalta, the Cuban ambassador in Dar es Salaam, both revealed important chunks of the story when being interviewed for these earlier books. Yet Guevara's account is unique, not just for the light it sheds on this otherwise obscure episode, but because he was writing with a political purpose.

The book was written over two months, in December 1965 and January 1966, in a small upstairs room in Rivalta's embassy. Guevara, then aged 37, pillaged his own reports and diaries and produced a book designed for the eyes of Castro and the leaders of the Cuban Revolution, to provide them with information and analysis that would help them avoid future pitfalls in their unfolding relationship with revolutionary movements around the world.

In her foreword to this book, Aleida March, Guevara's widow, reveals how Castro had found the text "extremely interesting", and subsequent events suggest that the Cubans took its lessons to heart. For in spite of the Congo disaster, Castro's government continued to provide political support and military assistance to revolutionary movements and radical governments in different parts of Africa – notably in the Portuguese colonies of Angola, Guinea-Bissau, and Mozambique, as well as in Eritrea and Ethiopia – and it did so with considerable success. The military victories won by Cuban soldiers in Angola in 1975–6 and in 1987–8, in support of the legitimate government and against the South African army, were an important factor in the ultimate collapse of white rule in Namibia and in South Africa itself.

Guevara, too, learnt lessons from the Congo, and he applied them in his expedition to Bolivia a year later. Indeed this book clears up some of the remaining mysteries of that catastrophic episode. In the Congo, the inadequate leadership provided by Laurent Kabila and other Congolese politicians stands out as one of the principal causes of the debacle, and after his experiences there Guevara was adamant that the political and military control of the guerrilla force should remain in his own hands. When he arrived in Bolivia in November 1966, he refused to play second fiddle to the febrile and indecisive leader of the local Communist Party.

Guevara himself indicated that his Congo book would probably not appear until "many years have passed". Yet he can hardly have imagined that Laurent Kabila, the 26-year-old anti-hero of his story, a man he describes as lacking in "revolutionary seriousness", would re-emerge some 32 years later, in exactly the same area of the eastern Congo where the Cubans had once fought. In 1997, in the aftermath of the upheavals caused by the genocide in Rwanda in 1994, Kabila's forces swept across the Congo to Leopoldville-Kinshasa, with support from Rwanda and Uganda. Within weeks, they had toppled the dictatorship of General Joseph-Desiré Mobutu, the man who had seized power in November 1965 in the very week in which Guevara had been obliged to withdraw from the country.

The excitement occasioned by the overthrow of Mobutu and the accession of President Kabila did not last long, although Aleida March describes how she was able to take part in the 1998 celebrations that marked the first anniversary of what she calls "the victory of the Congolese revolution". In subsequent years, the Congo has reverted to the state of civil war that characterized the early post-independence period after 1960, with soldiers from no less than six surrounding countries participating in this fratricidal conflict. "[Kabila] is young," wrote Guevara in 1966, "and it is possible that he will change. But . . . I have very great doubts about his ability to overcome his defects in the environment in which he operates." Anyone reading this book will reckon that Guevara had taken the true measure of the man.

★

Ernesto Che Guevara was born into a middle-class family in Argentina on 14 June, 1928. Although trained as a doctor, he also had ambitions to write. Travelling widely in Latin America as a young man, famously by motorcycle, he became familiar with the grim conditions in which most people lived. His early concern for the poor, and his later belief that their lot could be improved through violent revolution, fuelled his actions for the rest of his life.

Present in Guatemala during the CIA-assisted overthrow of the progressive government of Jacobo Arbenz in 1954, he acquired an implacable hatred of the United States. When he met Fidel Castro in Mexico the following year, he immediately signed up to his project to liberate Cuba and launch the Revolution. Such were his leadership skills that he became the senior commander in the rebel army, capturing the strategic town of Santa Clara on the eve of victory. His Cuban experience enabled him to develop theories of guerrilla warfare that he would later attempt to put into practice in the Congo and in Bolivia.

In Castro's new Revolutionary government, Guevara had a variety of senior roles, first and foremost as the economic czar and as the unofficial foreign minister. He was also tireless in organizing Cuba's political links with the newly emerging Third World. Yet his hopes of returning to a more active role in the revolutionary struggle did not decline with the years. In the course of 1964, he was clearly looking for an opportunity to leave Cuba. "Once again I feel under my heels the ribs of Rocinante," he wrote to his parents when he left for the Congo in 1965, conjuring up the image of Don Quixote and his horse.

"Many will call me an adventurer," he wrote, "and indeed I am". But he saw himself as an adventurer of an unusual type, to be counted among those "who put their lives on the line to demonstrate their truths". Therein lies the enduring appeal of Ernesto Che Guevara, a man who participated in one successful revolution and threw it all up to start again from scratch.

Guevara's expedition to the Congo has often been perceived as the personal whim of a professional revolutionary, a man bored with the tedium of a bureaucratized revolution who gathered together a group of friends to seek new challenges in distant lands. Yet this was only part of the story. His version of events in the Congo makes clear that some kind of Congo expedition was being planned by the Cuban government before his own involvement had been agreed. Aleida March includes a note from Castro to Che, in December 1964, in which the Cuban leader indicates that various choices were under discussion and that nothing would be decided until after Guevara had visited the Algerian president Ahmed Ben Bella, then Cuba's principal ally in Africa.

In the light of subsequent history, in which Cuba's continuing interest in Africa became clear for all to see, the intervention in the Congo can be seen as the first attempt by the Cuban Revolution to break out of the international straitjacket imposed on it by the United States. Denied support from governments in Latin America, who were all dragooned into opposing him by the United States, Castro made an imaginative leapfrog across the Atlantic. There he found a continent where post-colonial rhetoric was at its height, at least in some of the newly independent states, and where radical opposition movements existed in countries that were still under colonial control. After Guevara's death in 1967, when sponsorship of guerrilla movements in Latin America must have seemed a lost cause, Castro took an even closer interest in the cause of revolution in Africa.

Unlike the Bolivian episode of 1967, which was essentially a backroom operation supported by a few of Guevara's friends in the Cuban secret service and the ministry of the interior, the Congo expedition of 1965 was a major enterprise of the Cuban state. While one "column" of 120 men was sent to Tanzania in dribs and drabs, to be shipped across Lake Tanganyika into North Katanga, a second "column" of 200 men (the "Patrice Lumumba battalion") was sent to the other side of the continent, to a base near Brazzaville, the capital of Congo-Brazzaville, across the Congo River from Leopoldville-Kinshasa, the capital of the Congo-Zaire.

The eastern column, which arrived in Africa in April 1965, was commanded by Che Guevara, supported by several senior members of the Cuban government, while the western column, which came in September, was commanded by Jorge Risquet, a member of the central committee of the Cuban Communist Party. The deputy interior minister, Oscar Fernández Padilla (referred to in this book as "Rafael"), was the liaison officer between the two columns, and based himself in Dar es Salaam.

Guevara's task was to train the Congolese guerrilla forces in the east; Risquet's to train the embryonic guerrilla forces of Agostinho Neto in

Angola and in Cabinda, the Portuguese enclave at the mouth of the Congo River, and to assist a Congolese guerrilla force going to the aid of Pierre Mulele in Kwilu. He was also expected to stiffen up the army of Alphonse Massemba-Débat, the President of Congo-Brazzaville, against possible attacks from Leopoldville-Kinshasa.

Although the Cuban government assumed these very specific responsibilities in Africa, it would be a mistake to underestimate Guevara's own personal interest in promoting the "struggle against Yankee imperialism" that he described as "the great contemporary issue". The renewed Congo crisis of 1964 had coincided with the expansion of United States forces in Vietnam, and the start of the American bombing of North Vietnam, in the wake of the Gulf of Tonkin incident of August 1964. Guevara was to write a famous pamphlet, "Create Two, Three, Many Vietnams", published in 1967 when he was fighting in Bolivia. In his Congo book, too, he spelt out what he perceived to be the need to attack "Yankee imperialism" at the roots of its power: "in the colonial and neo-colonial lands that serve as the underpinning of its world domination."

★

The prolonged international crisis brought about by events in the Congo from 1960 to 1963 is now all but forgotten. Yet it once occupied the same role on the world stage as the events in former Yugoslavia did in the 1990s – with the added drama of Cold War tensions. The Congo's independence from Belgium was secured rather suddenly in June 1960 by a left-wing prime minister, Patrice Lumumba, and no one was prepared for the series of dramatic developments that followed: an army mutiny; the secession of Katanga, the country's richest province, organized by Moises Tshombe; the return of Belgian soldiers who had only just left; and the arrival of United Nations troops, at Lumumba's request, to protect the country's territorial integrity.

When Lumumba also asked for Soviet military assistance, he was promptly deposed by President Joseph Kasavubu, whose decision was supported by the commander-in-chief, Joseph Mobutu. Other notable moments in the Congo tragedy were the assassination of Lumumba (a murder planned by the CIA but executed by Tshombe) and the death in a plane crash of Dag Hammarskjöld, the UN secretary-general. This was no small crisis.

The Congo monopolized the world's headlines for more than three years, becoming a test case for the continent. Would the about-to-be-independent African nations really be independent, or would they fall back into the hands of "the imperialists"? Alternatively, were they about to be taken over by "the Communists"? These were the themes that exercised the Cold War capitals, and they were ones with which the Cubans themselves had already become familiar in the aftermath of their own revolution in January 1959. Yet by the end of 1963, the heat appeared to have gone out of the African crisis. The Congo was left in the hands of Cyrille Adoula, a weak and unpopular prime minister; the United Nations began planning to withdraw its troops; and international attention was focused elsewhere.

But history does not stop just because no one is looking, and a chain of rebellions throughout the Congo early in 1964 – invoking the name and the radical rhetoric established by Lumumba – seemed to herald new and significant developments more profound than the disorders of 1960. The rebellions were backed by an umbrella organization of leftist opposition groups called the "National Liberation Council" that established itself in Brazzaville in October 1963 after the Congolese parliament in Leopoldville-Kinshasa had been closed down by Adoula.

The rebellions sponsored by the Liberation Council took place in four specific areas of the Congo. The first, begun in January 1964 by 36-year-old Pierre Mulele, once Lumumba's minister of education and later the ambassador in Cairo, erupted in the west of the country in the province of Kwilu, east of Leopoldville-Kinshasa. Mulele, who said he was fighting for the Congo's "second independence", had spent time in China and secured promises of support from Peking. His deputy was Vitale Pascasa.

The second revolt was launched in the north-east of the country in February 1964 by a local politician, 43-year-old Gaston Soumaliot. He moved across the frontier from his base in the Burundi capital of Bujumbura, and spread out into the Uvira region in the province of Kivu. Like Mulele, he was supported by the Chinese, who had recently been able to open an embassy in Bujumbura.

A third rebellion was orchestrated by Soumaliot's lieutenant, Laurent Kabila, an articulate assembly member from North Katanga who had been a student in Paris and Belgrade. Kabila's forces, chiefly Babembe warriors from the area around Fizi, moved down the western shores of Lake Tanganyika in June 1964 and occupied the important town of Albertville-Kalemie. Here Kabila hoped to establish "a provisional government for the liberated territories in the east". This lakeside region was the area to which Guevara and his Cuban guerrillas were to come a year later. Among Kabila's supporters in 1964 were Leonard Mitoudidi and 30-year-old Ildephonse Masengo, who were to be Guevara's closest Congolese collaborators in 1965. For a few weeks in the middle of 1964, the rebel forces controlled much of the east of the Congo, even appearing to threaten the government's military complex at Kamina, in the heart of the country.

The fourth centre of revolt lay in the north, where a rebel force led by Nicolas Olenga marched on Stanleyville-Kisangani, on the upper reaches of the Congo River, and captured it at the beginning of August 1964. A "People's Republic of the Congo" was established there, presided over by Christophe Gbenye, a former minister of the interior in Lumumba's government in 1960, and a man with a strong claim to be regarded as Lumumba's political heir. Gbenye's "foreign minister" was Thomas Kanza, who had earlier been the Congo's ambassador in London.

By the middle of 1964, the old Lumumbist left – backed by China and the Soviet Union – controlled much of the Congo. Yet its triumph was by no means secure. Political divisions between the various political leaders continued to bedevil the revolutionary forces, as indeed they had done ever since 1960, and the rebellions soon came to the attention of the new government in the United States. President Lyndon Johnson had taken over after the assassination of John Kennedy in November 1963, and was to be faced at the presidential elections of November 1964 by an ultra right-wing Republican candidate, Barry Goldwater. Already embroiled in an escalating war in Vietnam, Johnson had no intention of being seen as "soft on Communism" in Africa.

The Americans expressed alarm at two African developments at the beginning of 1964: the multi-faceted rebellions in the Congo and the prospect of an imminent withdrawal of United Nations forces, and a left-wing revolution in Zanzibar, immediately perceived as a Communist bridge-head in the Indian Ocean. The Zanzibari revolutionaries were outspoken supporters of Castro's revolution, and saw their offshore island as a second Cuba.

To keep an eye on this potential threat, the Americans sent Frank Carlucci, a diplomat with experience in South Africa and the Congo (and later, in the 1980s, to be President Reagan's defence secretary), to be the US consul in Zanzibar in February. The following month Averell Harriman, a veteran diplomat of the Cold War appointed as President Johnson's African trouble-shooter, arrived in Leopoldville-Kinshasa to assess the situation.

Together with Cyrus Vance, the US deputy defence secretary, Harriman drew up plans for an American airlift to the Congo. Planes and helicopters, and T-28 fighter-bombers, secretly funded from the budget of the Agency for International Development (USAID), began arriving in May, expanding the existing stop-gap arrangement devised by the Central Intelligence Agency. Alarmed by the impact of Mulele's rebellion in Kwilu, the CIA station chief in Leopoldville-Kinshasa had suggested that T-6 training planes might be armed to help control it. These were Second World War planes brought to the Congo as part of a training programme for the embryonic Congolese airforce organized by the Italians. The Americans modified them to carry air-to-ground missiles and .30 calibre machine-guns.

The CIA recruited a number of pilots from the Cuban exile community in Florida, many of whom were veterans of the unsuccessful Bay of Pigs invasion of Cuba in 1961. The pilots were contracted at the rate of US$2,000 a month, with the promise that they would be rescued by helicopter should their planes be forced down in the jungle. The pilots established a base at Kikwit, the capital of Kivu, and had already begun operations against Mulele by the middle of February.

To provide support services for the Congolese airforce, and to look after the Cuban exile pilots, the CIA created a small unit, code-named WIGMO, or Western International Ground Maintenance Organisation, with a corporate headquarters in Liechtenstein. Guevara was to find traces of the existence of WIGMO when a number of mercenaries were ambushed by the Cuban guerrillas in October 1965.

A by-product of this renewed American interest in the Congo was a change of regime in Leopoldville-Kinshasa. Moises Tshombe, the old separatist leader from Katanga, seized power from Adoula in July 1964 and immediately sought external support to put down the rebellion that controlled half the country in the north and the east. United Nations troops had been withdrawn at the end of June, and what was left of the Congolese army was hardly reliable. The Americans suggested to Tshombe that he should recruit white mercenary soldiers from southern Africa, as he had done earlier in Katanga in 1960–61. These were to be organized and led by Colonel Mike Hoare, a veteran of the Burma campaign in the Second World War, who had helped Tshombe in Katanga in 1960. At that time the mercenaries had come to "save" Katanga from Lumumba; now they would return to save the Congo itself from "Communism".

The Americans worked through General Mobutu, the army commander-in-chief since independence, and Mobutu told Hoare to recruit 1,000 men in South Africa and Rhodesia. At the same time, the former commander of the Belgian paramilitary police force in the Congo, Colonel Frédéric Vandewalle, was brought in, together with a number of Belgian officers, to stiffen up the Congolese army. Colonel Vandewalle had been Tshombe's adviser between 1961 and 1963.

Tshombe's return to the political scene, coupled with his appeal for assistance to the United States, to Belgium, and to South Africa, left his government diplomatically isolated in Black Africa. A group of radical African states, notably Algeria, Egypt, Ghana, Guinea, Mali and Tanzania (which had formed a political union with Zanzibar in April), expressed their opposition to what looked like the re-imposition of colonial rule in the Congo – with Tshombe as a black puppet leader. They moved towards recognizing the government that Gbenye had established in Stanleyville-Kisangani, and taking practical steps to help it. At the conference of the fledgling Organisation of African States at Cairo in July, the Congo was high on the agenda, as it was at the second conference of non-aligned states in October, also held in Cairo, attended by a high-level delegation from Cuba.

The task of the army of white mercenaries assembled by Colonel Vandewalle and Colonel Hoare was to crush the rebellions. Recapturing Albertville with ease, they then began to advance from Kamina towards Stanleyville-Kisangani, in an operation code-named "Ommegang". As a counter-measure, the Gbenye government in Stanleyville seized as hostages many of the European expatriates, several of whom were missionaries, living in their zone. By the middle of November, as accounts of atrocities permitted by the authorities in Stanleyville spread, the Americans decided that they would have to take more extreme measures. They could not rely solely on the mercenary army marching up from the south.

A fresh plan was devised, "Operation Dragon Rouge", to drop Belgian paratroopers on Stanleyville from US transport planes. The paras were flown in from Britain's South Atlantic base on Ascension Island, with the permission of the recently elected British Labour government of Harold Wilson. They arrived, on the face of it, to protect the lives of Europeans being held "hostage", but their drop was purposefully timed to coincide with the arrival of the mercenary column, and thus to ensure the capture of Stanleyville. Ostensibly undertaken to save European missionaries, the Belgian and mercenary operation in and around the town left more than 200 Europeans and uncounted Africans dead.

The immediate result was to unite Africa's radical governments in yet fiercer opposition to the Tshombe regime. President Ben Bella of Algeria and President Nasser of Egypt announced that they would now supply the Congolese rebels with arms and soldiers, and they also asked others for help.

This was the spark that launched Cuba's direct involvement in the affairs of the Congo, for Cuba and Algeria had already been working closely together on revolutionary projects. Cuba had first helped the Algerian revolutionaries in 1961, sending them a large quantity of American weapons captured after the failed CIA operation at the Bay of Pigs. The weapons supply on that occasion was organized by Jorge Masetti, an Argentine friend of Guevara who had been instrumental in setting up the Cuban news agency Prensa Latina. Masetti had made plans subsequently to create a Cuban-style guerrilla movement in his native Argentina, and after Algeria gained independence in July 1962, he and Guevara secured Algerian help in the training of a group of Argentine guerrillas.

The Algerians provided many forms of practical assistance, even sending two agents with the guerrillas from Algiers to Bolivia in June 1963. The campaign never got properly off the ground, and it collapsed in April 1964 with the disappearance and unverified death of Masetti. Later that year, when the Algerians suggested that the Cubans might like to provide reciprocal assistance to their friends in the Congo, the Cubans were happy to oblige.

*

The Stanleyville paratroop landings caused an international furore, and early in December Guevara arrived in New York, as the Cuban delegate to the General Assembly of the United Nations. In an impassioned speech on 11 December that referred to "the tragic case of the Congo", he denounced "this unacceptable intervention". It was, he said, "a case without parallel in the modern world", and showed "how the rights of peoples can be flouted with absolute impunity and the most insolent cynicism".

At the root of the problem, Guevara went on, were "the Congo's vast resources which the imperialists wish to keep under their control". This, he said, was the explanation why "those who used the name of the United Nations in order to perpetrate the assassination of Lumumba are today murdering thousands of Congolese, in the name of the defence of the white race". How can we forget, he continued, "the way in which Patrice Lumumba's hopes in the United Nations were betrayed"?

The crowning insult, Guevara continued, were "the recent actions that have filled the world with indignation". Who were the perpetrators? "Belgian paratroopers, transported by United States aircraft, which took off from British bases." And he finished with a rhetorical flourish: "Free men throughout the world must prepare to avenge the Congo crime." Guevara himself was soon on his way to do just that.

Leaving New York, he embarked on a long tour of Africa, visiting the radical African states that were supporting the cause of the Congolese rebels. He flew first to Algiers to discuss the Congo with Ben Bella. In January and February 1965, he travelled on through the other radical states, calling at Mali, Congo-Brazzaville, Senegal, Ghana, Dahomey, Egypt and Tanzania. At each place he stopped, he was briefed on the situation in the various parts of the Congo by the different parties to the struggle. In Brazzaville, he met President Alphonse Massemba-Débat who asked for Cuban assistance to be provided to the forces of Pierre Mulele. In Dar es Salaam he saw Laurent Kabila, who sought help for what was left of his liberated area in the east of the Congo. In Cairo he had long discussions with Gaston Soumaliot, who wanted men and money for what had been the Stanleyville front. The only significant Congolese leader he failed to see was Christophe Gbenye, a man much mistrusted who was eventually to make his own deal with Leopoldville. In Brazzaville, Guevara also met the Angolan leader, Agostinho Neto, who asked the Cubans to provide help for the Angolan liberation army, the MPLA – the start of a long relationship.

It was not easy to weave a way through the various requests. The geographic dispersion of the Congolese revolutionary forces, and the different agendas of both themselves and their foreign backers, were to prove lasting problems in the months ahead. As his book reveals, Guevara was left in no doubt about the serious infighting within the Congolese leadership.

The Cubans had an agenda too, not always appreciated by those who required their help. They planned to construct a Third World alliance of all those opposed to American imperialism. In this context, they needed to know the attitude of the chief external supporter of the Congolese rebels: China. Early in February, Guevara flew from Cairo to Peking, accompanied by two senior Cuban figures who were to join him in the Congo later in the year, Osmany Cienfuegos, codenamed Bracero, and Emilio Aragonés, code-named Tembo. Both men were part of the inner group of Cubans making plans for the Congo expeditionary force.

The Chinese at that time were advocating the strategic notions of Lin Piao, the defence minister, who had famously advocated the encirclement of degenerate cities by radical revolutionary peasants. This of course was music to the ears of Guevara, though less attractive to the Soviet Union, then embroiled, over a wide range of issues, in the great Sino-Soviet dispute – an argument that was dividing the entire Communist world.

While the Chinese had initially been friendly towards Castro's revolution, they had become disillusioned after what they perceived as Khrushchev's "gamble" during the October missile crisis of 1962. By the time of Guevara's visit, they were additionally irritated by the Cuban failure to corral the Communist parties of Latin America into the Chinese camp. Over the course of 1965, they lost all interest in Cuba – for the next 30 years.

In Peking, Guevara's team met several officials specializing in African affairs, including Chou En-lai, who had made a long tour through Africa a year earlier. Between December 1963 and February 1964, the Chinese premier had visited Egypt, Algeria, Morocco, Tunisia, Ghana, Mali, Guinea, Sudan, Ethiopia and Somalia. Soon after his discussions with Guevara, Chou En-lai was to make a second visit to Algiers and Cairo in March 1965, possibly to meet Congolese leaders, and in June, when Guevara was already based in the Congo, he flew to Tanzania and held meetings with Kabila and Soumaliot.

Guevara left Peking to return to Cairo, and then flew south to Dar es Salaam. Tanzania was then a leading radical state, the government of Julius Nyerere moving leftwards after the union with Zanzibar, and Dar es Salaam was the headquarters of the various liberation movements recognized by the Organisation of African Unity. Guevara spent a week there in February, holding meetings with both Kabila and Soumaliot. He also met a number of the "freedom fighters" who were based there, with whom, as he describes in his book, he had fierce political arguments.

Flying back to Cairo early in March, he held discussions with Colonel Nasser, hinting for the first time that he might himself join the struggle in the Congo. Nasser proved less than enthusiastic about any such plans. According to the account of the meeting by Nasser's son-in-law, the editor and journalist Mohammed Heikal, Guevara told him that he was going to take charge of a group of black Cubans that would be fighting in the Congo.

"I shall go the Congo", Guevara said, "because it is the hottest spot in the world now . . . I think we can hurt the imperialists at the core of their interests in Katanga."

Heikal recalls that Nasser was astonished, warning Guevara not to become "another Tarzan, a white man among black men, leading them and protecting them . . ." Nasser shook his head sadly: "It can't be done."

But Guevara had made up his mind, and it only remained for him to return to Cuba to see how the preparations for the Congo expedition were progressing. He arrived in Havana after his extended two-month trip away on 14 March, 1965, to be greeted at the airport by Castro. This was effectively Guevara's last public appearance. From then on, he "disappeared", never to be seen in public again until his dead body was exhibited in Vallegrande in Bolivia in October 1967. This book reveals what he was doing in 1965, during the first year of his "disappearance".

*

The Cuban decision to intervene in the Congo had already been made before Guevara's return to Havana. An elite group of 150 guerrillas, all volunteers and all black, had been recruited at the beginning of the year and were undergoing training at three different camps in Cuba. They were not told of their destination, though the fact that they were all black had led several of them to suppose that it might be Africa. Black soldiers had been requested by Soumaliot in order that they should be differentiated from the white mercenaries employed by Tshombe. As Guevara admits in his book, this was neither a necessary nor a wise choice. Subsequent Cuban military expeditions to Africa employed both white and black soldiers.

The leader of the Cuban troops was Captain Víctor Dreke, code-named Moja, a participant in the Cuban war who was well known to Guevara. He had subsequently been involved in containing the long-drawn-out anti-Castro rebellion in the Escambray mountains – which finally ground to a halt in 1964. Years later, at the end of the 1960s, Dreke was to be part of the Cuban military mission to the forces of Amilcar Cabral in Guinea-Bissau.

The only question in the minds of the Cuban leadership, as they waited for Guevara to return, was whether Guevara would choose to lead the new revolutionary force. Although he had been involved in the planning of the various Latin America guerrilla projects of previous years, Guevara had not gone to Peru, Bolivia or Argentina himself. Now he had an opportunity to participate, and by the time he returned from his African trip, his mind was made up.

Captain Dreke had some perspicacious comments to add to this story, but his evidence – obtained in 1990, a quarter of a century after the event – sometimes reads as though it were made up of his subsequent thoughts; as though he were trying to explain to a later generation of Cubans what had actually been going on.

"I suppose that Che decided to participate in the project after his African trip. It went against his original idea to go and fight in Argentina. The assassination of Lumumba and the general situation in the Congo had led him to take an interest in the guerrilla struggle there. It enabled him to follow a double objective: to prepare a group for Latin America, and to create a third front [against imperialism], in Vietnam, Latin America, and Africa. These were the ideas that he wished to bring to fruition. Africa seemed easier than Latin America . . . The moment had come to act in Africa."

At the end of March 1965, a small advance guard of the guerrillas in training came to Havana from the camps in the country, and made their final preparations to leave Cuba. At the last moment, Dreke was taken aside by Osmany Cienfuegos, the minister of construction, and told that their destination was to be the Congo – and that Che Guevara was to be the leader of the expedition.

Guevara aside, the only other white member of the expedition at the start was 27-year-old José-María Martínez Tamayo, code-named Mbili, a Cuban secret service officer. He was already one of the most significant figures in Cuba's international military activities, and had been a close collaborator of Guevara over several years. Originally a tractor driver in Holguín Province, he had joined Castro's July 26 Movement and the Rebel Army in April 1958, at which time he came under Guevara's command. Subsequently he had worked with the embryonic Guatemalan guerrilla movement in 1962, and had gone to Bolivia in March 1963 to organize the base camp for the Argentine guerrilla movement organized by Guevara's friend Masetti, with the assistance of the Algerians.

In the year after the Congo expedition, Martínez Tamayo was to return to Bolivia in March 1966 to re-activate the revolutionary support movement there and to prepare the ground for Guevara's arrival. He was joined in Bolivia by his brother, Arturo, and both of them were killed there: Mbili (known in the Bolivian campaign as Ricardo) on 30 July, 1967, and Arturo on 8 October the same year, during the engagement in which Guevara was captured.

On the evening of 1 April, 1965, Fidel came round to the guerrilla base in Havana to say goodbye. Guevara had only been back in Havana for three weeks. Now he was to set off again. Although his leadership of the Congo expeditionary force had Castro's backing, no one was to know – not even the Congolese – that he was going to go back to Africa. His presence was to be kept absolutely secret. He flew off, heavily disguised, on a plane to Moscow. The small group of Cubans travelled on from there to Cairo, and then on to Dar es Salaam, where they arrived on 19 April.

Before he left, Guevara wrote his famous farewell letter to Fidel – which was to be read out publicly in Havana six months later in October. "I feel that I have fulfilled that part of my duty which bound me to the Cuban Revolution on its own territory ... I have no legal ties to Cuba ... Other nations are calling for the aid of my modest efforts ..."

It was a carefully constructed letter, suggesting that although Guevara was undoubtedly engaged on an operation supported by the Cuban state, his actions could be disavowed by the leadership should that be necessary. "I can do," he wrote to Fidel, "what you are unable to do because of your responsibility as Cuban leader". Guevara emphasized that both he and Castro were at one on this matter: "I have always identified myself with the foreign policy of our Revolution, and I continue to do so."

The letter was an important propaganda device, but at the very end of the Congolese venture, in the month after its publication in Havana, Guevara was to wish that he had not been so specific, or that Fidel had not released the text. His renunciation of his Cuban citizenship was to cause him serious difficulties with his guerrilla band.

★

Che Guevara's group of Cuban revolutionaries were greeted at the airport outside Dar es Salaam by the new Cuban ambassador, Pablo Rivalta, a schoolteacher by origin, who had set up the embassy in Tanzania a few months earlier. Rivalta had fought in the Cuban revolutionary war and been picked out at an early stage for duty in Africa. Fidel had asked him to take a message to Patrice Lumumba in 1960, although the trip had never materialized. As Cuban ambassador in Dar, Rivalta had had the full cooperation of the Tanzanian government. President Julius Nyerere had told him that if he ever had a problem he had only to put a flag on his car and drive round to State House. Rivalta had made contact with the various African liberation movements, as well as with Abdul Rahman Babu, the éminence grise behind the revolution in Zanzibar, who had become a minister in Tanzania. (Babu died in London in August 1996.)

Guevara was concerned that the arrival of such a large group of foreign blacks might alert the suspicions of the CIA, but he should not have worried. Frank Carlucci, the American diplomat appointed as consul in

Zanzibar, had been transferred to the US embassy in Dar and then accused by the Tanzanian government in January of being overly involved in Zanzibari affairs. He was expelled from the country (to turn up as the US ambassador in Lisbon during the Portuguese revolution in 1975), and the United States withdrew its ambassador from Dar in protest. The American intelligence agency in East Africa was working now under adverse conditions, and had inadequate resources to keep a check on airport arrivals. Indeed, so badly informed were the Americans about Guevara's movements that every reference to his Congo expedition until the 1990s suggested that he had entered the country through Brazzaville.

The group of Cubans was in some initial difficulty in Dar. No senior Congolese political figures were available with whom they could discuss future plans. Soumaliot and Kabila were away at a prolonged meeting in Cairo, as were their deputies Ildephonse Masengo and Leonard Mitoudidi. These men were supposed to be patching up the political differences within their revolutionary movement – a discouraging indication of what was to come. Since no one knew that Guevara formed part of the Cuban contingent, the Congolese in Dar initially paid him no great attention. The junior figure in charge, Antoine Godefroi Chamaleso, known to the Cubans as Tremendo Punto, was wholly without authority to make important decisions, though he did agree that the group should be allowed to make its way across Tanzania to Lake Tanganyika.

It was clear, from the start, that Che Guevara and the Africans were not going to see eye to eye. Guevara was to have similar difficulties the following year with the Bolivians. Local politicians, however hard-pressed, rarely like outsiders to come and tell them how to run their revolutions. The Cubans were internationalists in the purest sense: they had come to combat the American "imperialists" wherever they appeared, and to further the interests of the world revolution. The Congolese for the most part (and later the leaders of the Bolivian Communist Party) had no such large ambitions. They were circumscribed by their own petty nationalisms, their internal feuds, and their lack of knowledge about the politics of the wider world.

Pablo Rivalta had long discussions with Guevara about his intentions in Africa and gave an account years later of what he perceived to be Guevara's plan. "The Congo would serve as a base, as a detonator to set off revolution in all the African countries; it occupied, above all, a strategic position close to South Africa. The struggle itself, the training, and the impetus provided to the Congolese Liberation Movement, would be useful to all the other countries, and particularly South Africa. That was his idea."

Guevara's central plan was to take advantage of the existing liberated zone on the western shores of Lake Tanganyika and to use it as an enormous training ground, both for the Congolese and for guerrilla fighters from other liberation movements. The area was in the centre of the continent and was bordered by a friendly country (Tanzania). It seemed like a text-book case, and a year later he was to try to repeat the experiment in Bolivia, creating his own "liberated zone" on the edge of the Chaco where guerrillas from several nations could come for training.

It was not an outlandish ambition, indeed it was a mirror image of what the United States had already begun to do in the Panama Canal Zone. To the large American-owned "Zone" liberated from Panama at the turn of the century, and controlled by the Pentagon ever since, the Americans had brought officers from all over Latin America. There, in the local jungle conditions and using Spanish as the medium of instruction, these officers were taught the newly fashionable techniques of counter-insurgency that the Americans had developed in Vietnam. The Cubans, on the opposing side, could do no less.

★

On 22 April, 1965, Guevara's small group of 14 Cubans set off in three Mercedes-Benz cars on the road from Dar es Salaam to Lake Tanganyika. This was the dry season, hot in the day, cold at night. They were accompanied by a lorry carrying a motorboat purchased on the coast, to be used to ferry them over the lake to the Congo. They travelled in convoy across the country, passing through Dodoma to the lakeside town of Kigoma.

Adjacent to Kigoma stands the village of Ujiji, where the missionary David Livingstone and the American journalist Henry Stanley had an historic encounter almost a hundred years before, in 1871.

Before they left Dar, Guevara picked up his Swahili dictionary and gave each Cuban a pseudonym from the Swahili alphabet: Moja, one, for Captain Víctor Dreke; Mbili, two, for José-María Martínez Tamayo; and Tatu, three, for Guevara himself. Their code-names were to be the subject of some confusion. The Congolese got to know Guevara as Tatu, the number three in the group, the white man who was allegedly there as an interpreter. Yet Moja and Mbili, with numbers one and two, were clearly the leaders. So why, the Congolese wondered, was Tatu the man who always seemed to be in charge?

The little group established a supply base at Kigoma and then crossed the lake to the Congolese village of Kibamba, directly on the other side. They were welcomed there by a well-armed group of Congolese from the People's Liberation Army, dressed in khaki fatigues provided by the Chinese. Slogans were shouted, and songs sung. One of their number, fortunately for Guevara, spoke French. The Cubans were favourably impressed by the quality and quantity of the soldiers' equipment. Armaments, munitions, and clothing seemed always to be available. After the initial welcome, the Cubans made a camp for themselves outside the village. This was the start of a campaign that was to last seven months.

Guevara only had rather sketchy information about the terrain of the "liberated zone" in which his men would be expected to operate. Albertville-Kalemie in the south and Bukavu in the north had both been recaptured by Colonel Hoare's mercenaries more than six months earlier, but the towns of Fizi and Baraka were still in friendly hands. Colonel Hoare described the "mountain fastness" in which the Cubans now found themselves in his book *Congo Mercenary*, published in 1967: "The Fizi Baraka pocket of resistance covered an area twice the size of Wales. It stretched from Uvira at the top of Lake Tanganyika south along the coast for 150 miles to Kabimba, which was 30 miles north of Albertville, and inland to Kasongo on the Lualaba. It was a land of sudden escarpments, rushing rivers, and twisting tracks."

More surprising to the Cubans than the terrain was the presence in the area of thousands of Tutsis from Rwanda, of whom they had no prior knowledge. A group of some 4,000 Tutsis shared the defence of the region with the Congolese. Their Chinese-trained leader, Colonel Joseph Mundandi, was often involved in negotiations elsewhere, but he turned up with Kabila at Kibamba in the middle of June, after discussions with Chou En-lai in Dar es Salaam. Many of the Tutsi had lived in these parts for centuries, while others had taken refuge there after a Hutu massacre at the time of independence. Ousted from Rwanda, they were hoping to return to their country on the back of a successful revolution in the Congo.

Over the next few months, a fresh bunch of fighters arrived from Cuba every few weeks. The first group of 18 men arrived on 8 May, commanded by 35-year-old Santiago Terry Rodríguez, codenamed Aly, who had fought with Guevara in the revolutionary war in Cuba. (He survived the Congo, but was later killed in an accident in Cuba.)

A second group of 34 came at the end of May, accompanied by Osmany Cienfuegos, code-named Bracero, and a third group of 39 arrived on 24 June, with a man sent by Castro to act as Guevara's bodyguard. This was the 25-year-old Harry Villegas, known as Pombo, another veteran of Guevara's column in the revolutionary war, who had later worked with him in the ministry of industry. Pombo was subsequently to be part of the advance guard sent out to Bolivia in July 1966 and, after the death of Guevara in October 1967, he was the leader of the small guerrilla group that successfully avoided capture, escaped to Chile, and arrived back safely in Havana. He returned to Africa to fight in Angola in 1975, and again, between 1981 and 1990.

A fourth group arrived from Cuba at the end of September, led by Emilio Aragonés, code-named Tembo (the elephant), with whom Guevara had visited Peking in February, and Óscar Fernández Mell, code-named Siki, a doctor (later the Cuban ambassador in London) who had fought in the Cuban war and was one of Guevara's closest friends. Both were senior figures in the Cuban government, Aragonés being the organization secretary of the newly reorganised Cuban Communist Party.

The fifth and final Cuban group came at the beginning of October, accompanied by José Ramón Machado Ventura ("Machadito"), the minister of health, who had been sent from Havana to verify whether the Congolese request for 50 doctors was really justified.

In the middle of May, after the arrival of the first Cuban group, Guevara's small band moved from its lakeside camp at Kibamba to an "Upper Base" on the Luluabourg mountain, the highest in the chain of mountains along the lake, some five kilometres from Kibamba. This was a four-hour march from the lake, uphill all the way. "Quite unlike the hills of Cuba," noted one Cuban, "with a thick fog until ten in the morning that you could cut with a knife." The Cubans were unprepared for the mountains, having been told during their training in Cuba that the terrain would be flat jungle.

Guevara and Martínez Tamayo (Mbili) now formulated a plan with the two Congolese commanders, Leonard Mitoudidi and Antoine Chamaleso (Tremendo Punto), for exploring the zone. The Cubans would make a four-pronged probing expedition from their Upper Base: east to Lulimba, south to Bendera and Kabimba, north to Fizi and Baraka. The explorations, which lasted for two weeks, were led by Captain Dreke (Moja) and Mbili, while Guevara remained behind, to await the arrival of Laurent Kabila. The Cuban reconnaissance force encountered a number of friendly troops, but they noted that the forward bases of the enemy were well defended. In the Fizi sector, Moja thought that the morale of the Congo rebels was rather low, and when they moved forward to reconnoitre the Tshombe camp outside the town, they discovered a short landing strip for small planes and helicopters and saw a number of white soldiers for the first time.

When the exploring groups returned, Guevara summed up in two words what they told him they had found: incompetence and disorganization. Although the Cubans had been welcomed by the Congolese population, everyone had a low impression of the rebel leadership. Kabila and Mitoudidi were perceived as strangers, or more pejoratively as "tourists", since they were "never there when they were needed". The commanders most responsible "spent days drinking, and then had huge meals without disguising what they were up to from the people around them. They used up petrol on pointless expeditions." The Cubans diagnosed the basic problem on the ground to be lack of training. That was what they were there for. But how was it to be organized?

While waiting for the arrival of Kabila, the Cubans had to make do with Mitoudidi, the only senior Congolese leader with whom the Cubans had had any dealings. But on 7 June, in an unexplained accident, Mitoudidi was drowned in Lake Tanganyika. There were conflicting accounts as to how this happened, and questions about whether it was murder or an accident. It left the Cubans with inadequate political liaison with the Congolese revolution.

Instructions came from Kabila in Dar es Salaam in the middle of June, brought by Joseph Mundandi, that the Cubans should organize an attack on "Front de Force", a Tshombe garrison at Bendera on the inland road towards Albertville. The soldiers were there to guard a hydro-electric plant on the River Kimbi. The plan was for the attack to be led by Mundandi's Rwandan soldiers with the help of 50 Cubans. Guevara was told that the Bendera barracks was the largest in the area, with perhaps 300 *askaris,* and 100 Belgian mercenaries.

Guevara was unhappy about the project, for he could see that the hydro-electric plant was extremely well defended. Many of his men were still ill, and unprepared for combat, and he thought it would be a political error for the first major engagement to be conducted by soldiers who would be considered as "foreign" troops. The Congolese admitted that they had tried to capture the barracks twice before, but they explained that it was the nearest, and therefore the most desirable, target. Guevara's alternative strategy was to attack a smaller target, to take some prisoners, and to improve their information about the enemy, but after much heated discussion, it was decided that any action would be better than endless inaction.

On 20 June, a combined force of some 40 Cubans, with Tutsi and Congolese soldiers, set off to the west and made preparations to attack the plant and barracks at Bendera. The operation was doomed from the start, and made more difficult by the fact that the Tutsi soldiers did not speak Swahili. When it came to an actual battle, many of them ran away, the Congolese refused to take part, and four Cubans were killed. Their papers and diaries were captured. Guevara's worst fears were realized, for the Tshombe regime would now have concrete evidence that Cubans were participating in the rebellion.

Although the Bendera battle appeared to the Cubans to be a disaster, Colonel Hoare, the mercenary leader, was rather impressed. He reckoned that his task would not be easy. He had arrived in Albertville in early July, after visiting Johannesburg to recruit a further 500 mercenaries. With a fresh six-month contract from Tshombe and General Mobutu, he had orders to crush the eastern rebellion once and for all. He was aware of the presence of Cubans, but he had no inkling of the presence of Che Guevara. He writes in his memoirs that "observers had noticed a subtle change in the type of resistance which the rebels were offering the Leopoldville government. Whereas it had been of a reasonably passive nature – 'what we have, we hold' – now it was becoming more aggressive. The change coincided with the arrival in the area of a contingent of Cuban advisers, specially trained in the arts of guerrilla warfare . . ."

Any doubts about the presence of the Cubans, Hoare wrote, "vanished with the discovery of a dead Cuban" after the raid on Bendera. "His diary and passport confirmed that he had travelled from Havana via Prague and Peking, in both of which places he had undergone extensive training. An entry in the diary had the clarion ring of truth, where he described that the Congolese rebels 'were too damned lazy to carry the 76mm cannon and its heavy shells'."

The battle at Bendera, where the Congolese and the Tutsi soldiers had proved so inadequate, was a pivotal moment in the campaign, for it was followed for the first time by much defeatism in the Cuban camp. If the Congolese were not prepared to fight, what on earth were the Cubans doing there? Several members of the Cuban troop told Guevara that they would like to leave and return to Cuba.

There were additional reasons for gloom that month, for the international clouds were beginning to darken. The third Cuban group, travelling via Algiers in June, had only just missed being caught in a coup d'état. On

19 June, Ben Bella, Guevara's principal African ally, was overthrown in a military coup led by the army commander, Houari Boumedienne. With Ben Bella's downfall, the international support for the Congolese resistance movement slowly began to unravel.

Within the Congo itself, even before the arrival of Colonel Hoare's mercenary reinforcements, the Tshombe forces were already stiffening their defences. When the third group crossed the lake from Kigoma to Kibamba, they were caught by hostile aircraft operating out of Albertville. Several Congolese were killed, though the Cubans survived unharmed.

Outside the Congo, too, the differences between the various Congolese resistance movements were coming to a head. Gaston Soumaliot dislodged Christophe Gbenye as the official leader of the National Revolutionary Council at the beginning of August, accusing Gbenye of "betraying" the revolution. Gbenye had in fact given his support to efforts being made by the governments of the East African Community – Kenya, Uganda, and Tanzania – to negotiate an end to the conflict with Tshombe's government in Leopoldville.

Yet even at moments of maximum pessimism, the Cubans seemed to be able to pull off small coups. Captain Martínez Tamayo (Mbili) had been preparing ambushes on the road between Albertville and Bendera. Hoare's mercenaries and the Tshombe army were holed up in the two towns, while the guerrillas effectively controlled the road between them. In mid-August, four mercenaries in two Ferret scout cars, accompanied by a Belgian adjutant and his three assistants, were ambushed by the Cubans as they drove from Albertville to Bendera.

"The whole operation," recorded Hoare in his memoirs, "had been handled too lightly. Unsuspectingly, [Lieutenant] Graham [Hogan] and his boys rolled along, turrets open, almost at journey's end. Suddenly an enemy bazooka hissed through the air, to explode on the leading Ferret, while machine-guns opened up on one side of the road. Seven out of the eight people in the convoy were killed."

This was a valuable ambush for the Cubans, yet small-scale military successes were no substitute for political advance. The rebel movement was still faced with considerable disunity within the ranks, and if the divisions between the Congolese revolutionaries were causing problems within the Congo, they were also to create unexpected difficulties for Havana.

By the middle of the year, the Cubans on the ground in the Congo, including Guevara, were clearly demoralized. All of them had been ill at one time or another, and Guevara suffered from bouts of both asthma and malaria. This was an uncharted revolutionary experience that they were experiencing, with no sign of things getting better. In Havana, on the other hand, on the opposite side of the world, Castro had no reason to believe that the enterprise was not going well. Guevara was keeping his doubts to himself, and had not communicated the pessimism of his private diary to Castro. Nothing had been done to stop the regular monthly flow of newly trained guerrillas arriving in Tanzania from Cuba.

Early in September, the Cuban government had an opportunity to discover at first hand what was going on. Soumaliot was invited to Havana, and he spent two weeks being feted by the Cubans. Guevara had a poor opinion of Soumaliot and was hostile to the visit, but he had not been able to convey his anxieties to Havana.

Once in Cuba, Soumaliot gave Castro a glowing account of the progress of the revolutionary struggle, and the Cubans agreed to his request to send out 50 doctors. Having received a message from Rivalta, however, Castro must have had his doubts, and, as already mentioned, he decided to send out Machado Ventura, the health minister, to ascertain whether the doctors were really needed. When Machado arrived at the beginning of October, he agreed with Guevara that to send the doctors at this stage of the campaign would be a grave error.

A major counter-attack by Colonel Hoare's mercenaries was already well under way, threatening the entire Cuban position. Guevara had organized ambushes on the road to waylay mercenaries moving north from Albertville, but Hoare now ignored this route and, with superior mobility, advanced from the opposite direction. Sailing by night from Albertville at the end of September, his forces landed on the lakeside to the north of the Cuban positions. They had with them an 80-foot gunboat, half a dozen PT boats, twelve T-28s with a dozen Cuban exile pilots, four B-26s, and a Bell helicopter. Quite an armada! On 27 September, the mercenaries began a two-pronged attack against Baraka with two units of 100 men each. A third unit of another 100 men was to advance on Bendera and Lulimba from Albertville by land.

According to Hoare's account, this was by no means a walk-over for the mercenaries, for the Cuban training had begun to have some effect. "The enemy were very different from anything we had ever met before. They wore equipment, employed normal field tactics, and answered to whistle signals. They were obviously being led by trained officers. We intercepted wireless messages in Spanish. One of my signallers was a Spaniard and said the language used was very poor-class Spanish, and it seemed clear that the defence of Baraka was being organized by Cubans."

Yet the Congolese rebels, even with the stiffening provided by the Cubans, were no match for the mercenaries. By the end of October, after the Cubans had been in the Congo for six months, Major Hoare's men were drawing a tight circle around the Cuban positions. Baraka had fallen at the end of September, and the mercenaries captured Fizi ten days later. Soon they were moving south towards Lubondja and Lulimba. Preparing for a last stand, Guevara was forced to withdraw his troops to the Upper Base camp on the Luluabourg mountain, and it was made ready for a long resistance.

The drama was now drawing to a close, but military disaster on the ground was narrowly anticipated by diplomatic defeat at the conference table. On 13 October, aware that there would never be a rapprochement with a majority of the African states in the Organisation of African Unity if Moises Tshombe were to remain prime minister, President Kasavubu was persuaded to sack him, and his job was given to Evariste Kimba.

Guevara took this as a positive sign, and wrote of "the disintegration in Leopoldville". Yet this was not the case. The collapse of the Tshombe government was designed as the prelude to a political reconciliation that would undermine the rebellion and lead to the collapse of the support that it had been receiving from within Africa.

Ten days later, on 23 October, Kasavubu attended a meeting of African heads of state in Accra, presided over by Kwame Nkrumah. He announced that the rebellion in his country was virtually at an end, and that it would, therefore, be possible to dispense with the services of the white mercenaries and to send them home. This was the signal that the African presidents had been waiting for. If Kasavubu would end this affront to independent Africa – the reliance on foreign mercenaries – then they would agree to withdraw their support for Soumaliot's rebellion.

This was a major defeat for the radical African states. A new conservative tide now ran strongly through the continent that was to alter the balance of power in Africa for a decade. On 11 November, 1965, sensing that the climate was now favourable, the Rhodesian leader, Ian Smith, made his unilateral declaration of independence. The long resistance of the whites in Africa to the imposition of majority rule was turning to a fresh chapter. The Portuguese were to maintain their grip on Angola, Mozambique and Guinea-Bissau until 1975.

The radicals were being slowly eliminated: Ben Bella was toppled in June; Nkrumah was overthrown early in 1966, while on a visit to China; and Ben Barka, the Moroccan opposition leader who had been organising Cuba's Tricontinental Conference, a gathering of revolutionary movements from all over the world to be held in Havana in January 1966, was kidnapped and murdered in Paris.

For Colonel Hoare and his mercenaries, as for Che Guevara and the Cubans, these external developments seriously affected their positions. When Tshombe was dismissed, Hoare cabled Mobutu asking for a categorical statement that his men's contracts would be honoured. When he heard of Kasavubu's pledge in Accra a week later, he flew to Leopoldville to see Mobutu in person. "The general was furious", he wrote. "He had not been consulted about the withdrawal of mercenaries from his army and he felt bitter in consequence." Kimba, the new prime minister, was persuaded to make a statement to the effect that there was no intention of sending the mercenaries home until the Congo was thoroughly pacified. In practice, Hoare himself – as the most important and visible white mercenary – was sent back to South Africa at the end of October, although many of his men stayed on till the following year.

Guevara was in similar difficulties. On 1 November he received an urgent message from Padilla in Dar es Salaam. The Tanzanian government, as a result of the Accra meeting, had decided to pull the plug on the Cuban expeditionary force. President Nyerere, all too aware of the internal feuding within the Congolese leadership, and concerned about its implications within his own government, had no choice.

Guevara was under pressure from the mercenary advance, and had already envisaged the possibility that the rebel leaders might abandon the fight. If this were to happen, he noted, he had other plans. "I had already taken the decision to remain behind with twenty well-chosen men . . . I would have continued to fight until the movement developed, or until its possibilities were exhausted – in which case I would have decided to seek another front or to request asylum somewhere."

In the final weeks of the Congolese venture, according to Pablo Rivalta's evidence, Guevara wrote to Chou En-lai, asking for Chinese assistance. Chou En-lai replied, suggesting that he should remain in the Congo, forming resistance groups without entering into combat. Guevara reveals that he entertained the idea, at the end, of making a forced march across the Congo to join forces with Mulele's rebels in Kwilu, but he did not receive Cuban backing for so wild a notion.

What could we have done? asked Guevara unhappily on 20 November, as he sounded the final retreat and organized his men to cross the lake back to Tanzania from the tiny port of Yunga. "All the Congolese leaders were in full retreat, the peasants had become increasingly hostile." Castro, on the other side of the world, was less engaged. "In the end," he explained years later, "it was the revolutionary leaders of the Congo who took the decision to stop the fight, and the men were withdrawn. In practice, this decision was correct: we had verified that the conditions for the development of this struggle, at that particular moment, did not exist."

The hundred or so Cubans assembled on the shores of Lake Tanganyika and piled into three small boats to take them over to Kigoma. Some 40

Congolese rebels came too, but hundreds were left behind. It was an embarrassing and humiliating event for all concerned. The Cubans crossed the lake under enemy surveillance but without further disaster, and travelled back to Dar es Salaam in three lorries. After a few days in Dar, the bulk of the Cuban contingent returned home. They flew first to Moscow, and then two Soviet planes took them directly to Havana. Castro and his brother Raúl came to the house of the senior leaders to discuss in detail what had happened.

In the Congo itself, meanwhile, events had been accelerating. On 25 November, just five days after the Cuban withdrawal, General Mobutu seized power in Leopoldville with the overt encouragement of the United States. He overthrew the Kimba government, deposed Kasavubu, the President since 1960, and announced a fresh political programme that would end the war. Colonel Hoare's mercenary operation was gently wound up. The Belgian forces were asked to leave. The rebels ceased their operations. General Mobutu remained in power for 32 years, until toppled by Laurent Kabila in 1997, just 30 years after the death of Guevara in Bolivia.

★

In November 1965, Guevara had remained behind in the Cuban embassy in Dar es Salaam to write his account of the war. Early in 1966, still incognito, he travelled to Prague, and eventually he returned to Cuba to help prepare the expeditionary force that would establish itself in Bolivia.

In May 1966, Martínez Tamayo, the faithful Mbili, arrived in the Bolivian capital La Paz, to be joined in May by Pombo and Tuma, two other veterans of the Congo campaign. Guevara reached Bolivia in November, and a small band of Cubans and Bolivians established themselves at the base of Nancahuazú in eastern Bolivia, as they had once done in the eastern Congo.

In Bolivia, Guevara had a stalwart collection of both Cuban and Bolivian guerrillas at his disposal, many of whom had trained in Cuba, but it only became a useful military force once the weaker and more useless members had fallen by the wayside. Politically, there was almost a repeat of the Congo experience. There were no tribal divisions in Bolivia, but by 1966–67 the Sino-Soviet dispute had wreaked havoc on the Bolivian Communist Party. The traditionally combative Bolivian left was rife with schism.

With the Congolese experience fresh in his mind, Guevara insisted that he should be the leader. He could not endlessly wait around, as he had done in Kibamba, hoping that a local leader would eventually emerge to give instructions. When Mario Monje, the leader of the Moscow wing of the Bolivian Communist Party, turned up at the Nancahuazú camp in December 1966, Guevara told him that he, Guevara, would be running the show. Monje could not accept this and left the camp. From that moment on, the Bolivian guerrillas were bereft of any outside support – of the kind that had sustained Guevara in the Congo and Castro in the Cuban revolutionary war.

Three months later, in March 1967, the guerrillas' camp was discovered before the men were ready, and in April they were in action against the Bolivian army. With no friendly Tanzania across the border, and without contact with Havana, the guerrilla band slowly dwindled, motivated solely by Guevara's indomitable will. In October, he was captured one day and shot the next.

*

In his detailed account of the Congo expedition, Che Guevara blamed himself for abandoning the Congolese revolution, and wrote several pages explaining why he had not remained behind to continue the struggle. His morale had been adversely affected by the publication of his farewell letter to Fidel, written in April 1965 as he left Havana and made public by Castro in October. Its contents had become known to his guerrilla troops during the final weeks of the campaign.

The letter had emphasized his renunciation of "my positions in the party leadership, my ministry post, my rank of *comandante*, and my Cuban citizenship". It seemed a harmless statement, but its publication created an unexpected gulf between Guevara and the Cubans with him. Guevara wrote that it reminded him of the time nearly a decade earlier when he had first arrived in Cuba's Sierra Maestra. "Then, I was simply a stranger who happened to be in contact with the Cubans." Now he felt that he had become just such a stranger once more, and he knew that he could not ask his Cuban friends to remain with him in the Congo.

Less than two years later, when he found himself in a comparably disastrous situation in the jungles of eastern Bolivia, with a band of loyal friends, he forced himself to fight on. After the humbling experience of the Congo, it would not have been possible to have contemplated retreat.

In one sense, the Cubans did not retreat from Africa either. The strangest aspect of the Cuban adventure in the Congo is that this adverse experience appears to have encouraged the participants to try again. While Guevara returned to his earlier plans for Latin America and went off to Bolivia, Fidel Castro persevered as a major player in the politics of Africa.

Far from being deterred by Guevara's account of the Congo expedition, Fidel continued to assist African revolutionary movements all over the continent. First, he sent military experts to advise Amilcar Cabral in Guinea-Bissau in the late 1960s, in their struggle against the Portuguese. Then, in 1975, he organized a massive airlift of Cuban troops to Angola, to protect Agostinho Neto's MPLA from defeat at the hands of the South Africans, and he repeated this triumph in the 1980s.

From the irregular style of guerrilla warfare that they had championed so long, the Cubans moved towards military intervention of a more formal kind. In 1977 and 1978, Cuban troops were to turn the tide in the battles fought between Ethiopia and Somalia. United States officials estimated at that time that some 27,000 Cubans were either fighting or working in 16 African countries – a far cry from the 100 men led by Che Guevara who had tried to change the history of the Congo.

RICHARD GOTT

Bibliography

Alarcón Ramírez, Dariel ("Benigno") and Mariano Rodríguez, *Les Survivants du Che*, Editions du Rocher, Paris, 1995

Alarcón Ramírez, Dariel ("Benigno"), *Vie et mort de la révolution cubaine*, Fayard, Paris, 1996

Anderson, Jon Lee, *Che Guevara, a revolutionary life*, Bantam Press, London and New York, 1997

Cormier, Jean (with the collaboration of Hilda Guevara and Alberto Granado), *Che Guevara*, Editions du Rocher, Paris, 1995

Debray, Régis, *Loués soient nos seigneurs: une éducation politique*, Gallimard, Paris, 1996

Gálvez, William, *Che in Africa: Che Guevara's Congo Diary*, Ocean Press, New York, 1999

Guevara, Ernesto (with a preface by François Maspero), *Journal de Bolivie*, Editions La Découverte, Paris, 1995

Hoare, Mike, *Congo Mercenary*, Robert Hale, London, 1967

Kelly, Sean, *America's Tyrant: the CIA and Mobutu of Zaire*, American University Press, Washington, 1993

Schatzburg, Michael G, *Mobutu or Chaos: the United States and Zaire, 1960–1990*, University Press of America, New York, 1991

Stockwell, John, *In Search of Enemies*, W. W. Norton, New York, 1978

Taibo, Paco Ignacio, *Guevara, also known as Che*, St Martin's Press, New York, 1997

Taibo, Paco Ignacio (with Froilán Escobar and Félix Guerra), *L'Année où nous n'étions nulle part*, Editions Métailié, Paris, 1995

Vandewalle, Frédéric, *L'Ommegang*, Collection Témoignage Africain, Brussels, 1970

Verhaegen, Benoît, *Rébellions au Congo, Les Études du CRISP*, Brussels, 1966

Villegas Tamayo, Harry ("Pombo"), *Pombo, a man of Che's guerrilla: With Che Guevara in Bolivia, 1966–68*, Pathfinder Press, New York, 1996

Wagoner, Fred E., *Dragon Rouge*, National Defense University, Washington, 1980

FOREWORD

I was always told that I would have to start one day, but I was not warned how difficult it would be. This book was written by a man I have greatly admired and respected ever since I became conscious. Unfortunately he died, so he will not be able to give me his opinion about what I write, nor, worst of all for us, can he explain to you what he wanted to say then, and whether today, 30 years or more after the events described, he would add a note by way of clarification. This is why I say that my task is extremely difficult. To publish *Pasajes de la guerra revolucionaria: Congo* – a document preserved in Che's personal archive that contains stylistic corrections, incorporates various observations and eliminates a number of notes – involves a major obligation to history, for it is known that other versions, corresponding to Che's first transcriptions, have already appeared. Although he authorized editors to make the changes they considered necessary, we have respected in full the text that he actually wrote, since he composed it after the end of his mission in the Congo, when he subjected his notes on the struggle to a deep critical analysis that made it possible for "experiences to be extracted for the use of other revolutionary movements".

In the "Preface" he begins by saying: "This is the history of a failure." Although I do not agree with this, I understand his state of mind and can see how it could certainly be considered a failure. But personally I think it was an epic. Those who have lived for some time on the African continent will doubtless understand what I am saying. The degradation it has undergone over the centuries at the hands of so-called European colonizers still makes its effects felt within the African population: the imposition of a different culture and different religions, the paralysis of the normal development of a civilization, the exploitation of its natural wealth, the use of the physical strength of its people as slaves, torn from their habitat to be abused and humiliated – all this has left deep marks in these human beings. If we consider that it was caused by other men who still feel entitled to do such things today, and that in one way or another we allow them to happen, then we can begin to appreciate how people respond to certain events.

Nevertheless, many will wonder why Che Guevara took part in this revolutionary process, what motivated him to try and help this movement. And it is he himself who gives us the answer: "For, in relation to Yankee imperialism, it is not enough to be resolute in defence. It has to be attacked in its bases of support, in the colonial and neo-colonial lands that serve as the underpinning of its world domination."

Che always expressed his wish to continue the struggle in other parts of the world. A doctor by profession and a guerrilla by action, he was familiar with the limitations that life imposes on man and the sacrifices demanded by something as difficult as guerrilla warfare. It is therefore understandable that he felt anxious to make his dreams come true in the best possible physical conditions. We know of his deeply rooted sense of responsibility and his political maturity, as well as his obligation towards comrades who trusted in him to continue the struggle.

He had made a previous trip to the African continent, where he had the opportunity to meet some of the leaders of the revolutionary movements active at that time, and to familiarize himself with their difficulties and concerns. At all times he maintained contact with Fidel Castro, who, in an unpublished letter dated December 1964, told him of the measures that were meanwhile being taken in Cuba.

> Che:
> Sergio [Sergio del Valle] has just met me and described in detail how everything is going. There does not seem to be any difficulty

in carrying the programme through to the end. Diocles [Diocles
Torralba] will give you a detailed verbal account.
  We will make the final decision on the formula when you return.
To be able to choose among the possible alternatives, it is necessary
to know the opinions of our friend [Ahmed Ben Bella]. Try to keep
us informed by secure means.

It should never be forgotten that a group of Cubans took part in this
campaign alongside Che, and shared his conviction: "Our country, the only
socialist bastion at the gates of Yankee imperialism, sends its soldiers
to fight and die in a foreign land, on a distant continent, and assumes full
public responsibility for its actions. This challenge, this clear position
with regard to the great contemporary issue of relentless struggle against
Yankee imperialism, defines the heroic significance of our participation
in the struggle of the Congo."

Che, together with the group he led, aimed to strengthen as much as
possible the liberation movement in the Congo, to achieve a united front,
to select the best men and those prepared to continue the struggle for the
final liberation of Africa. He took with him the experience gained in Cuba
and placed it at the service of the new revolution.

Che was deeply affected by the harsh realities of the Congo – its
backwardness, the lack of political-ideological development among the
population against which it was necessary to struggle with firmness
and determination. There was no lack of moments of discouragement and
incomprehension, but rising above these adversities, like a prophetic vision,
was the enormous confidence and love that he felt for those who decided
to create possibilities of development and greater dignity for their people.

In Africa, history has been making a reality of these forward glimpses
for more than 30 years, as a developing education in military matters
has become part of revolutionary consciousness. This has resulted in
such major victories as Cuito Cuanavale [in Angola], Ethiopia, Namibia
and others, which have contributed to the sovereignty and independence
of the continent.

The Cuban revolution maintained absolute discretion for as long as possible about Che's internationalist activity in the Congo, firmly enduring for many months a deluge of slanders on the matter. But while he was still fully engaged in combat there, the first meeting of the Party's Central Committee decided to publish his letter of farewell, since it was no longer possible to refrain from explaining to the Cuban people and the world the absence of the man who had been one of the most solid and legendary figures of the revolution.

In his notes, Che comes to the conclusion that knowledge of this letter created a distance between himself and the Cuban fighters: "There were certain things that we did not have in common, certain longings that I had tacitly or explicitly renounced but which each individual holds most sacred: family, land, immediate surroundings." If this is what he felt at such moments, one can imagine how difficult it was for Fidel to get him to return to Cuba. He wrote several times trying to convince him, and achieved this by means of solid arguments. In June 1966, in an unpublished letter, he wrote:

Dear Ramón:

Events have overtaken my plans for a letter. I read in full the planned book on your experiences in the C. [Congo], and also again the manual on guerrilla warfare, with the aim of making the best possible analysis of these questions, especially bearing in mind the practical importance with regard to plans in the land of Carlitos [Carlos Gardel]. Although there is no point right now in my talking with you about this, I will just say that I found the work on the C. extremely interesting and I think it is really worth the effort for you to leave written evidence about everything. [. . .]

Concerning your situation

I have just read your letter to Bracero [Osmany Cienfuegos] and spoken extensively with the Doctor [Aleida March].

In the days when an act of aggression seemed imminent here,

I suggested to several comrades the idea of asking you to come back, an idea that turned out to be in everyone's mind. The Galician [Manuel Piñeiro] was given the job of sounding you out. From the letter to Bracero I see that you were thinking exactly the same. But at this precise moment I cannot make any plans on the matter, since, as I explained to you, our impression now is that nothing will happen for the moment.

It seems to me, however, given the delicate and worrying situation in which you find yourself there, that you should by all means consider the usefulness of making a jump over here.

I am well aware that you are particularly reluctant to consider any option that involves your setting foot in Cuba for the moment, unless it is in the quite exceptional case mentioned above. But on any coolly objective analysis, this actually hinders your objectives; worse, it puts them at risk. It is hard work to resign myself to the idea that this is correct, or even that it can be justified from a revolutionary point of view. Your time at the so-called halfway point increases the risks; it makes extraordinarily more difficult the practical tasks that need to be achieved; far from accelerating the plans, it delays their fulfilment; and it subjects you to a period of unnecessarily anxious, uncertain and impatient waiting.

What is the reason for all this? There is no question of principle, honour or revolutionary morality that prevents you making effective and thorough use of the facilities on which you can really depend to achieve your ends. It implies no fraud, no deception, no tricking of the Cuban people or the world, to make use of the objective advantages of being able to enter and leave here, to plan and coordinate, to select and train cadres, and to do everything from here that you can achieve only deficiently and with so much work from where you are or somewhere like it. Neither today nor tomorrow, nor at any time in the future, will anyone consider that a fault – and still less will your own conscience. What really would be a grave, unforgivable fault is to do things badly when you can do them well; to have a failure when all the possibilities are there for a success.

I am not remotely suggesting that you abandon or postpone your plans, nor I am letting myself be carried away by pessimistic considerations about the difficulties that have arisen. On the contrary, the difficulties can be overcome, and we can count more than ever on experience, conviction and the means to carry out those plans with success, and this is why I think we should make the best and most rational use of the knowledge, the resources and the facilities that we have at our disposal. Is it really the case that, since first hatching your now old idea of further action in a different setting, you have ever had enough time to devote yourself entirely to conceiving, organizing and executing your plans to the greatest possible extent? [. . .]

It is a huge advantage that you can use things here, that you have access to houses, isolated farms, mountains, cays and everything essential to organize and personally lead the projects, devoting 100 per cent of your time to them and drawing on the help of as many others as necessary, without any but a very small number of people knowing your whereabouts. You know perfectly well that you can count on these facilities, that there is not the slightest possibility that you will encounter difficulties or interference for reasons of state or politics. The most difficult thing of all – the official disconnection – has already been done, not without paying a price in the form of slander, intrigues and so on. Is it right that we should not extract the maximum benefit from it? Could any revolutionary count on such ideal conditions to fulfil his historical mission, at a time when it has particular importance for humanity and the most decisive struggle for the victory of the peoples is about to be acted out? [. . .]

Why not do things well if we have every possibility? Why do we not take the minimum time necessary, while working with the greatest speed? Did Marx, Engels, Lenin, Bolívar and Martí not perhaps have to endure sometimes waiting for decades?

And in those times there was no aeroplane or radio or other ways of shortening distances and increasing performance in each hour of a man's life. We ourselves had to invest 18 months in Mexico before returning here. I am not proposing that you wait decades or even years, only a few months, since I believe that in a matter of months, by working in the way you suggest, you can set yourself up in conditions incomparably more favourable than the ones we are trying to achieve at present.

I know you will be 38 on the 14th. Do you perhaps think that a man starts to be old at that age?

I hope that these lines will not annoy or worry you. I know that if you analyse them seriously, your characteristic honesty will make you accept that I am right. But even if you take a completely different decision, I will not feel disappointed. I write this to you with great affection and the deepest and most sincere admiration for your lucid and upright intelligence, your irreproachable conduct and your unyielding character of a whole-hearted revolutionary. And the fact that you may see things differently will not change these feelings by one iota or cool our work together in the slightest.

That same year Che returned to Cuba.

On the first anniversary of the victory of the Congolese revolution, I took part in the celebrations and had a chance to talk to some of the comrades who fought alongside Che. I also took the opportunity to discuss the publication of this book with them. Their opinions were a matter of concern to me, because Che is critical and direct in the hope that his document will make it possible to analyse the errors and ensure that they are not made again. He makes specific mention of several leaders, including Laurent Kabila, who is today the supreme leader of the Congolese people.

My contact with these men allowed me to feel the respect and affection with which they remember Che Guevara. Most of them were young at the time but, as they themselves put it, they cannot forget the image of simplicity and modesty which Che communicated to them, by offering his respect and placing himself under their command. For this reason, they are aware that his recommendations have always been useful to the great task they have ahead of them, the task of unifying the country and ensuring that for the first time in many years it is the Congolese people that benefits from its own riches.

Men do not die when their life and example can serve as a guide to others, and when those others succeed in continuing their work.

ALEIDA GUEVARA MARCH

June 1998

Clarification of Certain Names and Terms

Abdallah: Cuban sergeant.

Afende: Cuban soldier.

Agano: Cuban sergeant.

Anchali: Cuban sergeant; volunteered to rescue the comrades left behind in the Congo.

Arobaini: Cuban soldier; wounded and evacuated before our departure.

Arobo: Cuban soldier.

Azi: Cuban lieutenant; in command of various combat units.

Azima: Cuban lieutenant; deputy leader of the mixed Second Brigade.

Baati: Cuban soldier.

Bahaza: Cuban soldier; killed as a result of injuries suffered on 24 October, 1965.

Banhir: Cuban soldier.

Baraka: A small port on Lake Tanganyika on the road from Fizi to Uvira.

Bemba, Charles: Congolese soldier; worked with me as political commissar without holding this rank in the Congolese force.

Bendera, Feston: Political commissar of a Congolese formation.

Bidalila: Congolese colonel; head of First Brigade based in Uvira; promoted to general.

birulo: "Insect" in Swahili; for us synonymous with louse.

Bondo: Village on the shores of Lake Tanganyika.

Bujumbura: Capital of the kingdom of Burundi.

bukali: Congolese dish; manioc flour given the consistency of a paste through boiling with water.

Bukavu: Capital of the province of Kivu; 35,000 inhabitants.

Calixte: Congolese commander, head of the Makungo front.

Chamaleso: see *Tremendo Punto*.

Changa: Cuban captain; responsible for transporting supplies and messages from Kigoma.

Chei: Cuban soldier.

Compagnie: Rwandan fighter who joined our force.

Danhusi: Cuban soldier; my adjutant for part of the campaign.

dawa: "Medicine" in Swahili; a magic ritual protecting fighters from enemy bullets.

Duala: Cuban corporal.

Faume: Congolese leader of a guerrilla force in Katenga; we did not succeed in making contact with him.

Fizi: Town close to Lake Tanganyika, headquarters of general staff of Second Brigade; minor road junction.

François: Congolese commander killed in same accident that cost Mitoudidi's life.

Freedom fighters: Generic English term used for members of revolutionary organizations in exile.

Front de Force-Front Bendera: Fortified enemy position close to Albertville-Lulimba highway. There is a hydro-electric power station there.

Gbenye: Self-appointed president of insurgent Congo; as minister of interior in Adoula government, ordered the detention of Gizenga.

Gizenga: Former vice-premier of Congo; captured in Tshombe's time and released by Mobutu coup.

Hanzini: Cuban soldier.

Hindi: Cuban doctor.

Hukumu: Cuban soldier.

Huseini: Congolese commander; head of Congolese troops at Upper Base and Lubondja barrier.

Ila, Jean: Congolese commander; head of troops quartered at Kalonda-Kibuye.

Ilunga, Ernest: Congolese fighter; was my Swahili teacher until he fell seriously ill.

Ishirini: Cuban soldier; one of group who volunteered to rescue comrades left behind in Congo.

Israel: Cuban sergeant.

Jungo: Village on Lake Tanganyika, south of the lakeside base.

Kabambare: Village on Albertville to Stanleyville road. Area was dominated by revolutionary forces for a long time.

Kabila: Second vice-president of Supreme Council of the Revolution; head of the eastern front.

Kabimba: Village on Lake Tanganyika occupied by enemy; close to southern tip of our front.

Kaela: Village between Kasima and Kisosi.

Kalonda-Kibuye: Farming estate on Katenga-Lulimba road; a Congolese guerrilla unit was stationed there.

Kanyanja: Rwandan village on the altiplano between Nganja and Front de Force.

Kanza: Congolese politician; minister of foreign relations in Gbenye government.

kapita: Village political leader, a position below that of chairman, the title given to the leader of several settlements.

Karamba: Locality between Baraka and Kasima.

Karim: Cuban lieutenant; political commissar.

Karume: President of Zanzibar, first vice-president of Tanzania.

Kasabuvabu, Emmanuel: Responsible for supplies on general staff.

Kasai: Province of Congo where Mulele operated; large diamond deposits.

Kasali: Congolese commander assigned to general staff.

Kasambala: Cuban corporal.

Kasengo: River port on the Congo, road junction; strong revolutionary forces in the area.

Kasima: Village on Lake Tanganyika; only area with a small plain between mountains and lake. Occupied by enemy to threaten the base.

Kasulu: Cuban doctor and translator from French (Haitian nationality).

Katanga: The richest and most industrialized of Congolese provinces, situated to south of our zone of operations.

Katenga: Village on the Albertville-Lulimba road.

Kawawa: Cuban corporal, killed in action at Front de Force.

Kawawa: Second vice-president of Tanzania.

Kazolelo-Makungo: Location of Commander Calixte's camp.

Kibamba: Conventional name for place where base was situated on Congolese side of Lake Tanganyika.

Kiliwe: Tributary of River Kimbi; area where we suffered surprise attack on 24 October, 1965.

Kimba: Briefly prime minister of Congo; succeeded Tshombe.

Kimbi: Tributary of River Congo, rises in mountains of Lake Tanganyika.

Kisosi: Village located between Ruandasi and Kaela, on shores of lake.

Kiswa: Cuban lieutenant, Aly's second-in-command in Kabimba area.

Kivu: Province of Congo, northern part of our front.

Kiwe: Responsible for intelligence on general staff; student of journalism.

Kumi: Cuban doctor.

Lambert: Lieutenant-colonel; head of operations in Second Brigade.

Lubichaco: Small river and village on western slope of mountains of Lake Tanganyika.

Lubondja: Village between Lulimba and Fizi.

Lulimba: Village on Albertville-Bukavu road, from which a branch road went to Kabambare.

Mafu: Cuban lieutenant; in charge of group of fighters who left with Rwandans.

Maganga: Cuban sergeant.

Makambila, Jerôme: Former provincial deputy for Congolese National Movement.

Makungo: Village near Front de Force; no-man's-land until final enemy offensive.

Marembe: Cuban soldier.

Masengo: Chief of general staff of eastern front; succeeded Mitoudidi.

Maurino: Cuban soldier, disappeared during a retreat.

Mbili: Cuban fighter, led a number of actions; head of mixed First Company.

Mbolo: Village on Baraka-Uvira road on the shores of Lake Tanganyika.

Mitoudidi: Chief of general staff of eastern front; drowned in an accident.

Moja: Cuban comandante, member of Central Committee of Communist

Party of Cuba; was head of Second Company, as instructor of Cuban officers.

Morogoro: Cuban surgeon.

motumbo: A "canoe", generally made from a tree trunk hollowed out with fire and axe.

Moulane: Major-general, head of Second Brigade based at Fizi.

Muenga: Village on the Fizi-Bukavu road.

muganga: Swahili term designating both Western doctors and native sorcerers.

Mujumba: Delegate of CNL in Tanzania; later captured on his way to Mukundi area and interned in the country.

Mukundi: Area in Congo close to Albertville railway.

Mulele: Former minister under Lumumba; the first to take up arms; fought on in Kasai area.

Mundandi: Commander of Rwandan origin; captained a Rwandan group operating at Front de Force.

Mustafá: Cuban soldier.

Mutchungo: Public health minister in Supreme Council of the Revolution; remained in Congo until the end of operations.

Muteba: Head of communications on the Congolese general staff.

Nabikumbe: Small river and village between Lubondja and Nganja.

Nane: Cuban sergeant.

Nbagira: Foreign relations minister in Supreme Council of the Revolution; was in Uvira area until final moments and declared his willingness to return.

Nganja: Village on altiplano inhabited by Rwandan herdsmen.

Ngoja, André: Congolese fighter operating in Kabambare area.

Njenje: Cuban sergeant, appointed in closing stages as head of lakeside base.

Nne: Cuban lieutenant, killed in action at Front de Force.

Nor-Katanga: Province of Congo to south of our front.

Nyangi: Village near Front de Force; scene of enemy advance.

Nyerere, Julius: President of Tanzania.

Olenga: Congolese general; head of Stanleyville front.

Otto: Cuban corporal, retired sick before end of campaign.

Pascasa: Congolese colonel at Mulele's front; died in Cairo during a dispute between revolutionaries.

pombe: Fermented spirit distilled from manioc and maize.

Pombo: Cuban lieutenant; head of my group of adjutants.

Rabanini: Cuban soldier.

Rafael: Our delegate in Tanzania.

Rebocate: Cuban lieutenant.

Rivalta, Pablo: Our ambassador in Tanzania.

Ruandasi: Locality on shores of Lake Tanganyika, four kilometres from Kibamba.

Saba: Cuban soldier.

Salumu: Congolese captain; in charge of defence of Kasima area in final days.

Sele: Village approximately 15 kilometres south of Kibamba, from which we departed on our return.

Siki: Cuban comandante, member of Central Committee of Communist Party of Cuba; performed functions of chief of general staff (Óscar Fernández Mell).

simba: "Lion" in Swahili; title given to fighters in Congolese Liberation Army.

Singida: Cuban sergeant.

Sita: Cuban soldier.

Sitaini: Cuban soldier; withdrew on health grounds.

Sitini: Cuban sergeant.

Soumaliot, Gaston: President of Supreme Council of the Revolution.

Sultán: Cuban soldier.

Tano: Cuban soldier.

Tatu: "Three" in Swahili; my name in Congo.

Tembo: "Elephant", Swahili name of Emilio Aragonés, member of Central Committee of Communist Party of Cuba.

Thelathini: Cuban sergeant, killed in action at Front de Force.

Tom: Cuban soldier; political commissar of the troops until departure from Karim.

Tremendo Punto ["Top Guy"]: Nickname of Chamaleso, member of Masengo's general staff in final stages, previously delegate in Tanzania.

Tuma: Cuban lieutenant, head of transmissions unit.

Tumaini: Cuban sergeant; my adjutant.

Uta: Cuban captain.

Uvira: Village at extreme north of Lake Tanganyika and the northern limit of our front.

Zakarias: Rwandan captain who led troops of that nationality during absence of Commander Mundandi.

Ziwa: Cuban lieutenant, second-in-command of mixed First Company.

zombe: Congolese dish made from manioc leaves.

PREFACE

This is the history of a failure. It descends into anecdotal detail, as one would expect in episodes from a war, but this is blended with reflections and critical analysis. For in my view, any importance the story might have lies in the fact that it allows the experiences to be extracted for the use of other revolutionary movements. Victory is a great source of positive experiences, but so is defeat, especially if the unusual circumstances surrounding the incident are taken into account: the actors and informants are foreigners who went to risk their lives in an unknown land where people spoke a different language and were linked to them only by ties of proletarian internationalism, so that a method not practised in modern wars of liberation was thereby inaugurated.

The narrative closes with an epilogue which poses some questions about the struggle in Africa and, more generally, the national liberation struggle against the neo-colonialism that is the most redoubtable form of imperialism – most redoubtable because of the disguises and deceits that it involves, and the long experience that the imperialist powers have in this type of exploitation.

These notes will be published some time after they were dictated, and it may be that the author will no longer be able to take responsibility for what is said in them. Time will have smoothed many rough edges and, if its publication has any importance, the editors will be able to make the corrections they deem necessary (with appropriate indications) to explain the events or people's views in the light of the passage of time.

More correctly, this is the history of a decomposition. When we arrived

1

on Congolese soil, the revolution was in a period of reflux; then a number of incidents occurred which brought about its final regression, at this time and place at least, in the immense field of struggle that is the Congo. The most interesting aspect here is not the story of the decomposition of the Congolese revolution, whose causes and key features are too profound to be all encompassed from my particular vantage point, but rather the decomposition of our own fighting morale, since the experience we inaugurated should not go to waste and the initiative of the International Proletarian Army should not die at the first failure. It is essential to analyse in depth the problems that are posed, and to find a solution to them. A good battlefield instructor does more for the revolution than one who teaches a large number of raw recruits in a context of peace, but the characteristics of this instructor who fires the training of the future technical cadres of the revolution should be carefully studied.

The idea that guided us was to ensure that men experienced in liberation battles (and subsequently in the struggle with reactionary forces) fought alongside men without experience, and thereby to bring about what we called the "Cubanization" of the Congolese. It will be seen that the effect was the exact opposite, in that a "Congolization" of the Cubans took place over a period of time. In speaking of Congolization, we had in mind the series of habits and attitudes to the revolution that characterized the Congolese soldier at those moments of the struggle. This does not imply any derogatory view about the Congolese people, but it does about the soldiers at that time. In the course of the story, an attempt will be made to explain why those fighters had such negative traits.

As a general norm, one that I have always followed, nothing but the truth will be told in these pages – or at least my interpretation of the facts – although this may be confronted with other subjective evaluations or with factual corrections, should any errors have crept into my account.

At some moments when the truth would be indiscreet or inadvisable to relate, a particular reference has been omitted. For there are certain things that the enemy should not know, and some of the problems posed may be of help to friends in a possible reorganization of the struggle in the Congo (or in a launching of the struggle in another country in Africa or elsewhere whose problems are similar). Among the omitted references are our ways and means of reaching Tanzania, our springboard into the setting of this story.

The names given for the Congolese are their real ones, but nearly all men of our own contingent are mentioned by the names given to them in Swahili when they first arrived in the Congo; the true names of the comrades who took part will feature in an appendix, if the editors consider this useful. Lastly, it should be said that, in keeping to the strict truth and the importance it may have for future liberation movements, we have emphasized various cases of weakness on the part of individuals or groups of men, as well as the general demoralization that eventually came over us. But this does not in any way detract from the heroism of the gestures, while the heroic nature of the Cuban involvement derives from the general attitude of our government and the people of Cuba. Our country, the only socialist bastion at the gates of Yankee imperialism, sends its soldiers to fight and die in a foreign land, on a distant continent, and assumes full public responsibility for its actions. This challenge, this clear position with regard to the great contemporary issue of relentless struggle against Yankee imperialism, defines the heroic significance of our participation in the struggle of the Congo.

In this can be seen the readiness of a people and its leaders not only to defend themselves, but to attack. For, in relation to Yankee imperialism, it is not enough to be resolute in defence. It has to be attacked in its bases of support, in the colonial and neo-colonial lands that serve as the underpinning of its world domination.

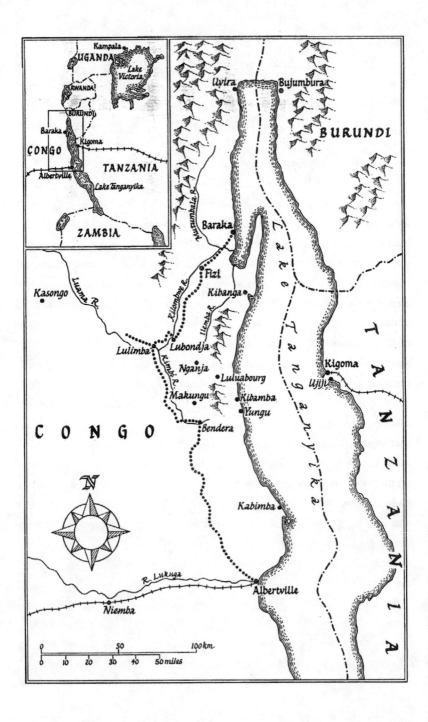

FIRST ACT

In a story of this kind, it is difficult to locate the first act. For narrative convenience, I shall take this to be a trip I made in Africa which gave me the opportunity to rub shoulders with many leaders of the various Liberation Movements. Particularly instructive was my visit to Dar es Salaam, where a considerable number of Freedom Fighters had taken up residence. Most of them lived comfortably in hotels and had made a veritable profession out of their situation, sometimes lucrative and nearly always agreeable. This was the setting for the interviews, in which they generally asked for military training in Cuba and financial assistance. It was nearly everyone's leitmotif.

I also got to know the Congolese fighters. From our first meeting with them, we could clearly see the large number of tendencies and opinions that introduced some variety into this group of revolutionary leaders. I made contact with Kabila and his staff; he made an excellent impression on me. He said he had come from the interior of the country. It appears he had come only from Kigoma, a small Tanzanian town on Lake Tanganyika and one of the main scenes in this story, which served as a point of embarkation for the Congo and also as a pleasant place for the revolutionaries to take shelter when they tired of life's trials in the mountains across the strip of water.

Kabila's presentation was clear, specific and resolute; he gave some signs of his opposition to Gbenye and Kanza and his broad lack of agreement with Soumaliot. Kabila's argument was that there could be no talk of a Congolese government because Mulele, the initiator of the struggle, had not been consulted, and so the president could claim to be head of government only of North-East Congo. This also meant that Kabila's own zone in the South-East, which he led as vice-chairman of the Party, lay outside Gbenye's sphere of influence.

Kabila realized perfectly well that the main enemy was North American imperialism, and he declared his readiness to carry the fight against it through to the end. As I said, his statements and his note of confidence made a very good impression on me.

Another day, we spoke with Soumaliot. He is a different kind of man, much less developed politically and much older. He hardly had the basic instinct to keep quiet or to speak very little using vague phrases, so that he seemed to express great subtlety of thought but, however much he tried, he was unable to give the impression of a real popular leader. He explained what he has since made public: his involvement as defence minister in the Gbenye government, how Gbenye's action took them by surprise, and so on. He also clearly stated his opposition to Gbenye and, above all, Kanza. I did not personally meet these last two, except for a quick handshake with Kanza when we met at an airport.

We talked at length with Kabila about what our government considered a strategic flaw on the part of some African friends: namely, that, in the face of open aggression by the imperialist powers, they thought the right slogan must be: "The Congo problem is an African problem", and acted accordingly. Our view was that the Congo problem was a world problem, and Kabila agreed. On behalf of the government, I offered him some 30 instructors and whatever weapons we might have, and he was delighted to accept. He recommended that both should be delivered urgently, as did Soumaliot in another conversation – the latter pointing out that it would be a good idea if the instructors were blacks.

I decided to sound out the other Freedom Fighters, thinking that I could do this by having a friendly chat with them at separate meetings. But because of a mistake by the embassy staff, there was a "tumultuous" meeting attended by 50 or more people, representing Movements from ten or more countries, each divided into two or more tendencies. I gave them a speech of encouragement and analysed the requests they had nearly all made for financial assistance and personnel training. I explained the cost of training a man in Cuba, the investment of money and time that it required, and the uncertainty that it would result in useful fighters for the Movement.

I gave an account of our experience in the Sierra Maestra, where we obtained roughly one soldier for every five recruits, and a single good one for every five soldiers. I put the case as forcefully as I could to the exasperated Freedom Fighters that most of the money invested in training would not be well spent; that a soldier, especially a revolutionary soldier, cannot be formed in an academy but only in warfare. He may be able to get a diploma from some college or other, but his real graduation – as is the case with any professional – takes place in the practice of his profession, in the way he reacts to enemy fire, to suffering, defeat, relentless pursuit, unfavourable situations. You can never predict from what someone says, or from his previous history, how he will react when faced with all these ups and downs of struggle in the people's war. I therefore suggested that training should take place not in our faraway Cuba but in the nearby Congo, where the struggle was not against some puppet like Tshombe but against North American imperialism, which, in its neo-colonial form, was threatening the newly acquired independence of nearly every African people or helping to keep the colonies in subjection. I spoke to them of the fundamental importance which the Congo liberation struggle had in our eyes. Victory would be continental in its reach and its consequences, and so would defeat.

The reaction was worse than cool. Although most refrained from any kind of comment, some asked to speak and took me violently to task for the advice I had given. They argued that their respective peoples, who had been abused and degraded by imperialism, would protest if any casualties were suffered not as a result of oppression in their own land, but from a war to liberate another country. I tried to show them that we were talking not of a struggle within fixed frontiers, but of a war against the common enemy, present as much in Mozambique as in Malawi, Rhodesia or South Africa, the Congo or Angola. No one saw it like that.

7

The farewells were cool and polite, and we were left with the clear sense that Africa has a long way to go before it reaches real revolutionary maturity. But we had also had the joy of meeting people prepared to carry the struggle through to the end. From that moment, we set ourselves the task of selecting a group of black Cubans and sending them, naturally as volunteers, to reinforce the struggle in the Congo.

SECOND ACT

The second act opens in the Congo and includes a number of episodes which, for the time being, still cannot be described in detail: my appointment at the head of the Cuban forces, even though I am white; the selection of future combatants; the organization of my secret departure, the limited possibility for leave-taking, the explanatory letters, the whole series of concealed manoeuvres that it would be dangerous even today to put on paper, and which can anyway be clarified at a later date.

After the hectic round of bittersweet farewells, which in the best of scenarios would be for a long time, the last step was the clandestine journey itself. That, too, it would be unwise to relate.

I was leaving behind nearly eleven years of work alongside Fidel for the Cuban Revolution, and a happy home, if that is the right word for the abode of a dedicated revolutionary and a lot of children who scarcely knew of my love for them. The cycle was beginning again.

One fine day I appeared in Dar es Salaam. No one recognized me; not even the ambassador, an old comrade-in-arms who had been with us in the initial landing and become a captain in the Rebel Army, was able to identify me.

We settled into a small farm, rented as temporary accommodation as we awaited the group of 30 men who were to accompany us. At that point there were three of us: Comandante Moja, a black man, who was the official head of our force; Mbili, a white comrade with great experience in these struggles; and Tatu – myself, pretending to be a doctor – who explained my colour by the fact that I spoke French and had guerrilla experience. Our names meant: one, two, three, in that order. To save ourselves headaches, we had decided to number ourselves by order of arrival, and to use the corresponding Swahili word as our pseudonym.

I had not informed any Congolese of my decision to fight in their country, nor did I now of my presence there. I had not mentioned it in my first conversation with Kabila, because I had not yet made up my mind; and once the plan had been approved, it would have been dangerous to reveal it until my journey through a lot of hostile territory had been completed. I therefore decided to present my arrival as a *fait accompli* and to go on from there according to how they reacted. I was not unaware that a negative response would put me in a tricky position (since I could no longer turn back), but I also reckoned that it would be difficult for them to refuse me. I was operating a kind of blackmail with my physical presence. An unexpected problem arose, however. Kabila was in Cairo with all the members of the Revolutionary Government, discussing aspects of combat unity and the new constitution of the revolutionary organization. His deputies, Masengo and Mitoudidi, were there with him. The only man left to whom authority had been delegated was Chamaleso, later to acquire the Cuban nickname "Tremendo Punto". Chamaleso accepted on his own responsibility the 30 instructors whom we initially offered, but when we told him that we had some 130 men, all black, ready to begin the struggle, he accepted this too on his own responsibility. This slightly changed the first part of our strategy, because we had thought we would be operating on the basis of 30 Cubans accepted as instructors.

A delegation set off for Cairo to tell Kabila and his comrades that the Cubans had arrived (but not that I was there), while we waited for the first of our contingents.

Our most pressing task was to find a speedboat with good engines, so that we would be able to cross in relative safety the 70 kilometres that was the width of Lake Tanganyika at that point. One of our fine experts had arrived in advance, to take charge both of buying launches and of exploring the way across the lake.

After a wait of several days in Dar es Salaam – a wait which, though short, made me anxious because I wanted to be inside the Congo as soon as possible – the first group of Cubans arrived at night on 20 April. Fourteen of us then set off, leaving behind four new arrivals for whom equipment had not yet been purchased. We were accompanied by two drivers, the Congolese Representative (Chamaleso), and someone from the Tanzanian police to clear up any problems en route.

Right from the start, we came face to face with a reality that would pursue us through the struggle: the lack of organization. This worried me because our passage must have been detected by Imperialism (which has power over all the airline companies and airports in the region), apart from the fact that the purchase of unusual quantities of backpacks, nylon sheeting, knives, blankets, etc. must have attracted attention in Dar es Salaam.

Not only was the Congolese organization bad; ours was too. We had not thoroughly prepared for the task of equipping a company, and had obtained only rifles and ammunition for the soldiers (all armed with Belgian FALs).

Kabila was expected to be two more weeks in Cairo, so that, unable to discuss with him my own involvement, I had to press on incognito and even to refrain from announcing myself to the Tanzanian government and requesting its acquiescence. To be honest, these problems did not bother me all that much, because I was eager to play a role in the Congo struggle and I feared that my offer might arouse excessively sharp reactions, that the Congolese – or the friendly government itself – might ask me not to enter the fray.

On the night of 22 April we reached Kigoma after a tiring journey, but the launches were not ready and we had to wait there all the next day for a crossing. The regional commissioner, who received us and put us up, immediately told me of the Congolese complaints. Unfortunately, everything indicated that many of his judgements were correct: the commanders in the area, who had received our first exploratory delegation, were now in Kigoma; and we could tell that they were granting passes for men to go there from the front. That little town was a haven where the luckiest ones could go and live away from the hazards of the struggle. The nefarious influence of Kigoma – its brothels, its alcohol, and especially its assurance of refuge – would never be sufficiently understood by the Revolutionary Command.

Eventually, on 24 April at dawn, we landed on Congolese soil and met a surprised group of well-armed infantry, who solemnly formed up into a little guard of honour. We were shown into a hut that had been specially vacated for us.

Our original information, obtained (I know not how) by our inspection agents, had been that on the Congolese side a plain stretched 16 kilometres inland to the mountains. In reality, however, the lake is a kind of ravine and the mountains, both at Kigoma and on the other side, begin right at the water's edge. At the headquarters location known as Kibamba, a difficult climb began ten paces or so from our point of disembarkation, all the more difficult given our lack of previous training.

FIRST IMPRESSIONS

Upon arrival, after a brief nap on the floor of the hut among backpacks and assorted tackle, we began to strike up an acquaintance with Congolese reality. We immediately noticed a clear distinction: alongside people with very little training (mostly peasants), there were others with greater culture, different clothes and a better knowledge of French. The distance between the two groups could hardly have been greater.

The first people I got to know were Emmanuel Kasabuvabu and Kiwe, who presented themselves as officers on the general staff: the former in charge of supplies and munitions, the latter of intelligence. Both were talkative and expressive young men, and what they said and what they held back soon gave you an idea of the divisions inside the Congo. Later, Tremendo Punto invited me along to a small meeting, which was attended not by those comrades but by another group comprising the Base Commander and several brigade leaders: there was the head of the First Brigade, Colonel Bidalila, who commanded the Uvira front;[1] the Second Brigade, under the command of Major-General Moulane, was represented by Lieutenant-Colonel Lambert; and André Ngoja, who was fighting in the Kabambare area, represented what seemed likely, from people's remarks, to become another brigade in the future. Tremendo Punto excitedly proposed that Moja, the official head of our forces, should take part in all meetings and decisions of the general staff, together with another Cuban chosen by himself. I watched the others' faces and did not notice any approval of

1 According to the latest information, he has been promoted general.

the suggestion; Tremendo Punto did not seem all that popular among the brigade leaders.

The reason for the hostility among the groups was that, one way or another, some men did spend a certain amount of time at the front, whereas others merely travelled back and forth between the Congo base and Kigoma, always looking for something not at hand. The case of Tremendo Punto was graver in the fighters' eyes, because, being the representative in Dar es Salaam, he came only occasionally to the Congo.

We chatted on amicably without mentioning the proposal, and I found out a number of things that I had not known before. Lieutenant-Colonel Lambert explained with a friendly, festive air that aeroplanes had no importance for them, because they had the *dawa* medicine that makes you invulnerable to gunfire.

"They've hit me a number of times, but the bullets fell limply to the ground."

He said this with a smile on his face, and I felt obliged to salute the joke as a sign of the little importance they attached to enemy weapons. Gradually I realized that it was more serious, that the magical protector was supposed to be one of the great weapons with which they would triumph over the Congolese Army.

This *dawa*, which did quite a lot of damage to military preparations, operates according to the following principle. A liquid in which herb juices and other magical substances have been dissolved is thrown over the fighter, and certain occult signs – nearly always including a coal mark on the forehead – are administered to him. This protects him against all kinds of weapons (although the enemy too relies upon magic), but he must not lay hands on anything that does not belong to him, or touch a woman, or feel fear, on pain of losing the protection. The answer to any transgression is very simple: a man dead = a man who took fright, stole or slept with a woman; a man wounded = a man who was afraid. Since fear accompanies wartime operations, fighters found it quite natural to attribute wounds to faintheartedness – that is, to lack of belief. And the dead do not speak; all three faults can be ascribed to them.

The belief is so strong that no one goes into battle without having the *dawa* performed. I was constantly afraid that this superstition would rebound against us, that we would be blamed for any military disaster involving many deaths. I tried several times to have a talk about the *dawa* with someone in a position of responsibility, so that an effort could be started to win people away from it – but it was impossible. The *dawa* is treated as an article of faith. The most politically advanced say that it is a natural, material force, and that they, as dialectical materialists, recognize its power and the secrets held by the medicine men of the jungle.

After the talk with the brigade leaders, I met Tremendo Punto alone and explained who I was. He was devastated. He kept talking of an "international scandal" and insisting that "no one must find out, please, no one must find out". It had come as a bolt from the blue and I was fearful of the consequences, but my identity could not be hushed up any longer if we wanted to make use of the influence I was able to exert.

That same night, Tremendo Punto set off to inform Kabila of my presence in the Congo; the Cuban officials who had been with us on the crossing and the naval technician left together with him. The technician had the task of sending two fitters – by return mail, as it were – since one of the weak points we had spotted was the complete lack of maintenance of the various engines and boats assigned to the crossing of the lake.

The next day, I asked for us to be sent to the permanent camp, a base five kilometres from the general staff, at the top of the mountains that rose (as I said before) from the shore of the lake. That is when the delays began. The Commander had gone to Kigoma to sort out some business, and we had to wait for him to return. Meanwhile, a rather arbitrary training programme was being discussed, and I came up with an alternative position: namely, to divide 100 men into groups no larger than 20, and to give them all some notion of infantry activity, with some specialization in weapons, engineering (mainly trench-digging), communications and reconnaissance, in accordance with our capacities and the means at our disposal. The programme would last four to five weeks, and the group would be sent to carry out operations under the command of Mbili; it would then return to base, where a selection would be made of those who had proved their worth. In the meantime, the second company would be in training, so that it in turn could go to the front when the first one returned. This, I thought, would allow the necessary selection to be made, at the same time as the men were being trained. I explained once more that, given the form of recruitment, only 20 would be left as possible soldiers out of the original 100, and only two or three of them as future cadre commanders (in the sense of being capable of leading an armed unit into combat).

As usual, we received an evasive response: they asked me to put my proposal in writing. This was done, but I never found out what became of the paper. We kept insisting that we should move up and start work at the Upper Base. We had counted on losing a week there to get things in shape for us to work at a certain rhythm, and now we were waiting just for the simple problem of our transfer to be resolved. We could not go up to the base, because the Commander had not arrived; or we had to wait because they were "having a meeting". One day after another passed like this. When I raised the matter again (as I did with truly irritating tenacity), a new pretext always arose. Even today, I do not know what to make of this. Perhaps it was true that they did not want to start preparatory work out of regard for the relevant authority, in this case the Base Commander.

One day I ordered Moja to go with some men to the Upper Base, on the pretext of training them for a march. He did this and the group returned at night, weary, soaked and chilled to the bone. It was a very cold and wet place, with constant mist and persistent rain; the people there said they were making a hut for us, which would take another few days. With patience on both sides, I set forth the various arguments why we should go up to the base: we could help build the shelter in a spirit of sacrifice, so that we would not be a burden, etc. etc.; and they sought new excuses to delay matters.

This enforced break saw the beginning of delightful talks with Comrade Kiwe, the head of intelligence. He is a tireless conversationalist, who speaks French at almost supersonic speed. In our various conversations, he made a daily analysis for me of important figures in the Congolese revolution. One of the first to be lashed by his tongue was Olenga, a general in the Stanleyville area and in Sudan. According to Kiwe, Olenga was little more than an ordinary soldier, perhaps a lieutenant, who had been charged by Bidalila to make some incursions in the direction of Stanleyville and then return. But instead of doing this, Olenga started his own operations during those easy moments of revolutionary flux, and raised himself by one rank whenever he captured a village. By the time he reached Stanleyville he was a general. The conquests of the Liberation Army stopped there – which was something of a solution, because if they had continued, all the grades known to the military world would not have sufficed to reward Comrade Olenga.

For Kiwe, the true military leader was Colonel Pascasa (who later died in a fight among the Congolese in Cairo); he was the man with real military knowledge and revolutionary attitude, and the representative of Mulele.

On another day, Kiwe very subtly broached his criticisms of Gbenye, remarking, as if in passing, that his attitude had been unclear at the beginning, that now, sure, he was president and a revolutionary, but there were more revolutionary ones, and so on. As the days went by and we got to know each other better, Kiwe's picture of Gbenye became that of a man more suited to lead a gang of robbers than a revolutionary movement. I do not have a record of all of Kiwe's assertions, but some are very well known: for example, what he said about the history of his involvement in the arrest of Gizenga, when he was interior minister in the Adoula government. Others are less well known, but if they are true, they cast a murky light on such matters as the attempts on Mitoudidi's life and connections with the Yankee embassy in Kenya.

On another occasion, the victim of Kiwe's tongue was Gizenga – characterized as a revolutionary, but a left-wing opportunist – who wanted to do everything by the political road, who thought a revolution could be made with the Army, and who, when given money to organize the revolutionary forces in Leopoldville, had even used it to form a political party.

The chats with Kiwe gave me an idea of what certain figures were like, but mainly highlighted the lack of solidity in this group of revolutionaries, or malcontents, who constituted the general staff of the Congolese revolution.

And the days passed. The lake was crossed by messengers with a fabulous capacity to distort any news, or by holidaymakers going off to Kigoma on some leave or other.

In my capacity as a doctor (actually an epidemiologist – which, if this illustrious branch of the Aesculapian tree will forgive me for saying so, gave me the right to know nothing about medicine), I worked for a few days with Kumi at the clinic and noticed various alarming facts. The first of these was the high number of cases of venereal disease, often caused by infection in Kigoma. What concerned me at that moment was not the state of health of the population or of the Kigoma prostitutes, but the fact that the opportunities for crossing the lake meant that so many fighters could be infected. Other questions also occurred to us. Who paid those women? With what money? How were the revolution's funds being spent?

From the first few days of our stay, we also had a chance to see some cases of alcohol poisoning caused by the famous *pombe*. This is a spirit distilled from the juice of maize and manioc flour, which is not high in alcohol yet has terrible effects. Presumably these arise not so much from the alcoholization *per se*, as from the amount of impurities, given the rudimentary methods of production. There were days when *pombe* washed over the camp, leaving behind a trail of brawling, poisoning, indiscipline, and so on.

The clinic began to be visited by peasants from the surrounding area, who had heard on Radio Bemba that some doctors were nearby. Our supply of medicines was poor, but a Soviet medical consignment came to our rescue. It had been chosen, however, not with the civilian population in mind, as was natural, but to meet the needs of an army in the field – and even then, it did not contain a complete range of requirements. Such imbalances were to be a constant feature of our time in the Congo. Highly valuable shipments of weapons and equipment always turned out to be incomplete; supplies from Kigoma inevitably featured guns and machine-guns without ammunition or essential components; rifles might arrive with the wrong ammunition, or mines without detonators.

In my view, although I have not been able to find an actual explanation, all these failures were due to the disorganized state of the Congolese Liberation Army, and to the shortage of cadres capable of minimally assessing equipment as it arrived.

The same happened with medical supplies, with the additional factor that they were stored in one big jumble in La Playa, where the reserves of food and weaponry also jostled one another in fraternal chaos. I tried several times to gain permission for us to organize the stores, and I suggested that some types of ammunition – such as bazooka or mortar shells – should be moved away from there. But nothing happened until much later.

Every day, contradictory news reached us from Kigoma. Occasionally, by dint of being repeated, some item eventually proved true: for example, that there was a group of Cubans waiting for a boat, an engine or something to get through; that Mitoudidi would cross over tomorrow or the day after, and then – when the day after tomorrow arrived – that he would be crossing in another day's time.

During this time, news also arrived from the Conference in Cairo, via Emmanuel on one of his frequent trips to Kigoma and back. The outcome had been a complete triumph for the revolutionary line. Kabila would stay for a while to make sure that the agreement was implemented, then he would go somewhere else to have an operation on a cyst (not very serious but a nuisance), and this would delay him a little.

We had to do something to avoid complete idleness. We organized lessons in French and Swahili, as well as classes in general culture, which were quite badly needed by our troops. Given the nature of the classes (and of the teachers), this could not add a lot to the comrades' cultural heritage, but it did have the important function of using up time. Our morale remained high, even though the comrades were starting to murmur that they watched the days pass to no useful purpose. Also hovering over us was the spectre

19

of malaria and the other tropical fevers that struck nearly everyone in one form or another; these often responded to special drugs, but left behind most troublesome after-effects, such as general debility or lack of appetite, which added to the pessimism creeping into the men's view of things]

As the days went by, the picture of organizational chaos became more evident. I myself took part in the distribution of Soviet medical supplies, and it resembled a Gypsy fair; each representative of the armed groups produced figures, and cited facts and reasons why he should have access to a greater quantity of medicine. There were several clashes as I tried to stop some medicine or special equipment being pointlessly carted off to the front lines, but everyone wanted to have something of everything. They started to bandy fantastic totals for the number of men in their group: one declared 4,000, another 2,000, and so on. These were inventions, which hardly had an objective basis even in the number of peasants living close to the Army and potentially recruitable to it. The real number of soldiers or armed men in the base camps was greatly inferior to such figures.

During these days, the various fronts were almost completely passive, and if people with gunshot wounds were nevertheless expected, it would be as a result of accidents. Since scarcely anyone had the faintest idea about guns, they tended to go off when they were played with or treated without care.

On 8 May, 18 Cubans headed by Aly finally reached us. Mitoudidi, the head of the general staff, arrived at the same time, but he had to return at once to Kigoma to search for guns and ammunition. We had a friendly conversation, and he left me with an agreeable impression of reliability, seriousness and organizational spirit. Kabila sent word that he had many reservations about my identity, and so I remained incognito as I went about my apparent tasks as doctor and translator.

We agreed with Mitoudidi that the transfer to Upper Base would take place the next day. This was done, but we left below Moja, Nane and Tano, who had gone down with fever, and the doctor Kumi in attendance at the infirmary. I was sent to the base as doctor and translator. There were barely

20 Congolese there, looking bored, lonely and ill at ease. I began the fight to break down this sluggishness; we began classes in Swahili (given by the political commissar at the base) and in French (assigned to another comrade there). In addition, we started building shelters against the intense cold. We were at 1,700 metres above sea level and 1,000 metres above the level of the lake, in an area where trade winds from the Indian Ocean condense and give rise to continual rainfall. We quickly set about the task of putting up some constructions, and fires were soon blazing to keep the nocturnal cold at bay.

THE FIRST MONTH

Some four hours from Upper Base on foot (the only possible means of locomotion), a group of hamlets each numbering no more than ten huts lie scattered over a huge area of natural pasture. The cluster of settlements, known by the general name Nganja, is inhabited by a tribe that originally came from Rwanda, and which, despite living in the Congo for several generations, retains the ineradicable spirit of its homeland. Its life is pastoral, though not nomadic, with cattle as the core that provides it with both food and money. Many a time we heard of the troubles of a Rwandan soldier, who did not have the number of cows required by the father of the woman of his dreams. For women too are bought, and to have more than one is a sign of economic power – quite apart from the fact that it is they who do the work in agriculture and in the home.

In the course of the war, this proximity enabled us from time to time to avail ourselves of the precious beef that is a cure – almost – even for homesickness.

The Rwandans and the various Congolese tribes treat each other as enemies, and the frontiers between ethnic groups are clearly defined. This makes it very difficult to carry out political work that aims towards regional union – a phenomenon repeated the length and breadth of Congolese territory.

In my first few days at Upper Base, I paid my tribute to the climate of the Congo by going down with quite a high, though short-lived, fever. Our doctor, Kumi, came up from the lake to visit me, but I sent him back as he was needed in the clinic and I was already feeling better. On the third or fourth day they brought in a man wounded in some skirmish at Front de Force; he had gone six days without medical attention, with one arm that had been fractured by a bullet and was now suppurating profusely. I got up to attend to him beneath a cold drizzle, and it may have been this that caused my relapse with a very high fever and delirium, and brought Kumi up to the base for a second time. For him it was like climbing Mount Everest, and according to eye-witnesses – because I was in no condition to appreciate the details – his condition after the long and steep ascent seemed worse than that of the patient.

The relapse did not last long either – some five days in total – but the effects may be judged by the extraordinary depression that overcame me and even took away the desire for food. During the first month, no fewer than a dozen comrades paid for their apprenticeship in this hostile land with raging fevers whose after-effects were equally trying.

Our first formal order, issued by Mitoudidi newly back from Kigoma, is to prepare for a two-pronged attack on Albertville in which we, presumably, will play a prominent role. The order is absurd; there have been no preparatory actions, we number only 30, and ten of these are sick or convalescing. But I explain the instructions to the men and tell them they should be prepared to go into battle, although I shall try to change or at least postpone the plans.

On 22 May we heard one of the many crazy reports that worried us so much: "A Cuban minister is coming across the hills; a whole load more Cubans are on their way." This was so irrational that no one could believe it, but I went down a few stretches of mountainside to get some exercise and, to my great surprise, came across Osmany Cienfuegos. After the embraces came the explanations. He had come to talk to people in the Tanzanian government and, in passing, had asked permission to pay a visit to the comrades in the Congo. He had been refused as a matter of principle, on the grounds that other Cuban ministers would then want to visit the centre of operations, but in the end the line had softened and here he was. I also discovered that my presence was not yet known to the Tanzanian government.

With Osmany came 17 of the 34 men who had arrived in Kigoma. In general, the news he brought was very good, but for me personally it included the saddest news of the whole war: telephone callers from Buenos Aires had revealed that my mother was very ill, in a tone that led one to suppose that they were simply paving the way for a further announcement. Osmany had not managed to get any more information. I had to spend a month in uncertainty, awaiting the outcome of something that was already suspected, but in the hope that there had been a mistake – until, finally, confirmation of my mother's death arrived. She had wanted to see me shortly before my departure, probably because she was already feeling ill, but the advanced state of the preparations for my trip had already made this impossible. Nor had she known of a farewell letter intended for her and my father that I left in Havana; it would only be delivered in October, when my departure was made public.

Mitoudidi came to Upper Base, and we discussed the various aspects of the military situation. He kept wanting to draw up a grand strategic plan for the capture of Albertville, but I managed to convince him that at this stage it was too ambitious, and therefore hazardous, to get involved with Albertville; that it was more important to acquire real knowledge of the whole zone of operations and of the means at our disposal, since at the general staff headquarters there was no clear picture of what was happening at each of the separate fronts. Everything depended on intelligence from the field officers, but they, in order to get something they wanted, inflated their figures, and, in order to escape blame, attributed disasters to a lack of arms or ammunition. We resolved by common agreement to send delegations to various localities, so that we could be clear about the respective positions of our men and the enemy, as well as about the relationship of forces.

Four groups were charged with the relevant investigations: Aly, with three other comrades, would go to the Kabimba area; Nne, with two others, to Front de Force; Moja and Paulu to the area of Baraka, Fizi and Lulimba; Mitoudidi and myself to Uvira. The last of these trips did not happen in the end: first there were the usual delays due to lack of boats, lack of petrol and unforeseen circumstances; then Kabila announced his imminent arrival, and I had to wait for him day after day – in vain.

The first reports of the inspections in Kabimba and Front de Force showed that there existed real armed forces there, seemingly with a will to fight, though with no training or discipline in the case of Kabimba, and only a certain amount in the case of Front de Force (where the same disorganization prevailed, moreover, in weapons maintenance, observation of the enemy, political work, and so on).

In an analysis carried out at the end of May, roughly a month after the first of us arrived on 24 April, I noted the following in my field diary:

> Until Mitoudidi's arrival it was time wasted; since then, we have been able to do reconnaissance and have found a receptive attitude to our suggestions. Tomorrow, serious training may begin with a group of men that have been promised me. It is almost certain that, in the course of June, we shall be able to show something for our efforts by joining combat for the first time.
>
> The main defect of the Congolese is that they do not know how to shoot, so ammunition has been wasted because it was necessary to begin with that. The discipline here is very slack, but one has the feeling that things change at the front, where the men are subject to acceptable discipline even if there is always a marked lack of organization.
>
> The most important tasks are: teaching them to shoot and to fight by laying ambushes (real guerrilla warfare), and certain military norms of organization that allow one to concentrate all one's strength at a point under attack.

Today we can say that the apparently greater discipline at the front was an illusion, and that the three things we had to establish as a priority – shooting, ambush technique, and concentration of forces for major attacks – were never developed in the Congo.

The groupings had a tribal character and adopted a criterion of positional warfare: that is, the fighters occupied what they called barriers or barricades, which were generally located in well-chosen places from a tactical point of view, in very high hills to which access was difficult. But the men led a camp life, without carrying out any military operations or even undergoing training, confident in the enemy's inactivity and relying upon the peasants to keep them supplied. In fact, the peasants had to bring them food, and suffered frequent vexations and mistreatment at their hands. [The basic feature of the People's Liberation Army was that it was a parasitic army: it did not work, did not train, did not fight, and demanded provisions and labour from the population, sometimes with extreme harshness] The peasants were at the mercy of groups who came on leave from the camps to demand extra food, and who repeatedly ate their poultry and little luxury items they kept in reserve.

The soldier's staple food is *bukali*, which is made as follows. Manioc root is peeled and left to dry in the sun for a few days; then it is ground in a mortar exactly like those used for grinding coffee in our mountain regions; the resulting flour is sifted, boiled in water until it forms a paste, and then eaten. If the will is there, *bukali* provides you with the necessary carbohydrates, but what was eaten there was semi-raw, unsalted cassava; this was sometimes complemented with *zombe*, cassava leaves pounded and boiled, and seasoned with a little palm oil or the meat of some hunted animal. (There was quite a lot of game in that region, but the meat was eaten only on occasion, not regularly.) It cannot be said that the fighters were well fed; very little was caught in the lake. But one of their bad habits was that they were incapable of marching to the base to look for food. On their shoulders were only a rifle, a cartridge-belt and their personal effects, which generally did not go beyond a blanket.

After a while, when we had begun living communally with this original army, we learnt some exclamations typical of the way they saw the world. If someone was given something to carry, he said: "*Mimi hapana motocari*" – that is, "I'm not a truck." In some cases, when he was with Cubans, this would become: "*Mimi hapana cuban*" – "I'm not a Cuban." The food, as well as the weapons and ammunition for the front, had to be carried by the peasants. Clearly, an army of this kind can have a justification only if, like its enemy counterpart, it actually fights now and again. As we shall see, this requirement was not met either. As it did not change the existing order of things, the Congolese revolution was doomed to defeat by its own internal weaknesses.

A HOPE DIES

From a technical point of view, the days that followed were much like the previous ones. It was a distressing time, because we were beginning to hate the angle formed by the two hills that ended in the lake, affording a glimpse only of the stretch of water that they defined as the horizon.

Mitoudidi, despite his goodwill, did not find the formula that would have allowed us to get down to work. He was probably blocked by some specific order from Kabila, whose arrival he anxiously awaited, as did we all. Meanwhile the days passed, one after another, without any change for our expeditionary force.

Moja returned from his inspection trip to Baraka, Fizi and Lulimba. The impression he brought back was really disastrous. Although he had been received enthusiastically by the local population, and quite correctly by the leading comrades, a number of dangerous symptoms were evident. The first was the open hostility with which people spoke of Kabila and Masengo, as well as of Comrade Mitoudidi, more or less accusing them all of being not only strangers to the region but mere drifters who were never where the people needed them to be. There were quite a lot of armed men in the area, but they were weakened by abominable organization, the effects of which, one might say, were not just similar but even worse than in other cases we had encountered. The big shots spent the day drinking until they got into the most incredible state, without even bothering to conceal it from the population because they considered it the natural thing for "men" to do. Given the facilities at that time for the transport of essential materials across the lake, they had access to enough petrol to keep travelling back and forth from one end of their extensive sector to the other, though no one could think of any actual purpose that might be served by these trips.

The "barrier" opposite the settlement of Lulimba was situated at a distance of seven kilometres, in the highest part of the mountains. It was a long time since the revolutionary forces had come down to launch an attack, or even to carry out any reconnaissance; their only activity was to fire off a recoilless 75mm gun. Without knowing the rules of indirect fire (that the gun can be used to hit a direct target only up to a distance of 1.5 kilometres), and without knowing the enemy's exact position, they specialized in massive rocketry training with 75mm shells.

I brought all this to Mitoudidi's attention, and he said that the envoys' impressions were correct, that Moulane, a self-styled major-general in charge of the area, was an anarchist lacking all revolutionary consciousness who should be replaced. Mitoudidi had called him in for discussions, but he had refused to come – suspecting that he would be arrested.

Since nothing else could be done, we kept insisting on reconnaissance missions and again sent Inne and Nane, at the head of little groups, to inspect the Front de Force and Katenga zones that seemed to offer certain possibilities. Aly also set off on a mission, to reconnoitre the area around Kabimba and the road from Kabimba to Albertville, and to find some practicable route between Front de Force and Kabimba. But he found himself powerless in face of the obstacles put in his way by the head of this sector.

Each morning we were given the same old tune: Kabila has not arrived today, but certainly tomorrow, or the day after tomorrow . . .

Boats kept arriving with plenty of high-quality weapons; it was pitiful to see how they squandered the resources of friendly countries (mainly China and the Soviet Union), the efforts of Tanzania, and the lives of some fighters and civilians, all to so little effect.

Mitoudidi, now committed to organizing the base, took the difficult step of cracking down on the drinkers and thus entered into conflict with 90 or 95 per cent of the people there. He also froze the delivery of arms and ammunition and, among other things, demanded that those who employed heavy weapons should show proof of their knowledge before he gave them any more items – which at least ensured that nothing more would be distributed. But there was too much to be done and he was only one man; his assistants gave him very little help in this task.

We became quite friendly with one another. He said that my weakest point was my lack of direct contact with non-French-speaking combatants, and he sent one of his aides to teach me Swahili, so that I could communicate directly with the Congolese. Ernest Ilunga, who was supposed to initiate me into the mysteries of the language, was an intelligent young man. We began our classes with great enthusiasm, at the rate of three hours a day, but the truth is that I was the first to reduce this to one hour, not for lack of time – I had too much of that, unfortunately – but because my character is completely incompatible with the learning of other languages. There was another difficulty that I was unable to overcome during my period in the Congo: Swahili is a language with quite a rich and advanced grammar, but in this country people speak it as what they call their national language, alongside the mother tongue or dialect of their own tribe, so that Swahili has to some extent become the language of conquerors or a symbol of superior power. Nearly all the peasants use it as a second language, but the backwardness of the region means that what they actually speak is a highly simplified "basic Swahili". Moreover, they adapted very easily to our halfway language, because they found it easier to communicate in this way. Caught up as I was in these contradictions, I did not speak either grammatical Swahili or the version that is peculiar to this region of the Congo, throughout all the time I spent there.

During these days I also got to know Mundandi, the Rwandan commander at Front de Force. He had studied in China and gave quite a pleasant impression of being firm and serious, but in our first conversation he let out that he had caused 35 enemy casualties in one battle. I asked him how many weapons he had captured as a result of the 35 casualties. He answered "none", explaining that they had attacked with bazookas and that the enemy weapons had been blown into tiny fragments. My diplomatic qualities have never been very acute, and I told him quite simply that that was a lie. He then exonerated himself, on the grounds that he had not been present at the actual fighting but had been informed by his subordinates, and so on. There the matter rested – but since exaggeration is the norm in that region, to call a lie a lie is not the best way to establish friendly relations with anyone.

On 7 June I set out to return to Upper Base, having had a talk with Mitoudidi about the truth behind Kabila's *mañanas.*

He tacitly gave me to understand that he was not expecting Kabila to return in the near future, especially as Chou En-lai was visiting Dar es Salaam just then and it made sense for Kabila to go there to try to discuss certain requests with the Chinese leader.

As I was making the difficult climb back to Upper Base, a messenger caught up with us and said that Mitoudidi had just drowned. His body remained underwater for three days, before being discovered on the 10th, when the lake returned it to the surface. Thanks to the fact that two Cubans had been in the boat at the time of the accident, I was able to reach the following conclusion from a series of personal conversations and enquiries.

Mitoudidi had been on his way to Ruandasi, the place where he had been thinking of moving the general staff. It was barely three kilometres from Kabimba base, but he went by water because of the state of the road. A strong wind was blowing and there were large waves on the lake. All the signs are that he fell into the lake by accident. From that moment a series of strange events occurred, which one does not know whether to attribute to straightforward stupidity, to extraordinary superstition (the lake being inhabited by all manner of spirits), or to something more serious. The fact is that Mitoudidi, who could swim a little, managed to remove his boots and – according to various witnesses – called out for help for some ten to fifteen minutes. People threw themselves into the water to save him, and one of these, his orderly, also drowned; Commander François, who was accompanying him on the journey, also disappeared (I never found out whether he fell in at the same time or threw himself in to save Mitoudidi). When the accident happened, they stopped the outboard motor,

31

which made it impossible to manoeuvre the boat in any way. Then they started it up again, but it seems that some magical force prevented them from approaching the spot where Mitoudidi was floundering. In the end, while he continued to call for help, the boat headed for shore and the comrades saw him go under shortly afterwards.

The structure of human relations among the Congolese leaders is so complex that one does not know what to make of this. What is certain is that the man in charge of the boat at that time, who was also an army commander, was later sent to a different front – the explanation given to me being that the comrade had been involved in a number of incidents at the base.

Thus, a stupid accident took the life of the man who had begun to implant some organization amid the terrible chaos of Kabimba base. Mitoudidi had been young (hardly more than 30), and had served as a functionary with Lumumba and a fighter with Mulele. According to Mitoudidi himself, Mulele had sent him to this area at a time when no revolutionary organization was functioning there. In our frequent conversations, he talked about Mulele's diametrically opposed methods, and about the completely different character that the struggle had taken on in that other part of the Congo, although he never hinted at any criticism of Kabila or Masengo and he attributed all the disorder to the peculiarities of the region.

I do not know the reason – perhaps it had something to do with race or former reputation – but when Kabila arrived in the region, Mitoudidi's field officer became the head of his general staff. The truth was that the only person with authority had now disappeared in the lake. The next day, the news was already known in the surrounding area, and Kabila gave signs of life by sending me the following brief note:

I have just heard about the fate of Brother Mitu, and of other brothers. As you can see, I am deeply hurt by it. I am worried about your safety; I want to come straightaway. For us, this sad story is our destiny. All the comrades with whom you arrived should remain where they are until my return, unless they want to go to Kabimba or to see Mundandi in Bendera.

I trust in your steadfastness. We will speed everything up so that we can move base on a precise date.

During my absence, I shall be sorting out some matters with Comrade Muteba, and with Bulengai and Kasabi.

Friendly greetings,

Kabila

Comrade Muteba, who was deeply affected by Mitoudidi's death, came to see me to find out exactly what our views were about what had happened. It was probably for superstitious reasons that they were contemplating the move to a different base; but I did not want to raise any objections, because it seemed a very delicate issue and I thought it wiser to avoid giving a clear answer. We talked about the most important problems that had brought us to the Congo; we had been there nearly two months and still had done absolutely nothing. I mentioned the reports I wrote for Comrade Mitoudidi that had disappeared with him, and then he asked me to do a general report for him about the situation to send to Kabila. I took on this task and wrote what follows. (I should place it on record that this text is slightly different from the original, since at a particular moment my macaronic French forced me to look for the word I knew and thus sacrifice the one I really intended. The letter is addressed to Comrade Muteba and is confidential.)

General considerations: Given that my experience of the Congo is limited to a month and a half, I cannot venture many opinions. I consider that we face one main danger: North American imperialism.

It is hardly necessary to analyse why the North Americans are a specific danger. The Congolese revolution is at a stage of regrouping its forces, after the recent defeats it has suffered. If the Yankees have learnt the lessons of other revolutions, now is the moment they should choose to strike hard and take pre-emptive measures such as a neutralization of the lake: that is, to do everything

33

necessary to close our main route for supplies of all kinds. On the other hand, world events such as the struggle in Vietnam and the recent intervention at Santo Domingo are somewhat tying their hands. Time is thus an essential factor for the consolidation and development of the revolution, which can be achieved only through heavy blows against the enemy. Passivity is the beginning of defeat.

But our own lack of organization hinders us from mobilizing all our forces and attacking those of the enemy. This may be seen in a number of inter-linked aspects.

1. There is no Unified Central Command with real power over all the fronts, which would confer what is known in military language as a unity of doctrine (I refer specifically to this area, not to the Congo in general).
2. The general shortage of cadres with a sufficient level of culture and absolute loyalty to the revolutionary cause results in a proliferation of local chiefs, each with his own authority and both tactical and strategic freedom of action.
3. The dispersal of our heavy weapons through egalitarian distribution leaves the Command without reserves – quite apart from the poor use to which those weapons are put.
4. There is a lack of discipline in the military units, which have been infected by the prevailing localism and have had no prior training.
5. The command centres are incapable of coordinating the movements of units beyond a certain size.
6. There is a general lack of the minimum training necessary to handle firearms, a lack all the graver in the case of weapons requiring special combat preparation.

All this produces an incapacity to carry out significant tactical operations, and therefore strategic paralysis. They are evils that any revolution has to face, and there is no reason to alarm ourselves. It is only necessary to take systematic measures to rectify them.

Cuban involvement: Our black population suffered the worst exploitation and discrimination in Cuba. Its involvement in the struggle was very important, especially in the case of the Eastern peasantry, most of which was, however, illiterate.

As a result, there were very few blacks among our principal military figures or properly trained middle cadres. When we were asked to send black Cubans by preference, we looked to the best elements in the army who had some experience of combat. As we see it, then, our contingent has a very good fighting spirit and precise knowledge of tactics on the ground, but little academic preparation.

The foregoing is by way of introduction to our proposals for action. Given the special characteristics of the soldiers, our involvement should mainly be in combat tasks or other matters related to the direct struggle.

We could do this in two ways:

1. We could split our contingent among the various units at the front, as instructors in the handling of weapons or as fighters with Congolese forces.
2. We could fight in mixed units initially under Cuban command, which would carry out clearly defined tactical missions and expand their radius of operations through the development and training of Congolese command cadres. (Given the small size of our force, the number of such mixed units should be no higher than two.) A central training base would be maintained, with Cuban instructors insofar as they were needed.

We are inclined towards this second proposal, for both military and political reasons: military, because it would ensure that things were conducted in accordance with our conception of guerrilla struggle (which we think is correct); political, because successes of ours could dispel the atmosphere that builds up around foreign troops with different religious, cultural and other conceptions, and would enable us to control our own forces better. A greater degree of dispersal could lead to conflicts, because it would weaken the understanding of Congolese reality that our commanders think they are acquiring.

We could perform (necessary) complementary work, such as unit training programmes, help in forming a general staff (services and, above all, weaponry are weak areas), the organization of public safety or military health, or any other task that might be entrusted to us.

Our assessment of the military situation: There is persistent talk of the capture of Albertville. But we think that, at the present moment, there is a higher task facing our forces – for the following reasons.

1. We have not been capable of dislodging the enemy from enclaves within our natural system of defence (these mountains).
2. We do not have sufficient experience for such a large-scale initiative, which would require the mobilization of units of at least battalion strength and their synchronization through an operational high command.
3. We do not have enough military equipment for an action of this scale.

Albertville should fall as the result of gradual, tenacious action on our part – perhaps it would be more appropriate to speak of its being abandoned by the enemy. First, we must completely deflate the enemy's fighting morale (which is relatively high at present), by means of systematic attacks on his communications and reinforcements; then annihilate, or force the withdrawal of, enemy forces from Kabimba, Front de Force, Lulimba, and so on, combining the above tactics with frontal assaults where the relationship of forces is more favourable, infiltration of all the roads leading to Albertville, frequent sabotage operations and ambushes and paralysis of the economy; then, finally, take Albertville.

For reasons that I shall develop in another report, the results of our reconnaissance lead me to think that Katenga would be the best place to start operations.

The reasons I can give today are the following.

1. Its garrison is relatively small.

2. We think we could organize the ambushing of reinforcements, since their supply line runs parallel to the mountains.

3. If Katenga were to fall and remain in our hands, this would isolate Lulimba as the gateway to Kasengo.

Following this letter, I sent the reconnaissance report on Katenga, the analysis of the situation and a recommendation to attack. At that moment it was relatively easy to attack Katenga, since the complete inactivity of our forces meant that the enemy's vigilance in the area was practically non-existent.

A DEFEAT

Mitoudidi's replacements embarked for Kigoma, and some of them – Comrade Muteba, for example, the recipient of my letter to Kabila – we did not see again during the war.

Chaos began to take over again at the base with an almost conscious frenzy, as if to make up for time lost during Mitoudidi's intervention. Orders and requests succeeded one another with no rhyme or reason. We Cubans were asked to man machine-guns strewn along the lakeside, thereby condemning a number of comrades to inactivity. Given the prevailing lack of discipline, it would have been impossible to use Congolese machine-gunners to defend the base from air attack: they did not know how to handle their weapons and did not want to learn (nor, with a few honourable exceptions, did they learn throughout our time in the Congo); indeed, they ran away from aircraft, instead of methodically doing something about them. Those machine-guns played a role in driving away enemy aircraft, whose crews (especially towards the end) mainly consisted of mercenaries. After one or two attacks, they lost interest in fighting against ground-based gunners and turned to the strafing and bombing of areas where there was no anti-aircraft defence. Nevertheless, I think that the fact that those men at the lake were inactive was a pointless waste of our combat strength, since the enemy was unable to mount an effective attack; four T-28s and two B-26s did the job for them.

We continued to face the same difficulties at Upper Base, only with many comrades suffering from the fevers of the Congo. Instead of the students promised by Mitoudidi, who never arrived, representatives of distant guerrilla groups showed up to take away arms and ammunition, which they would squander, waste or break for no purpose. Comrade Mundandi arrived around the middle of June, together with some letters from Kabila. One, dated 16 June, said the following:

> *Comrade,*
>
> *I have read and reread the report you sent to Brother Muteba for my attention. As I said before, comrade, I want to start some ambushes; Comrade Mundandi will talk to you about it. Please allow a good 50 Cubans with the rank of fighter to take part in the attack of 25 June, under the direction of Mundandi.*
>
> *You are a revolutionary and you must be enduring all the difficulties you find there – and, well, I shall arrive any moment now. You can also send a good dozen men to Kabimba.*
>
> *Friendly greetings,*
>
> *Kabila.*
>
> *P. S. I appreciated your plan concerning Bendera, which Nando showed to me. We had been contemplating almost the same thing. Courage and patience. I know that you are suffering because of the poor organization, but we are doing everything to improve it. It's the fault of our lack of leaders.*
>
> *Au revoir, Kabila*

Since Kabila said he was in agreement with the plan I had sent, we began discussing with Mundandi an attack, not on Bendera, but on Katenga a few kilometres away. Mundandi proved hard to pin down; he had no definite plan himself, just an order to attack on 25 June. Why on that date? Again he could not answer. We discussed our plan for attacking, not Bendera directly, but the village of Katenga, thereby drawing in reinforcements that we could destroy on the road, but he was uncertain. He seemed to be a simple soul, entrusted with a task beyond his capabilities; but in all this there was also a large dose of dissembling.

Evidently, Mundandi and Kabila decided between themselves to launch a surprise attack on Front de Force, perhaps in the hope that it might lead to a large-scale victory over the enemy army. I feared for the safety of the Cuban and Rwandan comrades who were supposed to take part in the action, if they directly attacked unknown positions in which there were trenches, natural defences and heavy weapons. My first reaction was to take part in operations myself; Kabila had specified that the men should put themselves under Mundandi's orders, thus cleverly rejecting my proposal that Cubans should lead the tactical actions involving mixed troops. I decided that this was not the most important aspect. My authority would, I thought, be able to push through solutions as they came up in future discussions, since Mundandi knew who I was and seemed to respect me. I therefore wrote Kabila a short note as follows:

Dear comrade,

Thank you for your letter. You can rest assured that my impatience is that of a man of action; it does not imply any criticism. I am able to understand things, because I myself have lived in similar conditions.

I, too, eagerly await your arrival, because I consider you an old friend and I owe you an explanation. At the same time, it is my duty to place myself unconditionally under your command.

As you ordered, the Cubans will leave tomorrow for Front de Force. Unfortunately, many are sick and the total number will be a little lower (40). There are four comrades in Kabimba. We shall send the others as they arrive.

I would ask you one favour. Give me permission to go to Front de Force, with no other title than that of my comrades' "political commissar", fully under the orders of Comrade Mundandi. I have just talked to him and he is in agreement. I think this might prove useful. I would report back within three or four days of receiving your call.

Best wishes,

Tatu

I had indeed discussed with Mundandi the possibility of my going along, and – on the face of it, at least – he had been in agreement. But he stressed that he would have to send the men without waiting for Kabila's reply, and this made me suspect that it would be negative.

The reply arrived a few days later and was not negative – more characteristically, it was evasive. But I had time to write a second letter, urging him to give me a frank "yes" or "no". This one did not allow of any beating about the bush, and he simply failed to answer it. So I did not go to Front de Force.

The men left on the appointed day, numbering 36 rather than the 40 I had mentioned. But shortly afterwards we sent another seven, making a total of 43. News came that all were well, but that the attack had been delayed – Mundandi had not yet appeared there. The men sent a request to have a doctor close at hand, and we were able to grant this because just then a group of 39 more comrades had arrived, including three doctors (one surgeon, one orthopaedist, and one general practitioner).

The first battle report said this:

Tatu or Kumi, the attack began at 5.00 a.m. today, 29 June, 1965. We are doing well. Apparently Katenga is under attack. Five of our comrades, Nane as group leader and two Rwandan comrades are around there.

Patria o Muerte,
Moja

And later:

It is 7.30. Things are going well. The men are very content and conducting themselves well. Everything started at the appointed time. We opened fire with guns and a mortar.

I'll send more information later.

41

Simultaneously with this note, however, alarming news arrived of dozens of casualties, Cuban dead, men wounded, which made me think that all was not well. Previously, a little before they set out, I had received a note:

On the 29th we did the business at Front de Force. Not possible to convince the man. We'll inform you about it later.

Comrades Mbili and Moja had long discussions to persuade Commander Mundandi not to attack in the way he had planned, but his position did not shift. He claimed to have orders from Kabila. Later, Kabila said he had given no such orders.

At Front de Force/Front Bendera, there is a hydro-electric power station on the banks of the River Kimbi; its water supply is effectively in the mountains controlled by the Rwandans, while the electricity lines pass across level ground (since the mountains fall sharply down to the altiplano of the Congo Basin). The village is divided into two: an old part, before one reaches the power station; and a newer part close to the turbines, where there is a military quarter with more than 80 houses. The River Kimbi, one of its natural defences, was suitably reinforced with trenches that had been very superficially reconnoitred before the attack. There was also a landing field for light aircraft. It was thought that an enemy battalion five to seven hundred strong might be there, plus a concentration of special troops four kilometres away, at the junction with the Albertville road, where there was said to be a cadet school or a military training college.

All we could get out of Mundandi was that Cuban officers had been placed at the main battle zones. The attached diagram [missing] gives a rough idea of the disposition of forces only on the northern side, with ambushes on both sides of the Lulimba to Albertville road. The plan was as follows:

A small group led by Ishirini would attack the so-called *chariot*, the channel supplying water to the hydro-electric turbine; below, across the River Kimbi, a group of men under Lieutenant Azi would attack the fortified positions closest to the mountain; and in the centre, Lieutenant

Azima and a group of Rwandans would capture the airfield and advance to link up with Azi; meanwhile Lieutenant Mafu and another group would be in the strongest position, preventing movement along the road from Lulimba with a 75mm gun and other heavy weapons; and Lieutenant Inne would lay ambushes on the road in from Albertville. The command post, where Moja and Mundandi would remain, would be on the other side of the River Kimbi, in the first of the mountain foothills. Mundandi originally proposed having two command posts, but he was persuaded that it would be better to have a single unified one.

This plan had some serious drawbacks. Inne had to march to an unfamiliar area that had not been reconnoitred. Mafu knew something about the area, as did Nazi, and Azima had made a superficial examination with binoculars from the mountains. But since we were expecting rein-forcements to be sent from Albertville, we should have planned for a very well-laid ambush, instead of setting one up blindly. There was a lot of discussion with Mundandi for the main effort to be directed at Katenga, and in the end he agreed to send an order to Captain Salumu to attack there. But, as later became clear, the order was given for the 30th, whereas Mundandi went ahead on the 29th.

At Front de Force, things did not go remotely as well as the first indications had led us to hope.

Ishirini, together with two other Cubans and seven Rwandans armed with rocket launchers and rifles, had the task of taking out the *chariot*, to silence a machine-gun nest and to cause some damage to the plant; but all that happened was that the lights went out for a couple of minutes. The Rwandan fighters stayed a couple of kilometres away from the scene of the action, which was carried out by the Cubans alone. To give some idea of the confusion, I shall transcribe in full the report by Lieutenant Azi, whose mission was to attack across the River Kimbi:

When I set off on the mission, I positioned the mortar, the gun, the anti-aircraft machine-gun and the terrestrial ones to fire directly at the enemy from a distance of 300 metres, except for the mortar that was at 500 metres, and followed up with 49 Rwandans and five Cubans. We crossed the river, which was 150 to 200 metres from the enemy mortars. Then, at 100 metres from the enemy position, a shot was fired at a Rwandan; the men became disorganized and five were lost, leaving 44. I organized the men into three groups, with two Cubans in mine and one in each of the others. By three o'clock on the 29th we had occupied the positions, some at 25 metres from the enemy, others further away. We could hear some bursts of enemy machine-gun fire. At five o'clock, as foreseen, the gun, the mortars, the anti-aircraft and other machine-guns opened fire, and we kept on shooting at the infantry. All the weapons hit the mark; firing went on uninterruptedly until six o'clock, by which time I had three wounded men in front of me. By seven, our troops could no longer be heard firing on our left flank. I moved a little and saw that many Rwandans were missing. Then I armed three Cubans with machine-guns instead of FALs: there were Anchali, Angalia and myself, plus a Rwandan captain. At 8.45 two Rwandans were killed; I went off to the left to look for Tano to send a message to Moja; the men in the centre and the group on the left, including the Rwandan officers, had retreated on their own initiative. I was left with 14 Rwandans, and one Cuban, Tano, was out there somewhere in the centre group. I sent Angalia with the first message to Moja. By ten o'clock I was left with four Rwandans, including one officer. I held out until twelve o'clock and then withdrew 25 metres, having two more dead and three wounded. I sent another message to Moja, held on there until 12.30, and crossed back over the river to the mortar and gun position. Before withdrawing, I looked for the position where Tano and Sita were, but neither came into sight – Sita appeared later. At the mortar position, I received orders from Moja to withdraw the mortar, the machine-guns and the gun, and to leave an ambush in case the guardsmen crossed the river. I maintained this position until six o'clock on 30 June, when I received the order to leave the place altogether. Only Cubans were left at the ambush: Anzali, Anchali, Agiri, Abdallah, Almari and Azi; there was not one Rwandan. The Rwandans were ordered by the command post to occupy the positions, and they went over the mountain to the camp. The Rwandan men abandoned their weapons and ammunition, and did not pick up their dead. Comrade Azima was under my orders, carrying out the mission of occupying the other side (right bank of the river, some 500 metres from our positions) together with Alakre, Arobo and 40 Rwandans. On the night when they moved to occupy the positions, the Rwandans heard a noise and said it was a tembo (elephant), and then left the two Cubans alone with it on the mountain; the Cubans thus had to return to the command post at seven o'clock on the 29th.

This was more or less the keynote of the whole operation. It began with a lot of gusto – even though men were missing at many of the positions even before the fighting started – and then turned into a rout.

Comrade Tano, who appeared seven days later, had suffered a wound and been abandoned by his comrades. He then dragged himself towards the mountain, where he was found by a patrol consisting of Rwandan soldiers. His wound healed and he was able to rejoin the struggle.

To complete the picture, here is another report from the same day:

We can report that the Rwandan comrades retreated in disorder all along the front, leaving behind weapons, ammunition, dead and wounded. These were picked up by our comrades, as Comrade Commander Mundandi can testify.

The mission of Comrade Inne, which was the principal one, was to occupy the Albertville to Force road and prevent the passage of enemy reinforcements, but according to the information we have at present, he did not reach the agreed place because the guide evidently became lost. Comrade Inne then made a wrong decision to attack the Military Academy, where – according to the reports we have from our Rwandan comrades who took part in the action – the only ones still there when it began were our own comrades and some Rwandan comrades who died or, in two cases, were wounded. Right at the start of the action, Comrade Inne actually asked them to set up the gun, given that the Rwandan comrades who had been carrying it made off in the same direction to the camp and left the shells and other parts to be collected by some of our own comrades.

When we learnt of Comrade Inne's death, we sent Comrade Mbili with 20 reinforcements to see how things really stood there, and they discovered that Comrade Mafu's ambush included Comrades Kasambala, Sultán, Ajili and others belonging to Inne's group. When Comrade Mbili saw the situation, he informed me of it and asked for some more men, so that, if I thought it appropriate, he could set off with them to the road. It was then 18.00 hours on the 29th.

When I discussed the problem with Commander Mundandi, he told me that the Rwandan comrades were refusing to go and fight. Thus we had no more men to send for the ambush, since the surviving Rwandan comrades from Inne's group had set off for the base, the 20 Rwandans with Comrade Mbili also refused to fight, and the men under Mafu's command were in the same situation. We therefore thought of sending word to Mbili that he should leave four or five of our comrades to look for dead bodies, while the others should return on the night of 30/06/65. But at 04.00 hours on the 30th, only he and the other Cuban comrades were left at Comrade Azi's position, and their situation was raised with Comrade Commander Mundandi. The decision was then taken that they should withdraw to a hill near the area.

The other problems that befell Comrade Mbili during this operation he will explain to you with a wealth of detail.

Our command post, where Commander Mundandi was also located, was some 800 metres from the front (beside the river). We had there: Moja, Mbili, Paulu, Saba and Anga.

We have not left any more at the command post, since we think that the ambushes should be strengthened because of the distances involved.

Bahaza and Ananane were too ill for combat and remained at the Front Base.

Moja

Nothing went smoothly for Comrade Inne. He had discussed his plan beforehand with Mafu, thinking that he would take part in the ambush and then return to attack the enemy position; he proposed this idea to the command and pressed it when he did not win their agreement. Once the battle was underway elsewhere, there was little possibility of returning to the appointed place, since the guide was so terrified that he would not take another step, and no one else knew the way. Inne decided to attack the position he had in front of him at the start of the fighting – that is, the Military Academy itself – but he was met with intense, well-coordinated fire from heavy weapons. According to eye-witnesses, Inne himself was soon wounded and handed over his machine-gun position to Kawawa, but then Kawawa was killed by a mortar, and another two comrades were lightly wounded and retreated. A scout sent out shortly afterwards found the body of Thelathini; Anzurume was missing, presumed dead. They had started the engagement at a point within the enemy's sights, at a distance of some 200 metres. In addition to the four Cuban comrades, at least 14 Rwandans were killed – including the brother of Commander Mundandi. The exact figure cannot be established, since the Rwandan counting was very poor.

In this ill-fated action, I assign much of the blame to the Cuban command. Comrade Inne, underestimating the enemy, waged an undeniably fearless operation to carry out what he considered his moral duty, but not his specific task; he launched a frontal attack and perished along with other comrades, leaving open the way from Albertville along which enemy reinforcements were expected to come.

As part of the contingency planning before the engagement, all the comrades had been instructed to leave behind any documents or papers that might allow them to be identified. They did do this, although Inne's group kept some documents in their packs and were meant to leave their belongings at a certain distance before joining the ambush. When the fighting started, however, they still had their packs with them, and the enemy found a diary which suggested that Cubans had been taking part in the attack. What they did not know was that four were killed at that place, since the newspapers always spoke only of two.

A very large quantity of weapons and ammunition was hastily abandoned, but we could not know exactly how much because there had been no previous counting. The wounded – as well as the dead, of course – were left to their fate.

Meanwhile, what was happening in Katenga?

One hundred and sixty men took part in the attack, with weapons greatly inferior to those of the Rwandans. (The best they had were sub-machine-guns and short-range rocket launchers.) The surprise factor was lost, since – for reasons that Mundandi never explained – the attack had been ordered for a day later, the 30th, when enemy aircraft were flying over the whole region and those in defensive positions were, naturally enough, on the alert.

Of the 160 men, 60 had deserted by the time of the engagement and many others did not manage to fire a shot. At the agreed hour, the Congolese opened fire on the barracks, nearly always shooting in the air because most of them kept their eyes shut and pressed the triggers of their automatic weapons until the ammunition ran out. The enemy answered with accurate 60mm mortar fire, which inflicted a number of casualties and immediately produced a rout.

The losses were four dead and 14 wounded, the latter during the disorderly retreat in which men ran away absolutely terrified. At first, they explained the defeat by saying that the medicine man was no good and had given them bad *dawa*. He tried to defend himself by blaming women and fear, but there were no women around there and not every-one was honest enough to admit his weaknesses. The medicine man was certainly in a tight corner and found himself being replaced. It became the main job for Calixte, the group's commander, to scour the whole area for a new *muganga* with the right qualities.

The result of this dual attack was great demoralization among the Congolese and Rwandans, but also a loss of heart among the Cubans: each of our fighters had glumly witnessed assault troops melt away at the moment of combat and throw away precious weapons in order to flee more quickly; each had also observed the lack of comradely feeling as they left their wounded to fend for themselves, the terror that had the soldiers in its grip, and the ease with which they dispersed without waiting for orders of any kind. Often it was the officers – including the political commissars (a blot on the Liberation Army of which I shall speak in a moment) – who took the lead in running away. The heavy weapons, which had mostly been handled by Cubans, were nearly all saved; the FM and DP machine-guns, handled by Rwandans, were lost in significant numbers, as were all kinds of rifles and ammunition.

During the days after the attack, a large number of soldiers either deserted or asked for a discharge. Mundandi wrote me a long letter, abounding as always in tales of heroism. Thus he lamented the loss of his brother, but stated that he had died after wiping out a lorry full of soldiers (a complete invention, since there had been no lorries). He regretted the loss of several of the more resolute cadres in his group, and protested at the fact that the general staff was in Kigoma while the men were fighting and laying down their lives in the Congo. He mentioned in passing that two-thirds of the enemy troops had been annihilated, but he could not have had any reliable source for this and it was, of course, false. In keeping with his inclination to fantasy, he could not refrain from making such assertions, while at the same time he apologized for his own weaknesses.

In short, Mundandi owned up completely to feeling discouraged. I had to send him a reply packed with advice and analysis of the situation, in an attempt to give him fresh heart. But his letters heralded the disintegration that would later overcome the Liberation Army and even catch the Cuban troops in its mesh.

On 30 June, when the engagement at Front de Force was already under way but no news of it had yet reached us, I wrote a monthly balance-sheet in my diary:

> It is the most meagre balance yet. When everything suggested that a new period was beginning for us, Mitoudidi died and the fog became denser. The exodus to Kigoma is continuing. Kabila has repeatedly announced his return but never effected it; there is a complete lack of organization.
>
> On the positive side, men have been going to the front; but on the negative side, there is the report of an attack that may be crazy or totally ineffective, and may alert Tshombe's forces.
>
> A number of questions have to be cleared up. What will be Kabila's attitude to us, and especially to me? Will he be the man for the situation? Will he be able to size it up and perceive that everything here is in chaos? It's impossible to tell until we meet each other in real life, but on the first question at least, there are serious signs that he is not at all keen on my presence. It remains to be seen whether this is due to fear, envy or hurt feelings about questions of method.

During these days I wrote a letter to Pablo Rivalta, our ambassador to Tanzania, and among other things instructed him to inform the government of my presence here, to apologize for the way in which I had arrived, to explain the problems resulting from the fact that Kabila had not then been in the country, and to stress that the decision had been taken by myself, not by the Cuban government. The bearer of the letter had first to meet Kabila in Kigoma and to discuss his views. But once Kabila learnt of my intentions, he flatly refused to say anything on the matter, arguing that we would talk it over when he returned to the Congo.

THE SHOOTING STAR

Before Kabila arrived, I received no fewer than four different messages from him, either in writing or by word of mouth. I no longer believed anything after all these promises, and was more preoccupied with a number of concrete problems.

Mundandi wrote a letter once in a while, each one more critical than the last and all heaping blame on the Congolese: their lack of fighting spirit would leave him without men to make the revolution in Rwanda; all his cadres were dying; he had thought of continuing as far as Albertville before heading for Rwanda, but by then he would no longer have any fighters left, and so on.

They had tried small-scale operations such as exploratory patrols at Front de Force, to pinpoint the enemy's location and to look for men who might have been abandoned by their comrades, since no one knew the exact numbers missing. But it was all to no avail, and the Rwandans refused to go beyond the first mountain slopes. Faced with our complaints, Mundandi explained that it was a political question; that his men would not act because they were disheartened by the lack of cooperation from the Congolese.

It was difficult to interpret these statements, since one of his concerns was to give the Congolese troops a wide berth. He had taken the initiative for the operation and was responsible for its failure; he might perhaps include us in the judgement, but he had no reason to implicate the Congolese from whom he had kept well clear.

Wounded men kept arriving from Katenga and Front de Force. It was the peasants who gradually brought them in, since the fighters were disinclined to carry anyone on a makeshift stretcher along mountain paths.

Once again I tried to speak to the men in charge. Major Kasali did not receive me because he had a "headache", but he sent Comrade Kiwe, an old acquaintance, to speak with me and pass on my views to Kigoma.

I did not have a lot to say.

a) What was being done with the 40 of our men who had arrived a short time ago? Where were they being sent?

b) I placed on record my disagreement with the way everything had been handled at Bendera.

At the same time I sent a short letter to Kabila, explaining that my presence at the front was becoming daily more necessary.

Symptoms of disintegration could indeed be observed among our troops. Even during the retreat from Front de Force, some comrades had said that they would no longer fight alongside such people and would withdraw from the struggle; it was rumoured that some would formally propose leaving the Congo. To maintain morale was one of my fundamental concerns. I had asked for an urgent reply to my above-mentioned note, but none arrived. I sent another letter via Commissar Alfred, in which I made an analysis of the defeat at Front de Force and added some further observations.

The attacks had not been coordinated: the Front de Force group attacked on the 29th and the Katenga group on the 30th, but Mundandi was not the only one to blame, since nothing had been done on the other front either.[2] He recommended the creation of a single command to unify operations across the whole front, and advised that it should contain one Cuban. As we could see, the conflicts made it impossible to transfer even a box of

2. It is necessary to stress this point, because the situation in which the Rwandans found themselves was very strange. On the one hand, they were given signs of confidence and appreciation greater than those shown to the Congolese, but, on the other hand, all the blame for the defeat was attributed to them. Both sides forgot about self-criticism and launched into a war of incredible insults. It is a pity that they did not keep these energies for use against the enemy. Mundandi told me that on one occasion Calixte went so far as to shoot at him, although I have no evidence for this. What is sure is that the one was as inefficient as the other.

bullets from one group to the other. He again insisted on the need for me to be present at the Front.

I went to Upper Base to explain the defeat to our comrades and to give the new arrivals a solemn warning. My analysis of our defects was as follows. First, we are underestimating the enemy, who have the same characteristics as the rebel soldiers opposed to them. We expose ourselves in the spirit of conquerors and think we can just sweep the enemy aside, without realizing that they have received military instruction and seem to be on the alert in well-protected positions.

Second, lack of discipline. I emphasized the need for rigid discipline. However painful it might be, it was necessary to criticize Inne's action, which, though heroic, had done a lot of damage by leading to the death not only of three other Cuban comrades but also of more than a dozen Rwandans.

Third, decline of fighting spirit. I stressed emphatically that it was necessary to keep morale high.

I publicly criticized Comrade Azima for making some defeatist statements and was explicit about what awaited us: not only hunger, bullets and all manner of suffering, but sometimes even death at the hands of comrades who had no idea how to shoot. The struggle would be very hard and long. I issued this warning because, at that point, I was willing to accept that the newcomers should express doubts and return if they so wished; later, it would no longer be possible. My tone was severe and my warning clear. None of the new arrivals showed signs of weakness, but to my surprise three fighters who had taken part in the attack at Front Bendera (and who were there with some messages) planned to leave. To cap it all, one of them was a member of our party. Their names: Abdallah, Anzali and Anga.

I took them to task and warned that I would ask for the severest penalties against them. I made no commitment because I was speaking with the new soldiers in mind, but I did promise to let them go at an unspecified future date.

To add to my pain and surprise, Comrade Sitaini – who had been with me since the war [in Cuba] and served as my aide for six years – said that he intended to return to Cuba. It was all the more painful because he used petty arguments and claimed not to know what everyone had been told about the length of the war: namely, that it was likely to last three years, with luck, or otherwise five years. It had been my constant refrain to predict a long and difficult struggle, and Sitaini knew this better than anyone because we had been together all the time. Refusing to accept his departure, I tried to make him see that it would harm the reputation of us all, and argued that he had an obligation to stay because of his closeness to me. He replied that this left him no choice but to agree, but he did so grudgingly and from then on he was like a corpse. He was ill with a bilateral hernia, and his condition worsened so much that it became necessary and justifiable for him to abandon the struggle.

My spirits were quite low during those days, but I cheered up on 7 July when I was told that Kabila had arrived. At last the top man was at the scene of operations.

He was cordial but aloof. I spoke of my presence there as a *fait accompli* and merely repeated the explanations I had given several times before about why I had arrived in the Congo without advance notice. I put it to him that he should inform the Tanzanian government of this, but he replied evasively and left the matter for another time. Two of his close assistants were there with him: Comrade Masengo, today head of the general staff, and Foreign Minister Nbagira (there were two foreign ministers at that time, because Gbenye had one of his own, Kanza). He was in a lively mood and asked me what I wanted to do. Of course, I repeated my old tune about wanting to go to the front: my most important task, the one where I could be most useful, was to train cadres; and cadres were trained in battle at the front line, not at the rear. He expressed his reservations, to the effect that a man like myself was useful to the World Revolution and should take care of himself. I argued that my intention was not to fight at the front, but to be at the front together with my soldiers. Besides, I was experienced enough to take care of myself; I was not looking for laurels but carrying out a definite task, and I thought it the one most useful to him because it could result in loyal and efficient cadres.

He did not reply, but he maintained a cordial tone and told me that we were going to make a number of trips; we would go to the interior and visit all the fronts, and our first move would be to leave that very night to visit the Kabimba area. For some reason, however, he was unable to go either that night or the next day, and on the day after that he had to speak at a rally about the Cairo Conference and clear up some doubts that the peasants had about it. For the moment, Aly was sent with ten men to carry out some unpretentious action in the Kabimba area. Lieutenant Kiswa went to Uvira for reconnaissance purposes.

The rally proved to be interesting. Kabila showed ample knowledge of his people's mentality, as he explained skilfully and elegantly in Swahili all the salient points of the Cairo meeting and the resulting accords. He made the peasants talk, then gave rapid answers in a way that satisfied them. At the end, everyone did a short slow dance to the sound of music and the sung refrain, "Kabila eh! Kabila va!"

His intense activity made it seem that he wanted to catch up for lost time. His aim was to organize the base's defences and he seemed to inspire everyone with fresh heart, so that the region sorely tried by indiscipline began to take on a different appearance. Sixty men were hastily assembled and assigned to three Cuban instructors in trench-digging and shooting, while we devised a plan to defend the little semi-circular bay in which we found ourselves.

On 11 July, five days after his arrival, Kabila sent for me and said that he had to leave that night in the direction of Kigoma. He explained that Soumaliot was there, and then criticized that leader for his organizational errors, his demagogy and his weakness of character. According to Kabila, just after the Tanzanian government had, on his advice, imprisoned some agents of Gbenye (or out and out enemy agents) who had been sowing discord, Soumaliot had shown up and released them. The division of labour with Soumaliot had to be clarified once and for all; he had been appointed Chairman so that he would spend his time travelling and explaining the Revolution and not interfere too much (because he was hopeless at organization), but now there had to be a clearer demarcation.

Kabila analysed Soumaliot's influence in this, his native region, and said that they needed to sort things out between them, because his activity could be harmful to the future of the Revolution. The trip would last a day, and he would be back on the morrow.

As we were talking, he let slip that Soumaliot had already returned to Dar es Salaam, so I asked him a little sarcastically how he was going to cross the lake, meet Soumaliot in Dar es Salaam and return the next day. But he replied that the news of Soumaliot's departure had not been confirmed, and that if it was true and he had to go to Dar es Salaam, he would return immediately.

When they heard that Kabila was leaving, the Congolese and Cubans again became downhearted. Kumi, the doctor, took out a piece of paper on which he had predicted that Kabila would stay seven days in the Congo – a mistake of just two days. Changa, our valiant "admiral" of the lake, was fuming: "Why did that man bring all those bottles of whisky if he was only going to stay five days?"

I shall not note what the Congolese said in protest, because I was not told it directly. But it was along the same lines, and it was transmitted to our own comrades.

Kabila would only be able to avoid falling further into disrepute if he returned at once. We had a final conversation in which I hinted at the problem as amiably as I could. We also talked of other matters, and he raised the question – obliquely, as was his wont – of what my position would be in the event of a split. I told him that I had not come to the Congo to interfere in internal politics and that it would be harmful if I were to do so; that I had been sent by the government to this region; that we would try to be loyal to him and above all to the Congo; and that, if I had doubts about his political position, I would present them to him first and foremost. In the end, I insisted, a war is won on the battlefield, not in committee rooms at the rear.

We spoke of future plans. He confided in me that he was arranging for the base to be moved further south to Kabimba, and that steps were being taken to ensure that weapons were not distributed in the zones of his political enemies. I explained that, in our view, Katanga's mineral wealth made it the key area of the Congo and the one where the toughest battles had to be fought. This was common ground between us, but for our part we did not think that the problem of the Congo could be solved on a tribal or regional basis; it was a national problem, and we had to get this idea across. I also argued that it was important to rely not so much on the loyalty of a particular tribe as on the loyalty of revolutionary cadres; we therefore had to create and develop cadres – which again made it necessary for me to go to the front (my usual refrain).

We said goodbye, Kabila left, and activity in the base, which had begun to improve through his dynamic presence, grew slacker the very next day. Soldiers whose task it was to dig trenches said they would not work today because the leader had gone away; others who were building the hospital also abandoned their labours. Again everything began to acquire the easy, pastoral rhythm of our general staff – the rhythm of a village far from all the vicissitudes not only of war but even of life.

WINDS FROM THE WEST,
BREEZES FROM THE EAST

It was clear to me that I had to do something to stop the rot – a process which, paradoxically, had begun with the only offensive operation we had seen the revolutionary movement undertake since our arrival. One thing followed another after the first Cubans proposed to withdraw from the struggle. Two more comrades followed suit – Achiri and Hanzini, one of them a Party member – and shortly afterwards two doctors who had only recently arrived, both Party members, made the same request. I was less stormy and much more cutting with the two doctors than with the ordinary soldiers, who had reacted to events in a more or less primal manner.

The selection in Cuba was obviously not good enough, but it is difficult to get it right in the present conditions of the Cuban Revolution. You cannot base yourself only on the great precedent of a man's record under arms, for later years of easier living have also changed people – and the revolution turned the huge majority into revolutionaries. Nevertheless, it is a mystery to me how such a selection can be made before the test of fire, and I think that every measure must take account of the fact that no one can be given the final approval until he has undergone selection in the theatre of battle. The reality was that, at the first serious setback (accompanied, it must be said in their defence, by the visible disarray of the forces in action), a number of comrades lost heart and decided to withdraw from a struggle for which they had come to die if necessary – as volunteers, moreover – surrounded by a halo of bravery, self-sacrifice, enthusiasm, in short, invincibility.

What meaning there is in the soldier's response: "Until death, if necessary!" It carries the solution to serious problems involved in creating our men of tomorrow.

Incredible things have been happening among the Rwandans. Mundandi's second-in-command has been shot, they say, but in reality brutally murdered. Thousands of conjectures are being spun around this event. The least favourable – which is not to say they are untrue – suggest it had something to do with women. The result is that Commander Mitchel, a soldier and a peasant have all gone to a better life. The formal charge against him was that he supplied a bad *dawa* which was responsible for the death of 20 of his comrades, but it did not specify whether the *dawa* directly caused their deaths or gave them inadequate protection, or whether operations outside the camp to find the *dawa* were the pretext on which he was denounced.

The incident had links to others taking place at the same time, which it would have been good to get to the bottom of. It came after a serious defeat for which Mundandi was the main person responsible, but another man was shot. And the whole thing happened at a time of virtual rebellion against Kabila and the high command of the Liberation Army, when the Rwandans, flatly refusing to carry out any military action, were either deserting or (in the case of those who remained at the camp) saying that they would go to fight only when they saw the Congolese doing the same. Even if Kabila were to go and see them, they would give him food without salt and tea without sugar, as they themselves took them, so that he would understand what it was to make sacrifices. (This was hardly a real threat, of course, because Kabila did not have the slightest intention of going there.)

A Congolese commissar, who was at the front on the day of the events, tried to intervene but was simply blocked and forced to leave the camp. This commissar was the same Alfred about whom I have already spoken, and his reaction was expressed in the following alternative: either Mundandi is shot for murder, or I withdraw from the struggle.

Some Rwandans who had grown close to us, and whom we had accepted as troops under Cuban discipline, were demoted and treated with hostility by their compatriots. This portended a cooling of relations, or something worse.

I talked these problems over with Masengo and stressed what, in my view, was the key point: that if we were to succeed in the struggle, we would have to integrate ourselves more and more into the Liberation Movement and come to be seen by the Congolese as other people who were just like them. Instead, we had limited ourselves to the circle of Rwandans, who were foreigners in the country and very eager to remain such, so that in their company we were condemned to the situation of perpetual outsiders. In reply, Masengo gave permission for some of our men to go and help Calixte in his work – and we quickly acted upon this.

Moja received instructions to organize fresh operations with any volunteers he could obtain, but on condition that it should be a mixed force, with the same number of Cubans and Rwandans. We had discussed with Mbili how to lay the ambush; my aim was for him to learn the basics of this type of warfare, and so he was ordered to attack only one vehicle in the first action.

This was set to take place on the road from Front de Force to Albertville, in an area scouted by Azi that had the right conditions for groups to harry the enemy or for a sizeable column to operate. There was thick forest on the mountainside, although it would be necessary to organize a supply system.

Aly arrived with news from the Kabimba front. On a reconnaissance trip, he had come across four enemy policemen on a mission to improve visibility by burning the nearby hills; three of them had been captured, while the fourth had been killed. Of the 20 Congolese who set off with Aly, 16 took to their heels; the only armed policemen had been the one who was killed. The soldiers' morale and combat readiness on this front gave no reason for envy among their colleagues at Front de Force or Calixte's front.

The base commander at Front de Force was now Captain Zakarias, and the idea was that he would come down with Mbili to carry out the action. Mundandi took quite a large force with him to the lakeside base: he looked threatening, but in fact he was afraid and wanted to make sure he would be safe when he went to Kigoma to talk with Kabila. Soon he fell ill (it was a real illness) and took the familiar month off together with some men loyal to him.

He visited me and behaved with solicitude, almost with humility. First we talked about general problems of the offensive, then moved on to the matter of the killing.

He explained the death of those comrades as follows. Commander Mitchel, trusting in the friendship of some local inhabitants, had confided the secret of the attack to them; one of them, however, was a spy who passed on the information to the enemy. When his comrades found out, it was necessary to shoot them; he, Mundandi, had disagreed, but he was in a minority at the meeting and had to carry out the wishes of the majority, given that the fighters were threatening to withdraw from the struggle.

I went over some aspects of the incident with him. First of all, the defeat could not be attributed to an act of betrayal, even if there had been one; it was due to the way in which the military action was carried out, to defects in the conception and execution of the attack – which was not to deny that we might also carry some blame as a result of Inne's attitude. Citing numerous examples from our own revolutionary war, I explained that it was highly negative to depend on soldiers' assemblies in cases such as this, that in the end revolutionary democracy had never been applied in the running of armies anywhere in the world, and that any attempt to implement it had ended in disaster. Finally, the shooting of a field commander who belonged to the Congo Liberation Army, without even informing the general staff and still less asking its views, was a sign of great indiscipline and complete lack of central authority; we all had to do what we could to ensure that such things never happened again.

When I commented to Masengo on the weakness of Mundandi's arguments, he replied that Mundandi had told him a different story but had been reluctant to speak frankly to me, because in reality it was superstition that lay behind the drama.

Mundandi was called to a meeting with leaders from various areas to try to improve relations between their groups. Apart from Mundandi himself, it was attended by Captain Salumu, Calixte's second-in-command, and Comrade Lambert, the head of operations in the Fizi zone, and a bevy of assistants.

Masengo, trapped by his lack of authority, could not get out of the crisis in the only way possible, by starting all over again and saying: "I'm in charge here!" He did not say that. Instead, he proposed to maintain the independence of action of the different fronts but to urge that no incident such as these should occur again – which left the problem unsolved and went right against my recommendation that a unified front should be formed under firm leadership.

Measures were taken with only a display of firmness, which then resulted in a multitude of weaknesses. Masengo had a list of weapons supplied to the various fronts, and not one figure coincided with the one given by the leader in question. No one doubted that the weapons really had been delivered, but assertions to the contrary were accepted and more military equipment was sent to the guzzling morass of the fronts. A commission had been set up to recover weapons from the large number of deserters all over the region, who were now lording it over others with the persuasive power of rifles they had taken with them from the front. There was even talk of capturing the parents of each man in question, if he could not be taken himself. But in the end they did not capture any deserters, nor recover any weapons, nor – as far as I know – imprison any lax parent among the peasantry.

When I suggested leaving for the front in a few days, Masengo refused and repeatedly invoked the excuse of my personal safety. I attacked him head-on by asking if he distrusted me in some way, since the reasons he gave were not valid. I demanded that he should treat me with greater frankness and say if he had any misgivings about me. The blow was too direct and he gave way; so we left it that we would make the trip together in five or six days' time, when a report would arrive from some men he had sent to carry out an inspection there.

There were misgivings, however, for the simple reason that neither Kabila nor Masengo had set foot at the various fronts for a very long time and the fighters were bitterly critical of them for this; the fact that the head of the Cuban expeditionary force could go and take part in life at the front, when those in charge of the war did not do the same, might give them fresh reason to feel censorious. Masengo was aware of this, but – apart from my concern to make a direct assessment of the situation – he also calculated that the Congolese leaders might feel obliged to make a journey around the fronts, and thus get to know and try to solve problems relating to the supply of food, clothing, medicine and ammunition.

To make ourselves more familiar with every aspect of the area in preparation for our planned trip, we went with the chief of staff to Kasima, 27 kilometres north of Kibamba. There too we found the scenes of indiscipline that have been a recurrent feature of this report, although Masengo was able to take some correct measures such as the replacement of a commander who spent the day sheltering in nearby mountains (afraid of aircraft) with the lieutenant who had been deputizing for him. Our own men, four machine-gunners, were laid low with malaria, and we took them to Kibamba for treatment.

We had advanced deep into the political territory of General Moulane, and the coldness toward Masengo was reflected in the attitude of the local population and the fighters, who were reluctant to accept what he wanted to be a central authority.

We pressed on and came to another place called Karamba. There we found one of the most original "barriers", manned by a group of Rwandans who were independent of Mundandi and had political-ideological differences with him that I would not know how to define. They had set up a recoilless 75mm gun on a hillock – the craziest place they could have found, because it had no strategic importance and all the gun could do was sink a boat that might pass nearby. It had, of course, already let loose some volleys without hitting the target, because the artillerymen did not know how to handle it and, in any case, the boats kept sufficient distance to remain out of range. It was another unit that was wasting its time. I recommended their immediate transfer to Kibamba, where there were no artillery pieces or training in how to use them, but this advice, as so often, fell on deaf ears. It was not that Masengo did not understand such matters, but simply that he did not have the authority. He did not feel that he had the power to impose decisions that went against the customary grain. A weapon that landed in a group of fighters was held sacred, and the only ones who could snatch it away (rather easily, in fact) were the enemy.

Masengo, wanting to changing the course of events through some offensive operations, suggested to me an attack on Uvira. I had to object to this, because inspections of that area had revealed the same general conditions, the same basic unfamiliarity with military methods, and a total lack of combat readiness. The scouts in that area had instructions to cross enemy lines and investigate the possibility of laying ambushes on the other side of the little town of Uvira, at the tip of Lake Tanganyika where the roads from Bukavu, and from Bujumbura in Burundi, come to an end. The idea, then, was to cross to the other side of Uvira and break the enemy's communications. Given the vast expanse of the Congo, it is quite easy to carry out such incursions. But not only had there been no one to take our men across the lines; they were even refused permission to go themselves, on the grounds that an attack was under preparation and they might alert the enemy.

During the days when all these diverse events were being recounted, we received news from Dar es Salaam – some of it good. A ship had arrived from Cuba with a cargo of weapons, provisions and 17,000 rounds of ammunition for our fighters; it would be sent by road very soon. I learnt that news of the Cubans killed in the Congo had appeared in all the newspapers, and that the ambassador had persuaded the Congolese formally to deny our presence there. This did not seem to me a wise course, because such things cannot be kept hidden and the only correct thing to do was to remain silent. I let Pablo Rivalta know this.

Along with the letter for the ambassador and the other reports, two comrades set off: Otto, who had been ill for some time, and Sitaini, whose bilateral hernia had become a medical case. I now had the opportunity to release him and to end the annoying situation that his reluctance to be there with us had brought about; I found it painful to do, but it was the best solution. Those who "cracked" and were forced to remain against their will tried to justify themselves by making negative propaganda, which found a ready echo among other comrades. In this case there was the justification of an illness, and that is why I allowed the escape.

My Swahili teacher, Ernest Ilunga, whom I already treated as a younger brother, was also due to leave in a few days' time. He had had some seizures of an epileptic kind, and the doctors suspected that a tumour was developing in his upper nervous centres. Masengo disagreed and explained to me that it was a fairly simple matter of evil spirits; the local doctors would cure him in Kigoma – and that is where he went, instead of to Dar es Salaam, where he had been advised to go for a cure, or at least for a diagnosis.

Following instructions, Moja visited Calixte's front and sent me a note which I have copied because it casts light on a number of questions I have already raised here.

Tatu:

I am writing to you from the Kazolelo-Makungo front, where the group of ten men were sent. I reached them yesterday, having learnt that a Congolese patrol had arrested a civilian with a Tshombe identity card in a settlement on the plain.

Today, the 19th, I met Commander Calixte, who personally interrogated the prisoner; he is kept locked up in a house far from the front, and has not seen any of the Cubans.

According to Calixte, the prisoner told him that he had been under arrest in Force at the time of the attack; that four officers had been killed there, with another two in Katenga, as well as a number of soldiers; that he did not know the dead officers by name, but had been able to see their rankings; that the prisoner's identity card was not an army card but of the kind issued to everyone going to Albertville; that in Nyangi there were 25 guardsmen, a mortar and an artillery piece, these weapons being located on the road to Makungo; that the prison where they had gathered the attacking revolutionaries was a kilometre from Force in the direction of Albertville, that the guardsmen had taken some of their watches and shoes, and that they had had to be buried by civilians.

Commander Calixte agrees that some men should be trained to go there with a mortar, a gun and anti-aircraft weapons, although he has none of these, and so we are awaiting the return of Captain Zakarias (Mundandi's replacement) to take these men to the Force front.[3] Today, the comrades at the Makungo front began to give classes to the rest of Commander Calixte's force. About Faume, I cannot yet tell you anything.[4] In a few days I'll send you more details about the situation - with a Cuban, as is natural for such details, and in a sealed envelope.

Moja

Shortly afterwards, the best news of these days arrived: the light breeze. The ambush had gone off quite successfully: 25 Rwandans and 25 Cubans, led respectively by Captain Zakarias and Mbili, but in reality under the latter's leadership, had carried out the engagement, if it deserves that name.

Azi's inspection had shown that the lorries passed there in single file, without protection. The 50 men attacked a lorry with five soldiers. A bazooka round from Sultán opened the proceedings, and for a few minutes the vehicle and the mercenaries (all of them black) were riddled with bullets. Only one was carrying a weapon, since the lorry was transporting food, cigarettes and drinks. From the point of view of gradually preparing for large-scale actions, the prize could hardly have been better - but a number of accidents were a blot on the record.

When the shooting began, the Rwandans ran backwards firing their weapons. This put our men in danger, and in fact Comrade Arobaini lost a finger when a bullet crushed the metacarpus of one hand.

3. Captain Zakarias refused to accept the Congolese at his front, on the grounds that they went to his camp to steal.
4. From what we knew, Commander Faume had split off from Calixte - apparently because of friction between them - and was on the plain with a lot of weapons. At that time, we were groping around in search of someone among the Congolese leaders.

Two examples will give some idea of the primitive mentality that still holds sway in the Congo. When Captain Zakarias learnt of the wound caused by the FM burst, he examined it and decreed that the guilty man should lose two of his fingers, in accordance with the principle of an eye for an eye; he took out his knife there and then and would have cut off the poor devil's extremities if Mbili had not very tactfully persuaded him to exercise pardon. The other example is of a Rwandan soldier who took to his heels almost as soon as he heard gunfire (our own fire, as there was no fighting); since each Rwandan was accompanied by a Cuban, our man in question caught him by the arm to hold him back, and the terrified boy, in order to shake off an attacker who was stopping him from protecting himself, gave the Cuban a huge bite on the hand.

These are two indications of the long road we will have to travel to make an army out of this shapeless mass of men. Unfortunately, the tragicomedy of this ambush did not end there. After the first moments of stupor, the brilliant victors realized that the greatest prize was on top of the lorry: namely, bottles of beer and whisky. Mbili tried to get the food loaded and to destroy the drink, but it was impossible. In a few hours all the fighters were drunk, under the astonished and reproving gaze of our men who were not allowed a drop. Then they held a meeting and decided they would not return to the plain for the other planned actions, but would return to base – they had done enough already. Mbili, diplomatically trying to avoid being left only with the Cubans, accepted the decision. On the way back, a drunken Captain Zakarias ran into a peasant and finished him off with a few shots, claiming that he had been a spy.

Strangest of all, when I explained to Masengo how dangerous it was to behave in this way with the peasants, he to some extent vindicated Zakarias, on the grounds that the tribe living in this region was hostile to the revolution. This meant that people were not to be catalogued according to their personal qualities, but to be incorporated in a tribal concept from which it was very difficult to escape; when a tribe was friendly, all its components were friendly; and likewise when it was unfriendly. Such schemas did not help the revolution to develop, but they were also clearly dangerous, because – as we saw later – some members of the friendly tribes were enemy informers, and in the end nearly all of them turned into our enemies.

We had had our first victory, and it was as if it had rid us of some of the bad taste left from before. But the problems posed by the things I have described were mounting up in such a way that I was beginning to change my time scale. If everything depended on the development of these armed groups into a fully fledged Liberation Army, then five years was a very optimistic target for the Congolese revolution to reach a victorious conclusion – unless something changed in the way the war was conducted. But that possibility seemed more remote with every day that passed.

BREAKING LOOSE

As usual, I analysed the past month (in this case, July) in my field diary.

A slight improvement on what has gone before. Kabila came, stayed for five days, and went away – which led to increased rumours about him. He doesn't like my presence, but he seems to have accepted it for the moment. So far, nothing makes me think he is the man for the situation. He lets the days pass without concerning himself with anything other than political squabbles, and all the signs are that he is too addicted to drink and women.

At the military level, since the disaster at Front de Force and the near-disaster at Katenga, there have been some small successes worth noting: two minor engagements at Kabimba, the ambush at Front de Force, the other one at Katenga where a bridge was set on fire. At the same time, some training has started and a search is on for better-quality men at the other fronts. The wretched method of strewing weapons all over the place, with no order and no co-ordination continues. My impression is that progress can be made, though at a slower pace, and that there is a chance Kabila will let me do something. For the moment, I'm still the scholarship boy.

News arrived of an ambush at Katenga. The men stayed there for four days and withdrew because the guardsmen did not travel along the road. Before leaving, they burnt and destroyed a bridge. The monthly analysis refers to this action.

The terrible thing is that the same conditions of indiscipline and lack of fighting spirit are to be observed in this area.

Azi arrived from Front de Force with 14 men, all Cubans, to find the food necessary for the laying of another, slightly less ambitious ambush. Given the conditions in the area, they needed to take some food along with them. The supply of provisions has been one of the sore points for the soldiers in the field. In the area where they had their fixed camps, it was possible to find some meat and manioc (which is the staple food), but the major plantations of this root are in the plain, where the peasants who cultivated it had their homes, and it was only the depredations of enemy soldiers that led them to leave and take refuge in the less hospitable uplands. To find manioc, it is necessary to make long and somewhat dangerous incursions. It was the Cubans who started these raids, because the Rwandans systematically refused to launch them, claiming that the high command had a duty to supply them with food. There were even days when the food ran short, and then they refused to attend the classes on heavy weapons or to do any kind of preparatory work, such as anti-aircraft defence or trench-digging. The phrase they used – another of the clichés we had to put up with during our time in the Congo – was "*Hapana chakula, hapana travaille*", or, more or less, "No food, no work".

Three new comrades, Sita, Saba and Baati, asked to return to Cuba. I was extremely tough with them, refusing point-blank to consider their transfer and ordering them to remain in the base for mess duties.

On 6 August it became known that Gbenye had been removed by Soumaliot. Two days later, Masengo came to tell me that he had been summoned by Kabila to Kigoma and would be back the next day. We talked about all the external problems of the Movement, and I remarked that I knew of Gbenye's removal by the Revolutionary Council. He said that, in his view, Soumaliot did not have the authority to decree a measure of that kind, but he would discuss all these things with Kabila and then explain better what had happened.

Masengo left, and the next day the group that was undergoing training at the lake was dissolved. It was the same group that had suffered a great

Above: Che's presence in the Congo had to be kept absolutely secret. Before leaving Cuba in April 1965, he transformed his physical appearance, and arrived heavily disguised in Moscow. From there he flew to Dar es Salaam.

Right: Che (*right*) in conversation with Fidel Castro (*left*) and Captain Víctor Dreke (*centre*), his deputy commander, shortly before he "disappeared".

Che teaching guerilla tactics to the Congolese forces. His plan was to use the liberated zone on the western shores of Lake Tanganyika as a training ground for the Congolese and fighters from other liberation movements. To his left is Santiago Terry (codename: "Aly"), to his right, Angel Felipe Hernández ("Sitaini").

Che, shortly
after arriving
at the camp,
with (*left*)
Víctor Dreke
(codename:
"Moja") and the
Cuban doctor
Rafael Zerquera
("Kumi").
Che gave each
Cuban fighter
a pseudonym
from the Swahili
alphabet. His
own codename
was "Tatu".

From left:
Ernesto, Che's
interpreter;
Rogelio Oliva
from the Cuban
Embassy in
Tanzania; Kiwe,
the Congolese
who was in
charge of
information,
and two others
who have not
been identified.

Throughout the seven-month campaign Che kept in touch
with news from Cuba.

From left: The Cuban guerrilla fighter Julián Contreras (codename: "Tiza"), Rogelio Oliva, and Godefroi Chamaleso , one of the two Congolese commanders, known to the Cubans as "Tremendo Punto".

From left: Pablo B. Ortiz (codename: "Saba"), Eduardo Torres ("Nane") and two unidentified Congolese fighters.

A Congolese fighter is put through his training. To his left is Santiago Terry Rodríguez (codename: "Aly") to his right are Rogelio Oliva (*seated*) and Julián Contreras ("Tiza").

Che at the base camp near Kibamba on the western shores of Lake Tanganyika, with local villagers and fighters. Squatting is the Cuban soldier Roberto Chaveco ("Kasambala").

Listening to a radio bulletin are (*seated from left*) Rogelio Oliva, José María Martínez Tamayo (known as "Mbili" in the Congo and "Ricardo" in Bolivia), and Che. Standing behind them is Roberto Sánchez ("Lawton" in Cuba and "Changa" in the Congo).

Second from the left is Godefroi Chamaleso ("Tremendo Punto"), followed by the Cubans Mario Armas ("Rebocate"), Roberto Sánchez, Osmany Cienfuegos (codename: "Bracero") and Ramón Armas ("Azima"). The others have not been identified.

Che in the Congo, 1965.
"When men are able to influence so many others through their life
and their example, they do not die" Aleida Guevara March

loss in numbers and morale on the day after Kabila's departure; work had stopped, the trenches had been half-dug, and we had gauged their spirit of combat and organization when the appearance of a small enemy boat raised the alarm. It had been impossible to form a second line of defence, as planned, because there were not the men to do it, while in the first line a number of the squad leaders were missing. A precarious line had been formed with the volunteers who came forward, in the half-dug and already half-collapsed trenches. Now, however, with Masengo gone, the group vanished into the pandemonium of Kibamba.

Arguments broke out again, because no one recognized the authority of the substitute officers. Sometimes it came to blows, or else guns or knives would glitter for a while. On one disgraceful occasion, an officer in charge sought refuge in the Cuban house, because a soldier had asked him for rice and, when refused, had threatened him with a cocked gun and sent him running to the "temple" of the (fortunately respected) Cubans. I think the soldier got his rice, and in any case there was no disciplinary sanction. Such was the demoralization that spread as soon as the top leaders left the general staff.

To avoid contamination, I cleared the useful Cubans out of the camp and left only those who had asked to return to Cuba, together with the lakeside machine-gunners, the sick and some instructors. I planned to wait a few days and, if nothing happened during that time, to head straight for the front without begging for further authorization.

From the tone of some notes and various conversations with comrades, I began to suspect the meaning behind certain phrases. In the small areas where some military or reconnaissance activity was reported, there came a moment after its basic failure when the explanation appeared: "The Congolese refused to go"; "The Congolese refused to fight"; "The Congolese, this and that". In analysing this, as well as the tension between those who planned to give up the struggle and those who remained, I composed a "Message to the Fighters", to be read at the fronts where we had troops. The maelstrom of the following months, and the unstable swings in my own situation, prevented me from issuing any more messages, although I do

71

not know if they had any effect. I shall copy out the only one that the men read; it will give an idea of the situation up to then, and of my views about the problems we were experiencing.

Message to the Fighters

Comrades:

In a few days it will, for some of us, be four months since we arrived in these lands, and a brief analysis of the situation must be made.

We cannot say that the situation is good. The leaders of the movement spend most of their time outside the country – which may be understandable in the case of political leaders whose activity has many aspects, but never in the case of middle cadres. These middle cadres, however, travel just as often and spend weeks outside the country, setting a wretched example. There is virtually no organizational work, precisely because the middle cadres do not know how to do it, and everyone lacks confidence in them.

Local leaders blackmail middle cadres whose tasks are similar to those of the general staff, and obtain weapons and ammunition without giving proof that they are using them properly. More weapons are given to more people who lack training and a fighting spirit, and there is hardly any progress in organization. It is a picture in which indiscipline and a lack of self-sacrifice are the main characteristics of all the guerrillas. A war is not won with such troops, of course.

One may wonder whether there is anything positive about our presence. I think there is. Many of our difficulties, including my own virtual imprisonment here, stem from the marked difference between the bodies of troops and from fear of conflicts between various types of leader. Our mission is to help them win the war; we should make the most of this negative reaction and convert it into something positive. That requires a greater stress on our political work. We have to show the differences through our own example, but without making ourselves hateful to cadres who might see us as the inverted image of all their faults.

For this, we must first try to exercise genuinely revolutionary comradeship among the rank-and-file; it is from there that the middle-ranking leaders of tomorrow will emerge. Generally, we have more clothes and more food than the comrades from here; we should share it to the maximum, selecting comrades who show revolutionary spirit and teaching them as much as possible. Our experience must be transmitted in one form or another to the fighters; the urge to teach should be paramount – not in a haughtily pedantic manner, but with the human warmth that goes with shared learning. Revolutionary modesty should guide our political work and be one of our basic weapons, complemented by a spirit of sacrifice that is an example not only to the Congolese comrades but also to the weakest of our own men. We should never look and see whether our own position is more dangerous than someone else's or whether more is being demanded of us; more should be asked of a genuine revolutionary, because he has more to give. Finally, we should not forget that we know only a tiny part of what we ought to know. We have to learn about the Congo in order to attach ourselves to the Congolese comrades; but we also have to learn the things we lack in general culture and even the art of warfare, without thinking that we are know-alls or that it is all we are required to know.

I would like to end this message with a couple of warnings.

1) Behaviour among comrades. Everyone knows that a group of comrades, by proposing to give up the struggle, did not honour their word as revolutionaries or the trust that had been placed in them. There can be no justification for this, and I will ask for the most severe moral sanctions against them. But we should not forget something else: they are not traitors, and they should not be treated with open contempt. Let us be clear. Of all the things a revolutionary can do, their action is the most open to repudiation.

*But you have to be a revolutionary for it to be repudiated –
otherwise it would not be serious but a mere flight like so many
others. Today these comrades are being cold-shouldered, and they
have united among themselves as a defensive measure to justify
an act that has no justification. But they will still have to spend
months here; and if the shame they are surely feeling (however
much they hide it) is exploited with comradeship we may save an
occasional one to share our fate here – which is a thousand times
preferable, whatever else may happen, to the fate of the moral
deserter. Without forgetting their faults, let us show them a little
warmth; let us not force them to justify themselves as a defence
against coldness.*

*2) It is noticeable in some reports, and especially in the expres-
sions used by comrades, that you feel contempt for the attitude
of the Congolese comrades in battle. There are two problems with
this. The first is that the Congolese are aware of it; watch two
people speaking in one of their languages that you do not
understand and you will see how you notice if they are speaking
about you and the sense of what they are saying. One scornful
gesture can wreck 40 positive actions. On the other hand, the
Congolese can turn into a* totí *[a black-feathered bird indigenous
to Cuba]; there are signs that the attitude of the Congolese is being
exaggerated – which may provide a justification for not carrying
out a particular task. Our primary function is to educate people
for combat, and if there is no real coming together this will not
happen. The education should concern not only ways of killing a
person but also, indeed, above all, the attitude one should have to
the sufferings of a long struggle. This is achieved when the teacher
can be taken as a model for the students to follow. Do not forget
this, comrades, and do not forget either that if any veteran of our
war of liberation says that he never ran away you can say to his
face that he is lying. We all ran and went through a dark period
when we were frightened of shadows. It is a stage that you have*

to help people overcome – and, of course, the conditions are more difficult here in terms of the development of consciousness, because the level of development is much lower than ours was in those days.

This message should be discussed among Party members and any suggestions communicated to me. Then it should be read out to the comrades and subsequently burned; it should not remain at the front. Nor should it be read in places where some comrades are giving up the struggle.

Revolutionary greetings to you all.

TATU

12 August/65

When neither Masengo nor Kabila arrived within the period I had set for myself, I went to Upper Base on the 16th and set off for Front de Force at dawn on the 18th, arriving there in the evening after a long, seemingly interminable hike through the altiplano that separated these two points. I felt a little like an escaped delinquent, but I was determined not to return to the base for a long time.

SOWING THE SEED

Scarcely had I arrived in Front de Force and thrown myself on the ground to relish my overwhelming tiredness, when the comrades started complaining about the attitude of the Rwandans, especially Captain Zakarias, who was inflicting corporal punishment on his men and who, they did not doubt, was capable of killing someone. For us, however, the reception had been cordial enough. The site chosen for the camp was at the edge of a mountain that rose from a gorge above hilly natural pastures which, in this dry period, were bare of grass. By day the temperature was pleasant, but at night it was quite cold and you had to have a fire going when you went to sleep. To protect myself from the rigours of the climate, I lay on a hide very close to the fire. I slept well, but immediately fell prey to one of the local fiends, the *birulo,* a louse that lives mainly in people's clothing and roams at will all over this region of relative cold and zero hygiene.

From the heights of our camp, it was possible to make out the town of Bendera with its electrical installations. As it lay spread out before me, I realized how foolish it had been to attack it frontally. At our present level of strength, it was a real bastion.

The latest news completed our general picture of the various fronts that made up this eastern sector of the struggle in the Congo. Although many more weapons had been distributed, the quantities actually available were as follows.

At Uvira, roughly 350, plus one artillery piece, a few anti-aircraft machine-guns, and a mortar.

In the huge region of Fizi, including Baraka, the number of armed men could be put at between 1,000 and 2,000, largely scattered among the local settlements. There were some anti-aircraft weapons, one artillery piece, and a few mortars.

At Lulimba, we reckoned that Lambert could count on 150 rifles, three anti-aircraft weapons, one artillery piece and two mortars. Further down the Kabambare road, Lambert had another small force with some 45 men, some light weapons and bazookas.

Various other groups were scattered along the Kabambare road, reportedly as far as Kasengo; most of them had little in the way of weapons – just a small number of rifles. There too, the authority of the general staff was treated with scorn. One of our men personally witnessed a discussion with someone sent from the lake, in which a man from the plains said that those who remained were unarmed and those who had run off to shelter in the mountains had all the weapons.

Between Lulimba and Front de Force, there were some other detachments that we did not know well: the one at Kalonda-Kibuye, which appeared to have some 60 weapons at that time; the group at Mukundi with roughly 150; the celebrated Faume (almost a legendary figure because he could not be located) also had 150 or so. Then there were the two groups in the mountains: Calixte had 150 weapons; while Mundandi had managed to get some 300, with three machine-guns, two artillery pieces and two mortars (although by now the number was much reduced because of the desertions, which usually happened with guns and equipment).

In the south, at Kabimba, there were roughly 150 weapons, two anti-aircraft machine-guns, one artillery piece and two mortars. And there was a profusion of weapons washed by the waters of the lake, including rifles, a number of anti-aircraft machine-guns, some reserve mortars, and an artillery piece whose original emplacement I have described before.

Satisfactory news arrived from Mbili's ambush. This time the booty was larger, but they did not complete the action because some peasants were passing down the road at the time and may have seen the tracks of this group of strangers and run off to report them at Front de Force, a few kilometres away. When it became clear that the peasants had spotted the ambush and fled, Mbili ordered everyone to remain alert and strengthened the positions on the Front de Force side, preparing to move by night if nothing else happened. At 10.00 a.m., however, a jeep with mini-tank escort came down the road from Albertville; Sultán was again responsible for opening fire, and he damaged the first vehicle and destroyed it with a second round. Comrade Afende, at a distance of barely ten metres, destroyed the jeep with a bazooka round whose fragments injured both Afende himself and Alakre. The comrades at the rear blew up the second mini-tank with hand grenades (they are armoured open vehicles, with a machine-gunner in a kind of turret, an assistant and a driver). In all they counted seven dead – including some with reddish faces who Mbili thought might be North Americans, but were later discovered to be Belgian. As they were going to collect all the equipment, enemy troops arrived from Front de Force (obviously having been tipped off by the peasants) and began shooting at one end of the ambush. The men had to withdraw at once and were unable to take the documents and weapons from the incident. Some lost their way in the first moments but appeared again later. Only one Rwandan did not return to base, and since the imperialist news agencies – which gave the correct figure of seven dead among the mercenaries – spoke of one guerrilla dead, it is logical to assume that he was hit by a stray bullet.

It would have been very useful to capture the documents, since, as we learnt from a couple of prisoners picked up on the road, those men had been assigned to make special plans for Front de Force, and probably also to devise a general plan of attack, or reconnoitre the sector with that in mind. The jeep had had a little trailer, carrying something that it had not been possible to identify. It may have been electrical equipment for microwaves, or it may have been documents. Everything suggests that the people killed there were pretty big fish, so any documentation would have been priceless to us.

As on the previous occasion, the Rwandans planned to return at once because of the lack of food, but Mbili had learnt his lesson and said that he and his people (the Cubans) were staying to the end and, after a long meeting, the Rwandans decided to remain as well. We had sent some food from the camp, and they had managed to kill an elephant (there are quite a lot in the region), so they were not constantly beset by hunger.

After the usual meetings, a new location was chosen for a second ambush. But the only ones who fell into our hands were two traders travelling on bicycle paths with food and two demijohns of *pombe*. (Mbili immediately had the drink poured away, to avoid scenes like those at the earlier engagement.) Once again the peasants spotted the ambush and went off to Force de Front, so that it was agreed with the Rwandans to lift it and return to base. Before leaving, they tried to bring down the electric cable with a bazooka round, but failed in the attempt.

I went to greet the people as they climbed the steep slopes with cheerful spirits and higher morale; the Rwandans had conducted themselves much better and, although there had again been no fighting because the Belgians had been taken completely by surprise, many of the men had stayed and done their share of the shooting. Then I met Captain Zakarias. Although these first interviews were not very cordial, his attitude began to change. They were holding the two traders captive, and since they were related to each other, I suggested keeping one hostage and sending the other to help our people establish some contact in Albertville. But Zakarias would not agree to this because they might be spies, and in the end they were sent to the lakeside base. They tried to escape from there, and at least one of them suffered a hair-raising death at the hands of his guards.

I sent another note to Masengo in which I stressed the need for a skilful and consistent policy toward the peasants, so that we could avoid the kind of problems encountered at the ambush. I proposed starting intelligence work with prisoners, and I also suggested that we involve the peasants in a plan for supplying the front and reward them with part of the goods they brought on the route that was still open from the lake. At the same time, I stressed the need for a single command at the front; the dispersion of independent forces was unacceptable, especially when one saw the tendency to anarchy and rivalry that led to extremes of violence among one or another of the groups.

We were convinced that the Rwandans, despite their recent progress, would not give much more and that we had to gear our training more to the Congolese; it was they, after all, who had to liberate the Congo. It was therefore decided to leave Comrade Mafu behind in charge of twelve men, so as not to hurt the Rwandans' feelings, and to send the rest of the troops to Calixte's front (where I would also go myself) for the time being. Before we left, it was further decided that Tom should make a political inspection at the lake, and then go to Kabimba to clarify the situation there, since I had some reservations about how Comrade Aly was behaving toward the Congolese.

Before Tom left, we had a Party meeting at which we again analysed all the problems and elected some members to help the "politico" in his tasks. The choice fell unanimously on Ishirini and Singida for the group that would continue with us, and on Alasiri for the small group that would remain with Mafu. Three wonderful fellows. We did criticize Comrade Singida at the meeting, however, for certain violent expressions toward the Congolese, and at a meeting of the general staff I criticized Azi and Azima for their discourteous treatment of the Rwandans.

Before we left for Calixte's front, the Rwandans asked me for a meeting that was attended by Captain Zakarias, the Party organization secretary, the youth leader, and a few others. We spoke about general issues of the war, such as the conduct of military operations and training, and practical problems of that kind. At the end, the organization secretary asked me to evaluate critically the work of the Rwandans up to that time, and I pointed out what I saw as two weaknesses.

First, the fatalistic attitude to food. The Rwandans relied on the peasants to bring them cows; the most they did was send some soldiers to look for food. (They had started to eat monkey meat – which ranges from tasty to merely edible as one's hunger decreases – and, except in the last few days, they had been incapable of going to look for manioc on the plains.) I explained to them that it was necessary to make the People's Army a self-sufficient army, in permanent communion with the people. It could not be parasitic – on the contrary, it had to be a mirror in which the peasants could look and see themselves.

Second, the excessive distrust of the Congolese. I urged them to unite with the Congolese, arguing that the outcome of the struggle in Rwanda depended on the outcome of the struggle in the Congo, since the latter involved a broader confrontation with imperialism.

In reply, they accepted the first criticism and gave some examples of how they were mending their ways; but they did not touch on the second point – which suggested that they did not agree with my remarks, or at least that they were not prepared to change their attitude.

I received messengers from the base, who had letters from Dar es Salaam and various pieces of news. A letter from Pablo explained some important points. It is dated 19 August 1965.

Tatu:

The trip was planned as you ordered it,[5] but a change was made because of a cable from Havana saying that a messenger was being sent here. The messenger is here, preparing and safeguarding the crossing, and will be with you shortly.

A couple of matters. A group of men are going there to organize a training base, where it will be possible to instruct comrades from Mozambique and from other movements in the region. This group was originally requested by the government of Tanzania for the instruction of Mozambicans and to carry out an action that Osmany will certainly have explained to you. Then, because of special circumstances, the plans were postponed and a request was made for the group to go to Tabera to take charge of the base there for the training of Congolese. But now, in agreement with Soumaliot, they have planned for the base to be inside the country, so they don't have to take men out from there and so they can also use it for the training of Mozambicans and members of other liberation movements in the region.

The other matter refers to various groups of Congolese who

5. This refers to the instruction to travel every fortnight from Dar es Salaam – which was never carried out.

have visited me in the last few days and who know you in one way or another. On the pretext that Kabila does not want to get involved, they are trying to carrying out work on his behalf. This is no more than a wish on their part, a little ambition to command and to seek the help of yourself and our men in creating their own group. I explained to them the danger that this will divide the movement, that they must first discuss any activity there with Kabila and yourself, and that that is how our obligations are established.

Kabila visited us and explained the situation, saying that he had expelled these comrades and spoken to the Tanzanian government so that, whenever anyone shows up claiming to be a fighter, he should be sent there. He also explained the situation to the embassies that these comrades had visited.

He went off promising that he would go there himself.

Yours, Pablo

I wrote back to Pablo that, although I did not have confidence in Kabila, all the others there were worse – they were not even intelligent and anyway had to hitch themselves to him; he should be given assurances that we here would work honestly to consolidate unity under his command; he should have no fears on that score. I expressed my doubts about the order to send instructors to be based here, because men from other movements would be so distressed to see the indiscipline, disorganization and complete demoralization that it would be a very cruel shock for anyone coming to be trained in the tasks of liberation. I expressed to Pablo my hope that the initiative had not come from him, because it was politically dangerous.

We set off for Calixte's camp, leaving behind the men we had agreed as well as Moja and a few more to wait for Zakarias, who had left on a supply mission. He had promised to bring ten men to take part in an action alongside the Congolese, and we were waiting for him to keep his word.

Calixte's camp is two and a half hours away by foot, at the end of the mountain chain where it drops down to the plains; it cannot be bettered from the point of view of defence, since the bare and extremely abrupt slopes make it easy to deny access just with rifle fire. The camp consisted of little straw huts that could hold four to ten people in cane bunks. We were allocated a few unoccupied ones. The place was more comfortable and less cold than at Bendera, but it had the same quantity of lice.

Calixte had been summoned by Lambert and was about to leave for Lulimba. He greeted me cheerfully enough and said he was glad we had come, but he did not like our being with the Rwandans. I explained that we had carried out orders by training that group, but that we wanted to work with him. Our conversation was amicable, although there was not the direct communication that we had had with the Rwandans; Calixte did not speak a word of French and my Swahili was still far from perfect, so that we had to rely on Cuban translators who did not appreciate every shade of meaning. It was very difficult to explain anything complex.

From the camp we looked down upon the whole nearby plain, the settlements of Makungo, Nyangi and Katenga, and even Front de Force. I told Calixte it was necessary to get closer to keep harrying the guardsmen and firing at the soldiers, and I suggested that this be done immediately. He agreed, and I sent Azi to explore the area with a group of men provisionally based in a village some four kilometres from Makungo. We prepared to go down at once with the help of Calixte's second-in-command, the temporary base commander, who called together his men and fought off the reluctance they felt when it was a question of approaching the enemy.

Taking advantage of the fact that it was a Sunday, the peasants held a festival in our honour before we left; men dressed in wood demon's clothes, or something like that, performed ritual dances and everyone went to pay worship to the idol, a mere stone placed near the top of the mountain and surrounded with a reed circle, which every now and then was sprinkled with the blood of an animal sacrifice. In this case it was a lamb, which everyone present then ate. The ritual seems complicated, but in essence it is extremely simple: sacrifice is made to the god, the stone idol, and the sacrificed animal is then consumed as people take the opportunity to eat and drink copiously.

The peasants were extremely friendly towards us, and I felt so much in their debt that I returned to my old profession as a doctor. Under the circumstances, though, I had to keep to the bare minimum of penicillin injections against gonorrhoea, the traditional disease in the area, and tablets against malaria.

Again we began the wearying task of teaching the elements of warfare to people whose determination was far from evident – in fact, we seriously doubted its existence. In this way did we desperately cast seed to left and to right, trying to ensure that some would germinate before the bad times arrived.

ATTEMPTED "PURSUIT"

In the Makungo area, with a new batch of aspiring guerrillas, we tried to resume the little classes in ambush that we had given on the road from Albertville to Front de Force. The men became more heterogeneous, as Captain Zakarias arrived with ten more Rwandans; we would try to draw them closer and thus establish a united front.

Enemy troops were located at: Front de Force, three or four hours on foot from our camp; opposite us at Nyangi; two hours away at Katenga, and 50 kilometres away at Lulimba. Our aim was to attack on the Katenga to Lulimba road and stop them if they tried to advance from Nyangi. The latter is a village on an abandoned road closer to the mountains, where Makungo is situated and we had our headquarters. Katenga is on the road that is currently used because it has modern bridges able to withstand flooding rivers.

We put Azi and a group of six Cubans and ten Congolese in charge of stopping any forces that might advance from Nyangi. The attack on the road would involve some 40 Congolese, ten Rwandans and 30 Cubans – more than enough to wipe out any enemy forces that might advance there.

During these days a group of ten Cubans had arrived who, it had been thought, would be the instructors at an international base for not only Congolese but also Africans from other movements. But, given the conditions, we had seen that it was impossible to keep a stable group studying these arts, and so, starting from this next action, we decided to incorporate the instructors in the struggle. It was not such a major reinforcement, because the comrades were theoretically prepared to give more or less orthodox weapons instruction but, with a few exceptions, did not have experience in guerrilla combat.

I personally accompanied the fighters. After crossing the River Kimbi, which in the rainy season has quite a strong current but could then be easily crossed waist high, we took up position in the area we had selected.

The tactic was simple. The centre of the ambush was the strongest point and was where the brunt of the fighting would occur. On both sides there would be enough men to stop any part of a large convoy that might remain outside the main ambush and to prevent any enemy troops escaping the trap – although ideally they would have no chance to defend themselves because of the surprise factor. As usual, we would begin firing with rocket launchers. A small group five or six kilometres down the road to Katenga had the task of smashing a wooden bridge after the lorries had passed and fallen into the ambush, to prevent their escape or the arrival of rein-forcements. Furthermore, since a lack of detonators (which never arrived) made it impossible to use anti-tank mines directly, we placed one on a little wooden bridge two or three metres wide at the very centre of the ambush and attached a grenade fuse and a piece of cord so that it would explode after five or six seconds. The device was unreliable because its detonation at the right moment depended on the user's skill and the speed of the passing lorry – so we kept it as a last resort in case nothing else could be used.

I set up the little command post by a well some 500 metres from the ambush. In actions of this kind, you must think of the supply of water and food, since you have to wait days and days for the vehicles to pass. The water was stagnant and dirty and, despite our use of disinfectants, there were many cases of diarrhoea during the time we spent there; the food was not varied but nor did it run short, because the ambush was right in the middle of an untended mountain of manioc, with roots to last us for years and years, tough but edible if you were really feeling hungry. Some rainfall made our stay less pleasant. But on the first and second days there were no greater inconveniences; the men were both tense and bored as the hours went by interminably, but at the same time any noise that broke the silence became the sound of an engine and immediately caused an alert. Even I, several hundred metres from the front positions, repeatedly suffered these aural hallucinations.

Until Sunday, the fifth day of our lying in wait, we managed to keep control of the men. Then the Congolese began to show signs of impatience and to invent ostensible information that lorries came here only once a fortnight, adding that, as the last convoy had passed the day before we laid the ambush, it would be best to pack up and leave. They did not insist too much, however, despite the fact that the forced idleness, the foul water and the manioc diet, occasionally varied with a tiny amount of tinned food or *bukali*, were not suited to keep up their fighting spirit. On the fifth day, a comical event revealed our weaknesses once again: as I was lying placidly in my hammock at the command post, I heard a sound as of stampeding elephants; the six or seven Congolese in charge of the food said to me with bulging eyes, *"Askari Tshombe, askari Tshombe"* (Tshombe soldiers). They had seen them at that very spot, some 20 or 30 metres from their position. I had scarcely had time to don my battledress, leaving hammock and rucksack to their fate, when one of the Cubans accompanying me also saw the *"askari Tshombe"*. The situation grew more complicated, for I could not rely on the Congolese and I had only four Cubans with me, one of them the ailing Singida, whom I quickly sent to Moja for reinforcements. I also got him to take away the Congolese, who in these circumstances were more of a nuisance, and walked a few metres towards the river to escape the strip of land visible to the enemy. Following the steps of those who were on their way back, I intended to withdraw along the same road after making contact with the guardsmen, but after a few moments the news came that the people they had seen were not enemy soldiers but local peasants, who had fled at the sight of us and had eventually been spotted by one of our men from afar.

We were discussing these incidents when a scout sent by Moja arrived at our rear to find out what was happening. He heard us talking and ran off to report that the guardsmen had already captured the command post and taken up position inside it. There was total chaos as it appeared that the ambushers had been ambushed. Moja, who was directly in command of the action, immediately called off the ambush and took shelter in a nearby area, giving orders for people to search for me in the direction of the River Kimbi (where I was reported to have gone).

After a couple of hours, we had started turning back but some of the Congolese were taking advantage of the situation to keep going until they reached the camp; we suffered a number of losses of this kind as a result of the confusion. The childish reactions of the Congolese, who ran off like ill-mannered kids, were compounded by the mistakes of some of our less battle-tried comrades.

We decided to move the site of the ambush by a few hundred metres, since the peasants had seen us and we did not know to which group they belonged. I myself felt compelled to return to the camp, as I had been told that Comrade Aragonés was on his way. The ambush lasted eleven days, from 1 to 11 of September, and several times, when the Congolese pressed more and more insistently to leave, Moja had to say that he would remain just with the Cubans – although, because of his attitude, they stayed at their posts in the end.

Finally the lorries arrived – all two of them. The first was destroyed, seven or eight soldiers were killed and the same number of rifles captured; they were carrying nothing other than their weapons, a plentiful supply of marijuana and some papers without importance (except for the Lulimba payroll). The second vehicle was not destroyed by the bazooka people, because it failed to fire, and the occupants (of whom there were more than in the first vehicle) took cover and put our left wing to flight. Most of those who fled were Congolese, but some Cubans got alarmed at this and also withdrew. Thus, instead of completely wiping out the two lorries, we were ourselves pursued at a certain moment and had to start retreating. As always happens at such times, the rout was complete. The Congolese quickly crossed the Kimbi, not stopping until they reached the general staff, and we were again almost reduced to the Cubans – although this time the Rwandans, who had more experience of battle, also stayed behind. One of them even fired his bazooka at the lorry, and another – who had joined our contingent – proudly displayed a dead soldier's boots he had appropriated because his own were falling apart. They also helped to recover the weapons.

What this action showed was how far off we still are from organizing forces that can wage even such minor battles, and how much more is needed to prepare some of the Cubans, who got alarmed at conditions different from those they are used to in their army (the conditions of guerrilla warfare) and did not manage to act with coordination and initiative.

On the enemy side, the way in which the soldiers defended themselves showed that they had had training and were making progress, because they did what they did after the first vehicle had been destroyed. They were all blacks, but we could see we were facing a far from negligible enemy – contrary to what the Congolese said when they blamed all the ills on white mercenaries and claimed that they had instilled terror in the blacks.

Before the fighting began, Calixte's chief lieutenant had told me that his men refused to fight alongside the Rwandans, because they ran off shooting wildly and were capable of killing their own comrades. We did not doubt that in the least, having suffered its effects on ourselves, but we had every reason to doubt the Congolese even more, since they never fired at the enemy and ran away at the first sound of gunfire. This did not worry us much, because the same had happened with the Rwandans at first, and already in this third audacious action – with a smaller number of men, it was true – they had shown a new attitude of mind. Nevertheless, any attempts to unite the two groups seemed doomed to fail. We were able to ward off the first crisis and persuade Calixte's people to fight alongside Mundandi's, but then a dispute broke out concerning weapons. I insisted that they be given to the Congolese as a gesture of goodwill, but the Rwandans argued that they were their weapons and that the Congolese had done nothing to deserve them. There was an attempt to resolve things by force, but after speaking to Captain Zakarias we were able to get the situation under control and the rifles were reluctantly handed over to them, without any show of friendship. The Rwandans, not wanting to stay there any longer, immediately went back to their part of the front. This happened a day after I told Masengo my views about Zakarias and the unity of the struggle.

The outcome of the fighting was satisfactory, in the sense that we had no wounded to feel bad about. Comrade Anzali, reconnoitring some hours later with Mbili, set fire to the enemy's abandoned lorry and suffered some quite serious burns when the petrol ignited.

Azi, for his part, had ambushed some enemy soldiers at Nyangi and perhaps wounded one or two, but the action had not had much effect.

Nevertheless, I still had the feeling that things might work out. I gave instructions for new ambushes to be laid on the road, and prepared to go to Lulimba to persuade Lambert of the need for action. Among the documents in the lorry, as I said before, we had found a payroll mentioning 53 men in Lulimba, and we thought this the ideal opportunity to attack there with Lambert's numerically superior forces and to open the road to Kasengo. If the ambushes between Katenga and Lulimba worked, they would give us a few days' breathing space to draw a circle around Lulimba and to assemble all our scattered forces from that large region.

In accordance with our principles, we got some action moving on social questions. Doctor Hindi, who had arrived from the base, began consultations for the local peasants and established a rota of visits to the mountain villages. I handed out seeds brought to me from the lake, so that some vegetables could be sown and cultivated and later distributed among us. We managed to create a different, more communicative atmosphere. Like peasants anywhere in the world, these ones were responsive to any human interest in them, thankful and very cooperative. It was painful to think that these same men who showed genuine trust in us and real interest in work could, when they joined the Liberation Army, become the undisciplined, battle-shy idlers we saw before us. The military formations, instead of being factors in the development of revolutionary consciousness, were a rubbish heap in which everything rotted away, as a result of the disorganization and lack of leadership we have already complained about so often in these notes.

THE PATIENT GETS WORSE

At the end of August I made my usual analysis, more optimistic this time than any of the others I had written during the seven months in the Congo.

> My scholarship has run out – which means a step forward. This month may be recorded as generally more positive, with a qualitative change in the men in addition to the action at Front de Force. The presence of Zakarias with ten men is a good indication of this, as is the fact that nearly all the men at the front are down on the plain. Now we need to come up with some results and to make the situation here more stable. My next steps will be to visit Lambert in Lulimba and to make a trip to Kabambare, then to convince them of the necessity of taking Lulimba and continuing from there. But for all this to happen, the ambushes and the subsequent actions must produce results.
>
> I don't know what Kabila will do, but I'll try to get him to come to Masengo and visit the fronts – that will change people's attitude to him. Then the peasants must be organized throughout the zone and given a single front-line command. In two months, if everything works out well, we could have Force encircled and be trying to cut off the electricity so that it loses its strategic importance. Everything is looking much brighter – today, at least.

A few days later, however, the dark colours were again taking hold of the situation. Aly had had some serious altercations with the leaders in his area and was now at the lake, unwilling to return though not saying as much. In the recently abandoned area at Front de Force, activity was completely falling off. We had sent someone to Kigoma to find a couple of oxyacetylene bags, with the idea of torching the overhead electric cable, but it was extremely difficult to transport them because of the weight and the men's negative attitude – in fact, they did not want to carry out any action if the Cuban people in charge were not there. The reconnoitring for a site from which to bombard the reservoir at the hydro-electric power station did not yield any positive results. And here, after the early euphoria, the soldiers tired of the active life and asked to return to the fun and games at their Upper Base.

The picture was at its gloomiest in the relations of Masengo and Kabila with the leaders in the Fizi area, and of the Revolution in general with the Tanzanian government. Kabila and Masengo went to Kibamba, but at once news arrived that the Tanzanian authorities were refusing to deliver a number of weapons we had requested, including the longed-for fuses for the anti-tank mines, and were demanding Kabila's immediate presence. We knew this for sure, because the man who had gone to get the weapons was Changa, our "admiral", and he had been personally told that nothing would be delivered and that Kabila himself should go and talk with the government. It was the only time Kabila had made a serious attempt to cross into the Congo (at least there was no proof to the contrary), and now he was obliged to go back out to discuss some problem or other.

At the lakeside base, they had arrested some members of Fizi's rival group who had been making liquidationist propaganda in the combat zone. Masengo did not have a proper prison there and sent them to be kept in Uvira. In fact, he decided to take them himself and to use the trip to carry out an inspection of the affected zone. They set off in a launch. Here is Aly's version of events; it gives a clear idea of the turn they now took.

8-9-65

From Comrade: Aly

To Comrade: Tatu

Re: Comrade Tom's trip to Kasima

   Comrade Masengo's trip to Changa and Aly's to Uvira

   We left on the 16th at 21.00 hours, intending to leave Comrade Tom at Kasima and to continue on to Uvira with the three counter-revolutionary prisoners, leaving some weapons there and inspecting the area – the latter to be done by Masengo.

   We reached Kasima at 24.30 hours. On arriving in Kasima, Comrade Masengo ordered the squad leader to come on board, but a soldier climbed up, found out that President Masengo was on board and started talking to him; he offered to bring him some cigars and various trifles on his way back.

   When he got off, the soldier asked for some soap and said that, if it was not forthcoming, the boat would not be able to leave. Comrade Tom got off and told the squad not to shoot – which they ignored once Comrade Tom was 100 metres away.

   Each of them fired a few shots and ran away; one of them was captured later.

   Comrade Masengo called the soldiers and officers to the shore and ordered them to capture the rest of the squad, saying that he would pick them up on his way back.

   We continued on towards Uvira, but on reaching Mubembe at 9.00 hours Comrade Masengo said we should stop there and travel through the night.

   We received rather a cool welcome in the village. Comrade Masengo talked with the headman there and a student comrade from China, asking them to call together the local population for a meeting at which they would be informed of the political situation.

   The meeting began at approximately 12.30 and lasted until 17.00. At that time Comrade Ernesto came up to us and told us to say nothing; they wanted to release the prisoners – otherwise there would be bloodshed.

At 17.30 Comrade Masengo said we should leave and go down to the shore. Once we were there, Comrade Masengo told us to go on board the boat, and when we dallied a bit, Ernesto called out again and said we were stupid, they were going to start shooting up the boat. They immediately began to take up positions and to speak in a nasty sort of way; they sent a squad to take the prisoners off the boat, and this was done without any response, until one of the sailors fired his rifle and made for the rebels, with Masengo and a few others following behind. They began to give blasts on the whistle to get men together and succeeded in capturing eleven soldiers, but not the prisoners, who seemed to have infected the soldiers with quite a campaign in favour of the opposing group.

The pressure exerted by these men and the advance reports made it impossible to continue to Uvira, since things were worse further on.

It is known that those who freed the prisoners came from Fizi and Baraka, and some other men were mentioned whose names I no longer remember, since I didn't want to take notes in front of them.

I want it to be known that at no time did Masengo come and warn us of the danger at that place; that he was aware of the danger since it was common knowledge, but we were not aware of it since we did not know the language well and it was all discussed at the meeting in which we did not take part but he did.

As far as we could tell from Ernesto, this situation has not arisen only now.

Bearing this in mind, I'd like to know what is to be done; what should be our attitude now that things are passing from words to deeds – dangerous deeds at that.

As far as you are concerned, you should be quite careful because they – that is, the rebels – are quite strong and are not familiar to us.

On the way back we stopped off at Kasima and picked up the politico, but not those who were supposed to be prisoners, because they had not been captured.

Back on a farming estate, although we made the signals we had taught them the night before, they opened fire.

Hoping for an early reply,

Revolutionary greetings,

Yours, Aly

Fortunately, it can be said that Aly's suspicions were unfounded, since Masengo himself had to go on board the boat and was exposed to the same dangers.

Almost at once, Masengo sent me a letter that indicated how insecure the comrades leading the Congolese revolution feel. It is dated Kibamba, 6 September.

> *To Comrade Doctor Tatu*
> *Makungo*

Comrade Doctor,

I greet you after our few days' separation. On military matters I have followed your advice: Comrade Lieutenant-Colonel Lambert will coordinate the activities of the Lulimba-Makungo and Kalonda-Kibuye fronts.

Comrade Kabila and myself were ready to visit you, but unfortunately the circumstances were such that we could not carry out the plan for the time being. Five days after we arrived in Kibamba, Comrade Kabila received an urgent call from President Nyerere of Tanzania. The political situation inside the country is not very serious, and we hoped that by an effort of ours we could overcome some difficulties that irresponsible people have caused. Today we arrested some members of the counter-revolutionary gang[6] and the population did not react in any way – which means that it understands their defects. The leader of this gang is the traitor Gbenye, who, having received several million, sent these agents everywhere with the aim of burying the revolution and then going off to negotiate with the people in Leopoldville.

The imperialists promised to let Gbenye form a government if he succeeded in burying the revolution and gathering all the agents of imperialism within his future government, with the aim of maintaining neo-colonialism in the Congo.

Gbenye used the meeting of East African heads of state (Tanzania, Uganda and Kenya) to state that we should solve our problems with Leopoldville, and promised that after the reconciliation with Leopoldville we would establish a federation with the East African states. This is why Comrade Kabila has just been called to Dar es Salaam; the intention may be to put pressure on us. They even refused to let Comrade Kabila be accompanied by one of our people to Dar es Salaam.

Despite all this, we shall never agree to such a reconciliation. We ask you to approach your embassy on this matter.

I would also point out that I am leaving today for Uvira, accompanied by the Cuban Captain Aly, and that after my return I shall also go to Kibamba. I hope to find your reply on these matters when I return – especially your good advice about the problem I mentioned above.

We consider that the major African leaders do not want the complete liberation of the Congo, for fear that when the Congo is completely independent, with genuine revolutionaries at its head, the whole of Africa will be in danger of following in the footsteps of the Congo.

Anyway the situation is not yet grave, and we are almost sure we can get through this period.

6. These were the three prisoners of whom Aly spoke.

On the basis of what I have just written, I hope that you will be able to give us some guidance on how to solve some problems of this kind.

The letter raised a number of interesting points: Gbenye's activity and his links with the imperialists, which were not as clearly demonstrated as Masengo indicated; his promises to African leaders, of which we were also not certain; and the pressure on Kabila from Dar es Salaam, which did indeed exist. It is worth mentioning his rapprochement with the Cubans at this point – which might have occurred in an earlier and more relaxed period, for now the enemy was about to unleash an offensive. I replied at once in the following terms.

Dear Comrade,

I have just spoken with your envoy Comrade Charles Bemba; he will be able to tell you how I see the situation, but I will make a little balance-sheet.

I feel we have now shown that it is really possible to remain on the plain. Following the actions at Mundandi's front, we have just laid an ambush that resulted in seven or eight enemy soldiers killed and six weapons captured.[7] We have placed ambushes on both the roads: the one from Nyangi to Lulimba, and the one from Force to Lulimba.

I think we should press harder in this area and try to drive out the Tshombists who are near Lulimba, so that we have a road open to the lake. I am aware of the problems in Baraka and Fizi, but it would be very important for us to have a direct supply route.

On the problems you have just described to me. First, you should rest assured that we will support you in relation to the Tanzanian government, and also – as far as we are able – in meeting your needs. I'd like to talk with you, but I understand your difficulties

7. In fact seven weapons were captured, but a Rwandan took one for himself. This caused a dispute when it was discovered, and he was ordered to hand it back.

in leaving the general staff. In a few more days, I shall be free to go and speak with you. I should like then to visit other parts of the same front and would ask you not to keep me at the lake; my job is what I am doing now.

Like you, I am optimistic in the long term, but it is necessary to pay more attention to political and military organization. We have made some progress but not enough, and we will be able to advance more by fighting more. Battle is the soldier's great school. Moreover, our great source of weapons is the enemy army; if we are not allowed to use the lake, we still have the battlefield.

I welcome your decision to appoint Comrade Lambert as co-ordinator, even though his role is becoming more difficult. His real task, in my view, should be as commander of the front. I would also draw your attention to the fact that the comrades from Rwanda have fought very well with us and have now done the same with the Congolese comrades. Captain Zakarias is a fine type, despite some flaws that can be corrected with time.

The point that needs underlining is our policy towards the peasants. Without the support of the people, we will not have any real successes. I hope to talk with you at greater length about this when we see each other.

Revolutionary greetings,

Tatu

I kept up an optimistic tone, which lasted a while longer. In spite of our difficulties, we had caused the enemy some losses and had the potential to wear them down and force them to give up certain positions as too costly to defend.

During these days, the long-awaited messengers arrived. They turned out to be Aragonés, Fernández Mell and Margolles, who had come to remain at the front. When I learnt of their identity, I feared that they might have a message urging me to return at once to Cuba or to give up the struggle, because it did not enter my head that the Party's organization secretary would relinquish his job to come to the Congo, especially in a situation where nothing was clearly defined and quite a few negative aspects were to be noted. Aragonés insisted on coming and Fidel gave his consent; the same happened with Margolles; and Fernández Mell, an old comrade-in-arms, was the man I had asked Cuba for to strengthen the command structure. Karim also joined us; he would replace Tom as the "politico", because of his greater ideological and cultural development.

The first three entered the country clandestinely, as doctors. We did not know if they would really be able to stay, given that they were whites, but our position was such that we could do virtually what we wanted in our own camp; the problems began when we tried interfering in the Congolese camp to organize things.

Comrade Aragonés, because of his size, was given the Swahili name "Tembo" (elephant), and Fernández Mell, because of his character, was called "Siki" (vinegar). The rest kept coming out of a vocabulary book. Tembo was given the number 120 on the list of members of our force. Taking into account our losses – four killed, two gone back to Cuba, and Comrade Changa (who, though on the list, operated at Kigoma and organized crossings of the lake) – we had 113 men or, not counting the four doctors, 107 fighters. The force was large enough to attempt something, but as we have seen, a number of circumstances that I could not or did not know how to avoid meant that they were dispersed over a wide area, so that we could never count on more than 30 or 40 men at the time of an action. If we add to this the fact that nearly everyone suffered an attack of malaria at one time or another – some much more than once – it will be agreed that the force was not capable of deciding the issue of a campaign. It might have formed the nucleus of a new-style army if the conditions of the Congolese comrades had been other than they were.

The morale of our troops had improved somewhat, as one may gauge from the fact that three of the comrades who had planned to return to Cuba were now asking to be put back on full duty: Abdallah, Anzali and Baati.

Apparently, the Liberation Army was also getting reinforcements in the shape of contingents trained in China and Bulgaria. The first concern of these men was to take a fortnight's leave to visit their family here; then they would stretch it out when it proved too short. After all, they were cadres trained for the revolution and it would be irresponsible to risk their lives in battle; they had come to infuse their comrades with the mountain of knowledge they had acquired in six months of theoretical studies, but it would be a criminal betrayal of the revolution actually to make them fight.

This position was taken by all the groups, regardless of whether they had been in China, Bulgaria or the USSR. Such were the consequences of training students from petty-bourgeois milieux in the Congo, with all their burden of resentment and their urge to copy the colonialists.

French-speaking students had been chosen, or else sons of political bosses who had absorbed everything negative in European culture and none of the revolutionary spirit born among the proletariat. They returned with a superficial gloss of Marxism, imbued with their importance as "cadres" and a huge desire to command that was expressed in acts of indiscipline or even conspiracy.

The humble ordinary fighters, capable of giving their lives for a cause they barely understood, were disregarded by leaders who kept away from the centres of fighting and lacked revolutionary cadres to assist them. We were determined to uncover these cadres among the fallen leaves, but time got the better of us in the end.

TAKING THE PULSE

It was necessary to keep up the action on the Katenga to Lulimba road, trying to prevent the arrival of reinforcements so that the number of isolated enemy troops would remain small enough for us to attack. We doubled the number of ambushes and put Pombo and Nane at the front of them. We also began a battle around a point where we broke through day after day but the enemy rapidly restored its position, until finally a strong garrison was placed there to stop us continuing.

After sending Azima and a small group on ahead to reconnoitre, I set off for Lulimba. It was a cloudy day, and intermittent rain slowed us down and forced us to seek shelter in some of the abandoned houses that were a frequent sight along the way. The road had also fallen into disrepair, even before the recent events convulsed the region. In mid-morning, there were sounds of fighting and many aircraft from the direction of the ambush; we learnt the outcome several days later, when Moja reported that the guardsmen had punctured our defences at the cost of a few mini-tanks and, probably, some of the men reinforcing Lulimba. Enemy troops also advanced from Lulimba to help their comrades at the point of break-through – which made us think that there had never been only 53 there, as the captured payroll indicated, but many more. For a moment we thought that the battle was for Lulimba itself, but in fact they were reinforcing the key points to launch an offensive. We later guessed as much because of the major work going on at Front de Force and Nyangi, but we had no intelligence from the enemy camp to keep us informed.

At midday we met Azima on his way back from the reconnoitre. He had gone along the road as far as a village that we called Lulimba, without coming across any guardsmen. The road runs parallel to the positions occupied by the rebels in the mountains, up to the point where it joins the highway coming from Front de Force and heads straight towards the hills, climbing them at their lowest and most negotiable point.

Azima told us how he scouted a kilometre beyond the junction, along the seemingly more important road to the River Kimbi, but found no trace of a human presence. They also explored the place known as the Mission, a former Protestant church that is now abandoned; as they crossed this no-man's-land, they were spotted by look-outs on the ridges six kilometres away, who fired at them 17 artillery rounds, a number of mortar shells and some other devices he could not specify. Their aim was accurate enough, but it would have been a titanic feat to score a parabolic hit on six men marching along a road; the upshot was a monstrous waste of projectiles, fired by hunch in an area that must have outposts all over the place.

With all this ahead of us, we decided to call a halt and get some sleep – for there was still a long distance to be covered, and it is very tiring to do it in one day. We also had to send someone ahead to tell the general staff at Lubondja that we were coming by the road across the plain. The next day, we made contact with advance parties which, on our advice, had been sent down to accompany us to the Lulimba "barrier" in the mountains.

As we moved along, we could see the large number of peasant villages in the forest at the foot of the mountains, two, three or four kilometres from the main road, at places where there was some water. The peasants had built primitive houses, and those willing to run the risk of an encounter with the enemy fed themselves from new or old fields close to the road – as well as from a little game-hunting. We spoke for a long time with the peasants; as we had no medicines with us, I asked Makungo to send a doctor for some sick people and I promised that one would drop by once a fortnight on his usual rounds.

Lieutenant-Colonel Lambert's barrier was a cluster of little huts (complete with lice) built of straw or zinc by the side of the road, without vegetation to conceal them, without trenches or shelters of any kind, and with the scant protection of a couple of anti-aircraft machine-guns. The soldiers' common defence, when aircraft appeared, was to run and hide in a nearby gully. But although the position was so visible, there had not been any major attacks from the air. There were no fortifications at the front-line defences either, only a few bazookas and look-outs. (Trenches are always a headache, since, for superstitious reasons, the Congolese soldiers refuse to enter holes in the ground that they have dug themselves and fail to construct any solid defence against attack.) The strength of the position was the height from which it overlooked the road winding among the hills; this made it easy to attack troops climbing towards them, so long as they did this only by road. If infantry were sent to advance at the edges, there was no one to attack them and they could take the position almost without losses.

There were very few men in the barrier and no officers. We thought of marching straight on to Lubondja, but they sent word that a commander would come up to meet us. When he arrived the next day, he told us that Lieutenant-Colonel Lambert was in Fizi because of a sick daughter; he had been at the lake before that, and it was now a month and a half since he last set foot in the camp. The person in charge of the men spent his time in Lubondja, which was described as the general staff, and only a lower rank remained in the barrier (which made no difference, because no one had any authority over the men). The food was provided by the peasants, who had to walk some 15 kilometres to the camp from the Lubondja area. From time to time they did some hunting nearby; there is a lot of game.

When the food arrived (essentially manioc root), they began the work of grinding it individually to make *bukali*, since there was no tradition of eating communally. Each had to prepare his own portion with what he had managed to obtain, so that the camp became a huge multi-kitchen where even the look-outs shared in the total disorder.

They asked me to speak to the men, a group of less than 100 who were not all armed, and I rattled off my usual "volley". Armed men, I said, are not soldiers but simply armed men; a revolutionary soldier is made in combat, and there was no sign of combat around there. I asked them to come down from the hills, with Cubans and Congolese sharing the same conditions, since we had come to endure together the hardships of the struggle. The war would be hard and peace could not be expected soon; you can't expect victory without making great sacrifices. I also explained that *dawa* is not always effective against modern weapons, and that death would be a common occurrence in hours of battle. All this in my elementary French, which Charles Bemba then translated into Kibembe, the native tongue in the region.

The commander was willing to come down with his men, but not to attack unless he received orders from his superiors. We would achieve nothing by bringing this motley little group to the plain if there was no order to attack Lulimba. I decided to go to Fizi and try to talk Lambert round. First we reached Lubondja in the great plain of Fizi, some 15 kilometres along the main road from the outpost. The peasants gave us a fine reception, which took material shape in food. The whole atmosphere was one of peace and security, as it had been a long time since the guardsmen last made a raid into the mountains, and the whole group enjoyed the relative well-being characterized by a variety of foods such as potatoes and onions and a more stable life. We left the next day and had already travelled ten kilometres when a lorry carrying troops to Lubondja appeared and, on its way back, took us to Fizi. Inside the vehicle was an individual with all the signs of alcohol poisoning, including dreadful vomiting. I found out the next day that he had died in Fizi's hospital – or receptacle would be a better word, since it had no doctors or medical assistance of any kind.

During the 40 or more kilometres on the road, we were able to observe a number of features of the region: first, the large number of armed men wandering around all the villages we passed, each with an officer who spent the time either in his own or in a friendly house, clean, well fed and well supplied with drink; second, the fact that the soldiers seemed to have a lot of freedom and to be very content with the situation, always walking around with a rifle on their shoulder; and third, the great distance between Lambert's men and Moulane's, who looked at each other like cats and dogs. They immediately identified Charles, Masengo's inspector, and everything turned cold around him.

Fizi is a small town, but still the largest I have seen in the Congo. It has two clearly defined parts: a small one with rubblework houses, some very modern; and an African quarter with the usual huts, impoverished and lacking water or hygienic facilities. This, the more populous of the two, had a lot of refugees from other regions; the other belonged to the big shots and army men.

Fizi lies at the top of the elevation that rises from the lake, 37 kilometres from Baraka in meadowland containing little vegetation. Its only defence was a single anti-aircraft machine-gun, worked by a Greek mercenary they had made prisoner in fighting around Lulimba, and they were quite satisfied with such a precarious instrument. General Moulane gave me a very cool welcome, for he knew the purpose of my visit and, given the tension between Lambert and himself, he thought it best to make his disgust obvious. My situation was a little odd: kept at arm's length by General Moulane, a polite and frosty host, and courted by an exuberant and enormously friendly Lambert, I was the field of a battle that never took external form. As a result, we were given two meals: one by the general, one by Lambert. They treated each other with respect, and Lambert excelled in his coldly official attitude to the general.

At a short meeting I informed the major-general of the work we had accomplished at the front, and of my intention to discuss with Lambert whether he could do anything in the Lulimba area without committing himself too much. The general listened to me in silence, then gave orders in Swahili to his adjutant (he did not speak French), whereupon the latter began to tell of the major battles at Muenga, a town some 200 kilometres to the north that they had just captured. The trophies were a flag and a shotgun, which they had taken from a Belgian priest. Apparently, they had been unable to advance any further and capture other villages, because of a lack of weapons and ammunition. They had taken two prisoners, but (to quote their very words): "You know, discipline is not very good and they killed them before reaching here." The patriotic forces had lost three men. Now they wanted to reinforce Muenga with heavy weapons and had sent someone to ask for them at the lake, along with more ammunition. Then they would begin a push towards Bukavu, through an area where they had some 300 weapons at their disposal. I did not want to ask too many questions because irony or distrust was visible on his face. I therefore let him talk away, although it did not seem very logical that 300 men, having taken the position after a furious battle, should have no other trophies than a flag and the village priest's shotgun.

That night the general's "adviser", together with a colonel from the Kasengo area, explained to me the special features of their vast territorial possessions. They referred to Uvira as a sector in their zone, although its commander, Colonel Bidalila, did not take orders directly from them; the colonel from Kasengo, on the other hand, was a loyal subordinate of the general's. Both complained that there were not enough weapons; the man from Kasengo had been waiting some time there for his equipment to arrive. I asked him why he had not made a trip to Kibamba, and he replied that he could expect the requested material to arrive in Baraka, from where he and his men would take it to Kasengo and begin the offensive.

Both of them – General Moulane and the colonel from Kasengo – were veterans who had begun the struggle together with Patrice Lumumba; they did not say so explicitly, but the "adviser" took it upon himself to explain that they had indeed launched the struggle and were genuine revolutionaries, whereas Masengo and Kabila had joined in later and now wanted to capitalize on everything. He made a direct attack on these comrades and accused them of sabotaging their own actions. In his view, since Kabila and Masengo were from Northern Katanga, they were sending arms and provisions there and keeping this area (which was loyal to Soumaliot) completely starved of supplies; the same was happening in relation to Kasengo. Furthermore, they did not respect the command hierarchy. There was a general there, and yet Lieutenant-Colonel Lambert – who was the brigade commander – was completely independent and settled matters directly with Kabila and Masengo, obtaining weapons and ammunition that they did not receive and thus undermining discipline and hindering the advance of the Revolution.

The people from Kasengo and from Fizi both asked me for Cubans.

I explained that I was trying to concentrate my scant forces and did not want to scatter them across the huge front, and that one or two Cubans would not change the situation. I asked them to go to the lake, where our comrades could instruct them in the handling of machine-guns, artillery and mortars, so that their own people would be able to use these weapons instead of having to rely upon a mercenary, as they were doing in Fizi. This argument did not convince them in the slightest.

The general invited me to go to Baraka and to Mbolo, his own village. I accepted diplomatically, but said that we would have to come back the same day since we were due to return to the Lulimba area. Before we left, they took me round Fizi and I had an opportunity to examine a wounded man from Kasengo. The bullet had gone through muscle, and the untreated wound had become infected and was giving off a nauseating smell (he had spent 15 days in these conditions). I advised that he be sent without delay to Kibamba for treatment by the doctors there, and suggested we could take advantage of our own trip to take him immediately as far as Baraka. They deemed it more important to put a large escort on the lorry and to leave the wounded man in Fizi; I heard no more about him, but I imagine he had a very bad time of it.

What mattered was to put on a "show". General Moulane donned his combat gear, consisting of a motorcycle helmet with a leopard skin on top, which made him look pretty ridiculous and led Tumaini to baptise him "the cosmonaut". Walking very slowly and stopping every few paces, we eventually reached Baraka, a small town on the shores of the lake, where we again felt the aspects of disorganization of which I have spoken so often.

Baraka displayed traces of its former relative prosperity, including a cotton-baling machine, but everyone had been ruined by the war and the little factory was bombed out. Mbolo lies on the lake some 30 kilometres to the north – you get there by a very bad road that runs parallel to the shore. Nearly every thousand metres we came across what they called a "road block", a stop signal as solid as the couple of poles and nondescript cord from which it had been improvised, where travellers were required to show their documents. The shortage of petrol meant that the only people travelling were functionaries of one kind or another, so that the effect of these groups was to disperse their forces instead of concentrating them. At Mbolo there was a change of personnel, the soldiers in the escort lorry replacing three who were due to go to Fizi on leave; they organized a military parade that culminated in a speech by General Moulane. It was so ridiculous that it had a Chaplinesque dimension; I felt I was watching a bad comedy, bored and hungry, while the officers uttered shouts, stamped on the ground and did imposing about-turns, and the poor soldiers came and went, vanished and reappeared, in the performance of their manoeuvres. The man in charge of the detachment was a former non-commissioned officer in the Belgian army. Any soldier who falls into the hands of one of these NCOs has to learn the whole complicated liturgy of barracks discipline, with all its local nuances – which is all very well for organizing a parade whenever a fly moves in the area, but never gets beyond that. The worst of it is that the soldiers are switched on more by all this nonsense than by lessons in tactics.

In the end, they all went off in different directions, while the general quite amicably took us to his home to recover from the day's exertions. That night we returned to Fizi and told Lambert that we wanted to leave at once. Apart from the iciness that dominated our relations, so different from the general attitude of the Congolese towards us, there were so many signs of disorder and languor that it was obviously necessary to take serious measures to clean things up. I said as much to Lambert when I saw him, and he modestly replied that General Moulane was like that but, as I had seen, such things did not happen in his sector.

We set off the next day in a jeep, but we soon ran out of petrol and were left on the road to continue on foot.

In the afternoon we stopped to rest at the house of a friend of Lambert's, who was in the *pombe* retail business. The colonel said he was going to see if there was any hunting around there and it was not long before the quarry arrived – a piece of meat that we ate with our usual appetite – but Lambert himself appeared much later, showing signs that he had had plenty of *pombe* yet kept all his wits about him (it's true his voice had some pleasing "notes"). We ran into a group of 15 or 20 of Lambert's recruits, who had decided to leave because they had not been supplied with any weapons. He gave them a good telling off, speaking with terrible emphasis because the state of euphoria had loosened up his speech, and they gathered together our equipment and accompanied us to Lubondja. I thought they were going back to the front, but in fact they were merely made to act as porters and then allowed to go free.

Later we talked over future plans with Lambert. He proposed leaving the general staff in Lubondja, but I argued that it was nearly 25 kilometres from the enemy. A force easily numbering 350 men could not have its general staff at such a distance; the impedimenta could be left here, but we ourselves had to be with our fighters at the front. He accepted this rather grudgingly, and we agreed to set off the next day. He took us to see his arsenal, at a well-concealed spot some five kilometres from Lubondja. It was really significant in the conditions of the Congo: a large quantity of weapons and ammunition, including some they had captured in the past when the enemy had been weaker; a 60mm mortar with its shells, US-type Belgian bazookas, also with some shells, and 50-model machine-guns. It was much better supplied than the dump at Fizi – which gave some weight to what those people had been arguing.

Our plan was to go straight down to the plain to meet Lambert's men, those at Kalonda-Kibuye and Calixte's troops, leaving only a few ambushes to intercept reinforcements. We would mount an elastic encirclement of Lulimba and use the men from Kalonda-Kibuye for the dual purpose of attacking by road and preventing the arrival of reinforcements. In reserve we would have the men from the barrier on the Lulimba to Kabambare road, who were also under Lambert's command.

We set off with all these good intentions, but we had not left the village of Lubondja (after the respective gatherings and the *dawa*) when two T-28s and two B-26s appeared and started systematically rocketing the village. After 45 minutes of this, two people had been lightly wounded, six houses destroyed, and some vehicles hit by machine-gun fire. A commander explained to me that the outcome demonstrated the strength of *dawa* – only two lightly wounded. I thought it best in such a case not to start a discussion about the relative efficacy of aircraft and *dawa*, and so we left it at that.

The meetings and assemblies started when we reached the barrier, until finally Lambert explained to me that for various reasons it was not possible to go down: he had only 67 rifles and his 350 men had scattered among the various groups of dwellings in the nearby area; he did not have the forces to carry out a proper attack; he would immediately go and look for the vacationists and impose the necessary discipline, and so on.

I persuaded him to send a group of men down to reconnoitre and keep our work moving; I myself would go with them. I went the next morning with the first group of men, telling myself that I would accompany them a little and then go to the Kabambare barrier to look for some more people – we would meet again down below.

When we arrived in the village we thought was Lulimba, nobody was there. We pushed on towards the River Kimbi and met all the people lying in ambush a couple of kilometres from the little town; the village we had been calling Lulimba was not Lulimba after all; the real one was some four kilometres away, on the banks of the Kimbi. Lambert had received some boastful news from Kalonda-Kibuye, claiming that all the enemy positions had been destroyed and the guardsmen driven into the forest. Trusting to this, he ordered the men there to advance calmly, and, when they arrived, they almost ran into the guardsmen, who were certainly behaving as nonchalantly as our own group. They were doing their drill in a camp close to the village, and there were a lot of them. A little ambush was set up, and some scouts went out and calculated their strength at between 150 and 300.

The key task was to concentrate and organize the greatest possible number of men, and then start a low-key attack that would attract enemy forces to that point. But first we had to establish a slightly stronger base and wait for Lambert to bring his famous 350 men. We withdrew to the Mission, four kilometres from Lulimba, and awaited the outcome of the parleys with each of the barrier leaders; Lambert was supposed to deal with that.

THE BEGINNING OF THE END

The impression one had at that Mission camp was of a group of kids on a weekend jaunt, without a care in the world. From some distance, people could be heard discussing in a loud voice, and the racket surrounding some funny incident was enough to bring down the roof of the church in which they were staying. It was an uphill struggle to keep the sentries at their posts. Lambert came and went all the time, giving the impression of great efficiency in the search for his men, but we were never able to increase the total above 40. When he did manage to get a few more, some others would return to their barrier or their little village out in the sticks. Nor was it possible to bring the machine-guns down to strengthen the position a little; they barely made it to the first hill overlooking the access to the mountains.

The reconnaissance I had entrusted to Waziri and Banhir showed that there were many more soldiers than the 53 original ones we had heard about. Their main camp was on the other side of the River Kimbi, but they also had another that we had not managed to locate precisely. The enemy freely crossed to this side of the river and fed on the large manioc fields once sown by the peasants on each side of the road. It would be possible to ambush them there with relative ease. Banhir, who had reconnoitred to the right of the road, thought there must be another camp, but he had not been able to see one before he was almost surprised by the soldiers. I sent him off again to some slight but commanding hills, where he could scour the plain for a second camp. He could not complete his mission, however, because he stumbled across some enemy soldiers out hunting – although fortunately they did not spot him. They obviously feel they can get away with anything, even a sortie to the foothills of the mountains. From where we were, we could hear them shooting in every direction. This made those manning our positions very nervous: already on the first day, they had rushed away from the ambush at the sound of hunters shooting nearby.

News reached us of Mbili's various engagements at the ambushes between Katenga and Lulimba; they had caused some enemy casualties but not in the desired amount, and reinforcement columns had been able to get through. Moja pointed out that our own men were the only ones left at the ambushes, since the Congolese stayed at best for two or three days and it was more and more difficult to replace them; they were going back up to their high-level camp, having completely lost the little enthusiasm with which they had started out. Aeroplanes had bombed the peasant villages of Nganja and Kanyanja, also dropping leaflets with a fuzzy picture of some dead people and a caption explaining that this was the result of raids by "*simbas*". Below this, an appeal in Swahili and French urged people not to let themselves suffer or be killed to enrich the Chinese and Cubans, who were here only to steal gold. And among such stupidities were such truths as the fact that the peasants had no salt or clothing, could not hunt or sow, and were threatened with starvation – things that the peasants felt most acutely. The bottom part of the leaflets consisted of a safe-conduct signed by Mobutu, which would enable them to return to a normal life; Tshombe's army would guarantee their life and liberty.

It was the same as the method used by Batista during our war. It was capable of making some weak individuals crumble, but it did very little damage in Cuba. My fear was that here the weak were a majority in every sense. Of course, the people who dropped the leaflets were as stupid as Batista's men: they did it immediately after terror bombing. It seems to be a stock in trade of repressive armies.

I went exploring the nearby area for places where weapons could be installed and effective ambushes laid. I spent the morning in this way and had it in mind to continue when Danhusi, one of my aides, came running

112

to tell me that the guardsmen had been hunting very close to the Mission and fired a few shots; the sentries left posthaste and everyone was soon scattered around. I had to make my way back and start the tiresome business of looking for the men. It was difficult, because their cohesion lasted only until the moment of an alert, when they all managed to race to safe shelter in the mountains. This disorderly flight meant that scarcely 20 or 25 Congolese remained with me.

The next day Lambert arrived from his trip to the barrier on the Kabambare road and said that the men were now four kilometres from Lulimba. He had given them instructions to be ready for any eventuality; there were not 120 of them but only 60, although they were in good fighting spirits. I no longer had much faith in Lambert because of his frequent acts of irresponsibility, but we could calculate 60 men as a first approximation. I gave him an account of what had happened and said that we could not attack with the men remaining to us. The latest reports were that Lulimba had been seriously reinforced, and so I proposed that we organize three little ambushes just to give the enemy a few scratches: two where the manioc grew (and the enemy was off his guard), one on the main road. I would move my command post to the Kiliwe, a stream to the left of the barrier, and try to organize my men there. In reality, I was looking for a way to detach myself from Lambert and organize the mixed force – an ambition I had never been able to achieve, since I had not had the necessary nucleus of Congolese. Lambert said that he would discuss this new tactic with his men and let me know, but his reply never came – both because of the sort of person he was, and because we were overtaken by events.

On one of his anarchic excursions from one side to the other, Lambert came across an enemy soldier out hunting and killed him. This caused more anxieties for me: the Tshombists would certainly have heard the shooting and known that the soldier in question only had a Springfield; nor had he been buried or taken away from the spot where he fell. I pointed out to Lambert that he should bury the body so as not to leave any trace and to keep the enemy uncertain about his fate, but it was all too difficult as everyone was too terrified of the dead to do anything about it. I had to struggle hard to convince them that the corpse should be made to vanish; I don't know if they did it, but at dusk they reported that it had been buried in a concealed place.

It was not advisable to spend more time there, since the sentries dashed off at the least hint of danger and sometimes did not even report anything before heading straight for the mountains. I proposed pulling back a kilometre, but although Lambert agreed in principle he did nothing about it.

I ought to have looked in Makungo for the men I would command and form into the nucleus of a guerrilla army, free from the harmful influence of these undisciplined soldiers. But I could not leave Lambert alone in that madness and we agreed that I would send him Moja with ten men; in exchange he would give me ten selected volunteers to undergo training. Lambert half kept his promise; he gave me ten men, but they were not volunteers and certainly not selected – in fact, they were good for nothing.

At the stream, five kilometres from Lulimba, I caught up with the group that was arriving with Tembo at its head; the men had endured the tiring march with great dignity and won the respect of the untrusting Cubans. We now numbered 35, including the men who would go with Moja to help Lambert; a tiny force. The rest of our contingent of 120 men was scattered at the lake, at the Upper Base, at Front de Force or at Calixte's front. Each time we advanced there were fewer of us and it was proving impossible to concentrate our force. I did not dare leave any position completely without Cubans, since I knew there would immediately be a return to the past. There were some new faces in this group: a lieutenant, Azima's brother, whom we called Rebocate; a Haitian doctor, Kasulu, who was very useful to us (I would say, without wishing to run him down, more useful for his command of French than for his medical knowledge); and Tuma, the head of the wireless communications group. I discussed Tuma's instructions with him (which were that he should remain in Dar es Salaam) and modified them so that he would set up his base on the higher part of the lake and try to make contact with Dar es Salaam and Kigoma from there; I also instructed him to look for a powerful radio capable of communicating directly with Cuba. The war could not be conducted from the Congo (which is what I intended) if we had to depend for everything on Dar es Salaam.

We agreed on the equipment that would be necessary. We also had the same views about a very good Chinese apparatus, which had been distributed with absurd egalitarianism, one to each of the fronts, with no consideration for the fact that they did not have the slightest idea of how to use it or that, even if they had, the limited range of the transmitter would not have allowed them to use it to communicate with each other. Nevertheless, it was impossible to take it away from them; each was kept guarded and there was no way they could be made to give it up. We would try to form a solid communications unit to train Congolese operators. I also instructed him to examine the long-wave apparatus in Fizi, which was still intact despite a number of air raids, and to see if we could not establish a revolutionary radio station for the region.

I sent with the comrades to Masengo a letter full of the usual pieces of advice; this time I stressed that we had to discuss seriously with the people in Fizi so as to clarify our relationship with them, and to use the radio that already existed there, under a central control to avoid self-serving propaganda. In passing, I made a few criticisms of the newspaper edited by Kiwe. Without referring to its generally poor quality – nothing more could be demanded of it – I objected to the lies it told about battles. They were terrible; any fabricator of reports from the Batista age could have learnt a thing or two from Comrade Kiwe's feverish imagination. No doubt he would explain that it was all due to his correspondents.

These days were used to try to locate the enemy's exact position, and to find a provisional camp that would allow us to begin reorganizing our force and get out of the roadside huts that would give us shelter for a while. Aircraft were active in the area, but they did not bother with the abandoned houses and instead machine-gunned the area around Lambert's barrier. We had become anxious as a result of this attack, when two of Moja's men arrived and told us that they had been sent to carry out reconnaissance but had run into advancing enemy troops spread out over a wide area; they had managed to hide but not to make their way back to the Mission. The attached report describes what the action was like.

28 September

Tatu:

At about 10.30 hours today, the guardsmen began a sweep on foot along the road from Lulimba to the Mission, firing mortar shells and with planes bombing from the air. I met the colonel and some of our other comrades at the anti-aircraft machine-gun; we gave the order to fire the gun to prevent the guardsmen from surrounding the comrades at the Mission; there was no fire from the containing ambushes where the Congolese were, and they have not appeared up till now. Comrades Tiza and Chail, who were at the Mission cooking food, were able to retreat to our position; Comrades Banhir and Rabanini set off at 4.00 to reconnoitre, and we do not know anything about them at the present moment – we think they have pulled back to where you are.[8] Nearly all the Congolese are a lost cause; my idea is to count on our own people to shoot at the guardsmen from this position, since the Congolese moved the anti-aircraft machine-guns when the planes started shooting, and fired into the ground when I told them to put them back in position. I put a Cuban on the machine-gun, and I sent another of our comrades to take charge of the artillery piece, which is located two hills to our rear. The colonel was told to bring the piece here yesterday already, but so far this has not happened. Comrade Compagnie,[9] who was with Comrade Tiza at the Mission, retreated with the Congolese and his present position is not known, so at the moment there are eight of us. If we do not manage to stop the guards, we think we will retreat to higher

8. These were, in fact, the two comrades to whom I referred.
9. A Rwandan soldier who had been incorporated into our force.

ground, because this hill is very bare. We have also heard shooting from the region of Fizi – which is very strange.

The Comrade Colonel assures me it is our people, but I take such an assurance with a pinch of salt. The guardsmen stopped at the Mission and are still there at the moment.

Moja

News arrived from Mbili to the effect that he had attacked two mini-tanks and destroyed one, but the enemy got through and the aircraft pounded them and caught them in a clearing; they did not suffer any losses, however. The end of the report was full of pathos; Mbili had a number of Cubans down sick and only three Congolese (the rest having gone back to their base). The guardsmen again broke through the ambush – this time with relative ease, as the fighters were deeply demoralized.

The next day, the radio broadcast a report from Mobutu's general staff that a force of 2,400 men under Lieutenant-Colonel Hoare was attacking in the Fizi-Baraka area, with the aim of destroying the last rebel stronghold, and that Baraka had already fallen into their hands.

Lambert, for his part, announced that Baraka had indeed been attacked, but that they had fought off the enemy and killed 20 whites and countless blacks. As we see, the Congolese themselves did not bother to count the dead blacks; what mattered was the number of whites. Meanwhile, another report from Lambert's front.

29 September

Tatu:

Yesterday we talked with the colonel: we asked him to bring the gun and mortar down to fire at the concentration of guardsmen this side of Lulimba, and discussed the fact that they had occupied the Mission. Lambert therefore went off to get the gun and mortar, taking Nane with him to make sure that he did not go away. I also suggested that, after shooting at the concentration, we should withdraw to the other hillock so that the aircraft are not able

117

to inflict any casualties today; yesterday they flew quite low and the guardsmen indicated with their mortars where they should bomb. Comrade Nane returned at about 17.00 hours yesterday with two mortars and a gun, and we set up our firing positions. The colonel returned not with Nane but later, at about 18.00 hours, completely drunk and dragging along some men from the camp. He suggested that, after we had fired off the gun and mortars, we should go down to the Mission with the men he had there and our own men, since the guardsmen would retreat before the gunfire. We told him that would be very dangerous, since the enemy certainly had ambushes and we would be virtually placing ourselves inside their circle; moreover, the confusion would lead our own men to start killing one another. But he said this was not true; we had to do it, and anyway he had spoken to you and you had both agreed to attack Lulimba. So I told him that our men would stay here, on my own responsibility. He further said that the guardsmen would keep the blankets they had taken at the Mission, and that that could not be allowed to happen.[10] After the attack he was going to go to China. We fired the gun and mortar rounds and withdrew to his camp, together with him and all his men.

When we talked back at the camp last night, we did not discuss the matter any further, since he was still drunk. I decided to wait for a better opportunity to talk. We have the gun at a different position from the one they had it at. At the place where we fired it yesterday, we have left an observation outpost. One of our comrades is at the gun, to stop the guardsmen advancing if they try to do so. All the signs are that the guards have set up a camp at the Mission, while others have returned to their camp – since their lorries are going back that way. Virtually the only thing we

10. The previous day, the retreat had been so abrupt that the belongings of some men not there at the time – the lieutenant-colonel, Moja and some others – had been left behind.

do is take measures to halt the guardsmen if they try to advance again. My idea is as follows.

We should fire some shots at the Mission during the night and wait a few days to reconnoitre a little around there, as it is possible that the guardsmen will keep out of the way and not be seen. I am keeping an eye on our men, except for the comrade who is at the gun emplacement. Today we told the colonel to get his men out of the houses early because of the aircraft – which is what he did. We are thinking of building a few shelters. Our relations with Lambert have not suffered any cracks, because the thing he had was due to his being "sozzled" with *pombe*. We can have some contact here in the camp, for even if we go to another position we'll always leave someone behind.

Waiting for some instructions from you,

Moja

The lieutenant-colonel's irresponsibility was terrible. The news I had been given about Baraka was false; it had been lost almost without a struggle, so that the situation was growing ever more difficult and the planned army, with all its arsenal of weapons, men and ammunition, was becoming more and more diluted. Still imbued with a kind of blind optimism, I was unable to see this and wrote in my monthly analysis for September:

Last month's analysis was full of optimism; now it is no longer possible to be so optimistic, even though some things have moved forward. Clearly we cannot encircle Force within a month. In fact, we cannot now set a date for this. Whatever the truth is about Baraka, the mercenaries are going onto the offensive and Lulimba has been turned into a strongpoint. It does have a communi-cations weakness, but it is almost impossible to make this group fight in present conditions, and the Cubans have to do it all them-selves. However, Masengo appointed our friend Lambert as front coordinator (a man who is no use for anything, though he is respected by the others and respects me). Masengo wrote me a conciliatory letter,[11] asking me to write back about a number of specific problems. My struggle has to focus on the creation of an independent column, perfectly armed and well equipped, which will be at once a shock force and a model for others. If this comes to pass, it will have significantly changed the picture; if it does not happen, a revolutionary army will be impossible to organize – the quality of the officers precludes it.

In sum, it has been a month with some advances, but optimism has receded. A month of waiting.

11. The word "conciliatory" appears in my diary but it is not the right one. For there was never either a breach or close contact between Masengo and us.

BATTLING AGAINST TIME

Our position had little to recommend it, and it would have been very bad indeed if the enemy had launched an offensive there. As fighting was then taking place over towards Lulimba, however, there were reasonable grounds for thinking that we would not be disturbed for a while. The location was on the banks of the Kiliwe, near the first of the mountain foothills. Our main worry was food; we occasionally hunted some game, but there was less and less of it and we ran a risk in doing this. It should be remembered that we were in no-man's-land and any hunting had to be done right there, so that the shots would have been heard quite clearly by the guardsmen. Despite everything, though, they maintained an apprehensive, almost defensive attitude.

We had a meeting with the headman of one of the nearby villages. Each small village has its *kapita* or chief, and the large ones – or a group of hamlets – have a headman. Our man spoke French and was quite sharp. In the course of a long conversation, I presented our requests: we needed some loaders to go to the lake and find some tinned food and other supplies; the peasants would provide us with general assistance, some vegetables they might produce, and raw tobacco. What we could offer was some of the food and provisions brought up from the lake, payment for the food they gave us, medical assistance and free medicine within our capacities, and vegetable seeds (whose produce we would share). The headman noted everything down and held a meeting with his comrades; after two or three days, he ceremoniously brought me a signed typewritten reply bearing a number of stamps, which said that he would look for men to send to the lake, that they would guarantee us food and try to find tobacco, but that he could not accept payment because it was a norm of the revolution that the peasants were to feed and support the army.

More news came from Mbili. Again the soldiers had passed through his lines and again some mini-tanks had come to grief in the action. This time they had used an ingenious device: the mine was buried in the road and the same grenade fuse suspended by a cord as a detonator, but now the pressure of the vehicle falling into a little trap released the safety catch and set off the explosion within six seconds; at least one mini-tank was blown up thanks to this "crude device".

I sent Siki to work as a doctor in the area of the barrier, as well as to help Moja in his tasks. His first reports from there, like Moja's, laid it on thick and complained of the extent of the disorganization. He was amazed by a custom they kept unchanged even as they waited for the enemy to attack; every night when they went to sleep, they dismantled their gun and took it away with them. They were incapable of digging trenches to protect themselves, of sleeping in them with their weapons, or simply of leaving someone to guard them while they slept. The gun, like a personal object, went with its master, who did not deign to sleep anywhere other than in his own home. Every morning saw the ordeal of mobilizing people so as to be early at their fighting post.

They too said they had heard some loud explosions in Lubondja. When they went to investigate what they thought was an enemy attack, they noticed that a whole ammunition dump was ablaze, with its large stock of mortar and artillery shells and machine-gun bullets.

While I was waiting for Comrade Masengo to arrive, Mujumba suddenly appeared – the man who, until a short time ago, had been the Revolutionary Council's representative in Dar es Salaam. He had come to take charge of sabotage operations against the Albertville railway in the Makungo area, and he wanted to take six Cubans with him. I reacted sharply and told him that I was waging an uphill battle to concentrate my men and forge a strong mixed army; that I constantly had to fight this kind of dispersal of our forces. (It was the first time I used the term "Congolization" in reference to the Cubans, meaning contagion by the prevailing spirit.) Such dispersal did more harm than any benefits it might bring; we had to discuss this very seriously, because I did not give much for the future of the revolution if it kept going along this road. Our discussion, and especially my account of what was happening, made a great impression on him; he said he was willing to stay there with me and find 20 peasants for training, and that he would return after making an inspection of the Mukundi area. When he asked whether the recruits should be peasants without any military training, I replied that it was much better that way; I preferred a thousand times people who were fresh and had had no contact with bivouac habits, rather than these soldiers already corrupted by camp life.

When Masengo arrived the next day, I spoke openly with him too and clearly expressed my view of the problems we were facing. I stressed that he needed to make a decision to build a powerful and disciplined army – otherwise, they would remain at the level of scattered groups in the mountains. We agreed that we would establish a front in this area under Lambert's command, but that I would have an independent column. I specified that it would have to be independent of Lambert too, because the consequences of his irresponsibility were already weighing me down.

We would create a kind of combat academy. I preferred the students to be peasants. But although Mujumba undertook to increase the number to 60, it would be necessary to add some soldiers from the various fronts – which I was not very keen to do. Furthermore, we would organize a more rational general staff that could conduct operations on all the fronts, and I agreed that we would send as advisers Siki (for the work of the general staff), Tembo (for the work of political organization), and Doctor Kasulu (as a French translator). Masengo asked me to write to our ambassador in Tanzania to intervene with the government there, because the difficulties were increasing every day. Lastly, he asked for some more Cuban cadres. I said yes in principle, but the selection would have to be done with care; this was a special kind of war, in which the quality of individual cadres mattered a lot and could not be replaced with numbers.

The next day, while we were discussing how to lift the Liberation Army from the ruins, a tragicomic accident occurred. One of the men dropped a lighted match and – the rainy season having only just begun – those dry straw huts caught fire like torches. A number of things were lost, but what annoyed me most was the danger to people from the grenades exploding inside, and above all the impression of disorganization and carelessness that we gave to Masengo and his comrades. Agano, the cause of the disaster and one of our best comrades, was sentenced to go three days without eating.

When we were at the fiesta of exploding bullets and grenades, accompanied by my own higher-calibre explosions, Machadito (our health minister from Cuba) arrived with some letters and a message from Fidel; he had with him Mutchungo, the health minister in Soumaliot's revolutionary government. They were lost and had been guided to the camp by the light and noise from the explosions. I knew of the long conversations that Soumaliot and his colleagues had had with Fidel. The people from the Revolutionary Council had not been truthful in their account of things – partly, I suppose, because that is always how it is in such cases, and partly because they had been outside the country for a long time and were ignorant of what was happening inside. I imagine that, faced with a wave of lies from the soldiers that spread ever larger until it finally reached the top, they could not form, even with the best of wills, a clear idea of what things were really like there. The fact is that they painted an idyllic picture of military units present on all sides, forces in the forest, constant battles – all very remote from what we could see and feel. Besides, they got a considerable sum of money to travel all over the African continent explaining the features of their Revolutionary Council, exposing Gbenye and his clique, and so on. They also requested support for a number of foolhardy enterprises; it was rumoured that they had asked friendly countries for as much as 5,000 rifles, torpedo boats for the lake and a variety of heavy weapons; and totally false plans were concocted for attacks and breakthroughs. They had extracted a promise of 50 doctors from Cuba, and Machadito had come to look at the conditions on the ground.

I had already sensed from Tembo that people in Cuba thought my attitude very pessimistic. This impression was now reinforced by a personal message from Fidel in which he urged me not to give up hope, asked me to remember the early stage of the struggle in Cuba, recalled that such obstacles always occur, and spelt out that these were fine men. I wrote a long letter to Fidel, from which I shall quote the paragraphs that set out how I saw things.

Congo, 5/10/65
Dear Fidel:
I received your letter, which has aroused contradictory feelings in me – for in the name of proletarian internationalism, we are committing mistakes that may prove very costly. I am also personally worried that, either because I have failed to write with sufficient seriousness or because you do not fully understand me, I may be thought to be suffering from the terrible disease of groundless pessimism.

When your Greek gift [12] arrived here, he told me that one of my letters had given the impression of a condemned gladiator, and the minister, [13] in passing on your optimistic message, confirmed the opinion that you were forming. You will be able to speak at length with the bearer of this letter, who will tell you his first-hand impressions after visiting much of the front; for this reason I will dispense with anecdotes. I will just say to you that, according to people close to me here, I have lost my reputation for objectivity by maintaining a groundless optimism in the face of the actual situation. I can assure you that were it not for me this fine dream would have collapsed with catastrophe all around.

In my previous letters, I asked to be sent not many people but cadres; there is no real lack of arms here (except for special weapons) – indeed there are too many armed men; what is lacking are soldiers. I especially warned that no more money should be given out unless it was with a dropper and after many requests.

12. Tembo.
13. Machado.

None of what I said has been heeded, and fantastic plans have been made which threaten to discredit us internationally and may land me in a very difficult position.

I shall now explain to you.

Soumaliot and his comrades have been leading you all right up the garden path. It would be tedious to list the huge number of lies they have spun, and it is preferable to explain the present situation by the attached map. There are two zones where something of an organized revolution exists – the one where we ourselves are, and part of Kasai province (the great unknown quantity) where Mulele is based. In the rest of the country there are bands living in the forest, not connected to one another; they lost everything without a fight, as they lost Stanleyville without a fight. More serious than this, however, is the way in which the groups in this area (the only one with contacts to the outside) relate to one another. The dissensions between Kabila and Soumaliot are becoming more serious all the time, and are used as a pretext to keep handing towns over without a fight. I know Kabila well enough not to have any illusions about him. I cannot say the same about Soumaliot, but I have some indications such as the string of lies he has been feeding you, the fact that he does not deign to come to these godforsaken parts, his frequent bouts of drunkenness in Dar es Salaam, where he lives in the best hotels, and the kind of people he has as allies here against the other group. Recently a group from the Tshombist army landed in the Baraka area (where a major-general loyal to Soumaliot has no fewer than 1,000 armed men) and captured this strategically important place almost without a fight. Now they are arguing about who was to blame – those who did not put up a fight, or those at the lake who did not send enough ammunition. The fact is that they shamelessly ran away, ditching in the open a 75mm recoilless gun and two 82 mortars; all the men assigned to these weapons have disappeared, and now they are asking me for Cubans to get them back from wherever they are (no one quite knows where) and to use them in battle. Nor are they doing anything to defend Fizi, 36 kilometres from here; they don't want to dig trenches on the only access road through the mountains. This will give you a faint idea of the situation. As for the need to choose men well rather than send me large numbers, you and the commissar assure me that the men here are good; I'm sure most of them are – otherwise they'd have quit long ago. But that's not the point. You have to be really well tempered to put up with the things that happen here. It's not good men but supermen that are needed . . .

And there are still my 200; believe me, they would do more harm than good at the present time – unless we decide once and for all to fight alone, in which case we'll need a division and we'll have to see how many the enemy put up against us. Maybe that's a bit of an exaggeration; maybe a battalion would be enough to get back to the frontiers we had when we arrived here and to threaten Albertville. But numbers are not what matters; we can't liberate by ourselves a country that does not want to fight; you've got to create a fighting spirit and look for soldiers with the torch of Diogenes and the patience of Job – a task that becomes more difficult, the more shits there are doing things along the way.

The question of the launches deserves a new paragraph. For some time, I have been requesting a couple of technicians to stop the landing-stage at Kigoma from becoming even more of a rubbish tip for used vessels. Of three Soviet ferries that arrived a little over a month ago, two are already out of service and the third, in which the emissary crossed the lake, is leaking all over. The three Italian launches will go the same way unless they have a Cuban crew. But this and the artillery business require the consent of Tanzania, which is not easy to obtain. These countries, unlike Cuba, are not going to stake everything on one card, however big (and the card now being played is pretty feeble). I have given the emissary the job of clarifying how much support the friendly government is prepared to give. You should know that almost everything which came on the ship has been impounded in Tanzania, and the emissary will also have to talk about that with them.

The business with the money is what hurts me most, after all the warnings I gave. At the height of my "spending spree", and only after they had kicked up a lot of fuss, I undertook to supply one front (the most important one) on condition that I would direct the struggle and form a special mixed column under my direct command, in accordance with the strategy that I outlined and communicated to you. With a very heavy heart, I calculated that it would require 5,000 dollars a month. Now I learn that a sum 20 times higher is given to people who pass through just once, so that they can live well in all the capitals of the African world, with no allowance for the fact that they receive free board and lodging and often their travel costs from the main progressive countries. Not a cent will reach a wretched front where the peasants suffer every misery you can imagine, including the rapaciousness of their own protectors; nor will anything get through to the poor devils stuck in Sudan. (Whisky and women are not on the list of expenses covered by friendly governments, and they cost a lot if you want quality.)

Finally, 50 doctors will give the liberated area of the Congo an enviable proportion of one per thousand inhabitants – a level surpassed only by the USSR, the United States and two or three of the most advanced countries in the world. But no allowance is made for the fact that here they are distributed according to political preference, without a trace of public health organization. Instead of such gigantism, it would be better to send a contingent of revolutionary doctors and to increase it as I request, along with highly practical nurses of a similar kind.

As the attached map sums up the military situation, I shall limit myself to a few recommendations that I would ask you all to consider objectively: forget all the men in charge of phantom groups; train up to 100 cadres (not necessarily all blacks) and choose from Osmany's list plus whoever stands out most over there. As for weapons: the new bazooka, percussion caps with their own power supply, a few R-4s and nothing else for the moment; forget about rifles, which won't solve anything unless they are electronic. Our mortars must be in Tanzania, and with those plus a new complement of men to operate them we would have more than enough for now. Forget about Burundi and tactfully discuss the question of the launches. (Don't forget that Tanzania is an independent country and we've got to play it fair there, leaving aside the little problem I caused.) Send the mechanics as soon as possible, as well as someone who can steer across the lake reasonably safely; that has been discussed and Tanzania has agreed. Leave me to handle the problem of the doctors, which I will do by giving some of them to Tanzania. Don't make the mistake again of dishing out money like that; for they cling to me when they feel hard up and certainly won't pay me any attention if the money is flowing freely. Trust my judgement a little and don't go by appearances. Shake the representatives into giving truthful information, because they are not capable of figuring things out and present utopian pictures which have nothing to do with reality.

I have tried to be explicit and objective, synthetic and truthful. Do you believe me?

Warm greetings,

Machado and I share the view that it is impossible to have 50 doctors here, unless we organize them along guerrilla lines. He also agreed with me about the really alarming features of the present situation, since he witnessed all the depraved goings-on at the fronts and got a feel for the spirit in which the revolution is being conducted.

I had hopes that some comrades, such as the public health minister, might help to put a little order into things – especially as he came from the Fizi area and had some authority. But he proved to be a nonentity. He was there up to the end, except for a brief time when he left for something to do with his work, but he kept completely aloof from Masengo (I don't know who is to blame) and even more aloof from reality. Of course, he could not occupy himself with people's health; he had only the Cuban doctors, and the few medicines that arrived were for the fronts or for some elementary medicine in the areas where our force was camped. We had once spoken with Masengo of the need to concern ourselves more with Fizi, to impose authority on the general and pay him some attention (as far as doctors and the radio were concerned, for example), but that was now history since Fizi had gone over to the enemy.

Moja arrived from Lubondja, where he had been to inspect the aftermath of the explosion at the dump. He brought news of the loss of Baraka (without a fight, he thought); the gun and mortars had been abandoned by the men in charge of them. In this case, I think it was the brand-new Bulgarian instructors.[14]

With all this information, we called a meeting with the leaders for whom a search had been made and who had finally reappeared. Up to then we had not managed to get any coherent action from either Calixte or Jean Ila (the commander at Kalonda-Kibuye); I don't know whether they themselves were to blame for this, or rather Lambert, whose sloppy working methods precluded any proper organization. In the end, the meeting was attended by Masengo himself, Comrade Mujumba, the public health minister, Commanders Ila Jean and Calixte, Lieutenant-Colonel Lambert, other commanders from Lambert's front, and the usual political commissars and onlookers. Word had been sent to Zakarias but he had not replied, so the Rwandans were not represented. What I had to say was more or less as follows.

First, an introduction of those now there: the public health minister from Cuba, who had been to examine healthcare needs; Siki, the chief of staff of a Cuban army; Tembo, the Party organization secretary who had given up his post to come and fight here; Comrade Moja, Comrade Mbili, with a long

14. I follow the established practice in the Congo of awarding students the nationality of the country where they trained.

record of struggle. My points were more or less the same as the ones I had made to Masengo, but I added an analysis of each leader's conduct. Lambert was undoubtedly a dynamic comrade, but he had to do everything himself; he had not formed an army; people did things when he was present, but did not advance when he wasn't – I referred to the dead comrade as an example. He was at the front line because his comrades had insisted that he go and stay there. Calixte, on the other hand, had never appeared at the line of battle. Both attitudes were bad: a leader should not stay so close to the front line that he cannot survey, and take decisions about, the whole of his sector of the front; but nor should he be so far back that he loses all contact. To the representative from Kalonda-Kibuye, I objected that the barrier which they claimed to have on the road was an illusion, since there had never been one clash with the army; there was no reason to keep 150 men there in such circumstances. Then I analysed the acts of indiscipline, the atrocities and the parasitic features of the army; it was a real diatribe, and although they politely weathered the storm, no one was in agreement with the "discharge".

In his remarks to me about the meeting, Comrade Tembo said that in his view I had offered virtually no way out of the problems of the Congo; I had spoken of all the negative aspects, but not of the possibilities offered by guerrilla warfare. It was a fair criticism.

I also had a meeting with my comrades, since rumours had reached me of certain expressions that reflected the growing despondency; some men were saying that the Cubans remained in the Congo because Fidel did not know of the real situation in which they were living there. I said to them that the situation was indeed difficult; the Liberation Army was falling apart and a struggle had to be waged to save it from ruin. Our work would be very hard and thankless, and I could not ask them to have confidence in victory; I personally thought that things could be sorted out, although it would take a lot of work and a lot of partial defeats. Nor could I demand confidence in my leadership capacities, but I could call on them to trust my quality as a revolutionary and to have respect for my honesty. Fidel was fully informed about the fundamentals of the situation, and nothing of what had happened was being covered up. I had not come to win glory for myself in the Congo, nor was I going to sacrifice anyone for my personal honour. If it was true that I had not communicated to Havana the view that all was lost, it was because I honestly did not hold it. But I had expressed the men's state of mind, their vacillations, their doubts and weaknesses. I reported that there were days, as in the Sierra Maestra, when my despair was total at the lack of faith among the new recruits, who, having affirmed their unshakable resolve in the name of all the saints, "cracked" the very next day. That's how things were in Cuba, at our level of development and with the strength of our revolution. So what could not be expected in the Congo? The Congolese soldiers were there among the masses; it was our basic task to examine them one by one until we found them.

The need for this explanation shows the ferment that has been dissolving the morale of our troops. It was difficult to get the men to work; quite disciplined comrades would formally follow the guidelines, but there was nothing creative in what they did; everything had to be said several times over and strictly checked; I had to use my proverbial volleys (which are not very delicate) to get certain tasks performed. That romantic time when I could threaten to send someone back to Cuba was long past; if I did that now, I would be reduced to half the present numbers, with luck.

Tembo wrote a long letter to Fidel in which he set forth – mainly in the form of anecdotes – the situation as it is at the moment. Machado is now on his way back to Cuba, carrying all this material and analysis.

As a result of the meeting with the commanders, some modifications have been made to the composition of the academy: it will now have 150 soldiers – 50 from each of the three fronts (Lambert, Kalonda-Kibuye, Calixte) – plus 60 to be recruited by Mujumba from among the local peasants.

As regards Baraka, I again spoke with Masengo and agreed to send Siki there with some men to organize a defence of Fizi – a defence which, after some planning, would make it possible to bring all the forces there and to attack at the first point. But Siki would demand as a precondition that things were done seriously and that the command was completely in the hands of Cubans; then we could undertake to send all the men to fight there. This ultimatum was necessary. Recently, at the time of the failed attempt to mount an attack on Lulimba, the grumbling among our comrades had been such that, if the Cubans were again left to fight alone and die pointlessly, many would plan to give up the struggle – because things could not go on like this.

I could not risk an attack on Baraka unless we had all the weapons in our hands and made a serious analysis of the situation. We did not know how many men the enemy had there, but their positions posed a lot of problems for us; there was a beachhead surrounded by mountains, in hostile territory, and other things might have been done. In the end, I almost begged Masengo to use his authority to make the people at Fizi see sense, and to write officially again to Kabila urging him to enter the Congo. It was not possible to talk badly of Soumaliot and his people, and at the same time to keep up the spectacle of constant promises to come to the Congo, amid binges in Kigoma and Dar es Salaam. (I was told of drunken sprees by people from the other group; it does not appear to be true.) I wavered a lot before saying such delicate things, but I thought it my duty to tell them to Masengo so that he could transmit them directly to Kabila. It was not our intention to play the governess, but there are sacrifices that a revolutionary leader has to face up to at a certain moment.

Masengo promised to write to Kabila; I don't know if he did. He left with Siki for the Fizi area, while Mujumba left for the Mukundi area with the promise to send the 60 peasants within seven days – a promise which, for reasons I do not know, was never kept, since he did not show any more signs of life.

Lambert sent me a letter in which he reported rumours that Fizi had already fallen and he asked for authorization to set off with 25 men; he would find another 25 on the way and recapture Baraka or (if already lost) Fizi. I replied that I was not entitled to give such permission, but that, in my view, there were many weaknesses in his sector of the front, that the enemy was about to attack and his own presence was indispensable there. Besides, it was unthinkable that with 25 or 50 men he could recapture what had been lost when they had several hundred. He was kind enough to send me a reply as he set off for Fizi with his little band.

For all these reasons, the chances of even harassing the enemy in the Lulimba area were virtually nil; the men at the main barrier were not coming down to the plain; a contact group was sent to the barrier on the Kabambare road, with the aim of crossing the River Kimbi and reconnoitring the soldiers' positions from the other side, and the report was that it was at the same general level; the lieutenant in charge of the barrier declared that he could not keep his men at the position (only 25 were left); they did not obey him but did what they liked, and would desert if they were taken away for some military action. It was also a barrier only in theory, and the group there could be written off as a fighting force.

VARIOUS ESCAPES

Despite all the fears, we kept trying to incorporate Congolese into our little army and to give them the rudiments of military training, so that this nucleus might save the most important thing: the soul, the presence of the revolution. But the Cubans charged with imparting the divine breath had an ever weaker grip on it themselves. The effects of the climate were still being felt, as gastro-enteritis was added to the endemic malaria. Until the rigours of the job got the better of my scientific spirit, I noted in my field diary the statistics of my own case: I had the runs more than 30 times in 24 hours. Only the scrub knows how many more there were after that. Many comrades suffered from the same malady; it did not last long or fail to respond to strong antibiotics, but it did serve to undermine a morale that was already ailing. Nor did anything happening outside our camp help to raise our spirits; not one high-minded gesture, not one intelligent action.

The few Congolese we had managed to recruit went to get a *dawa* in a nearby camp, or to be examined by a Congolese doctor (sorcerer), and then simply deserted. This made me feel the impotence that comes from a lack of direct communication. I wanted to instil into them everything I felt, to convince them that I really did feel it, but the translation transformer – my skin as well, perhaps – undid everything. After one of the frequent transgressions (they had refused to work – another of their characteristics), I spoke furiously to them in French; I rattled out the worst things I could find with my poor vocabulary and, at the height of my rage, said that they should be made to wear skirts and carry manioc in a basket (a female job), because they were good for nothing and worse than women; I preferred to have an army of women than people of this kind. But while the translator turned the "volley" into Swahili, all the men looked at one another and guffawed with a disconcerting simplicity.

Perhaps the most constant enemy was *dawa* and the various things it required. I called in a *muganga*, probably one of those considered second-rate, but he immediately sized up the situation; he settled into the camp and happily idled away the time in a way appropriate to a first-rate *muganga*. He was certainly intelligent. The day after he arrived, I told him that he ought to go off with a group of men who were to spend several days at an ambush, because *dawa* lost its effect with time and people did not remain at their position. But he answered with a flat refusal; he would prepare a stronger *dawa* for them that would last a fortnight. Such a forceful argument had to be accepted from someone with his authority, and the men left with the stronger *dawa* which, combined with the speed and smoothness of the road, gave excellent results.

Several days before, I had spoken with Masengo about practical training in the Kalonda-Kibuye area, so I started making preparations to send a team of Cubans who, operating in two groups, would select the best Congolese fighters on the basis of their actions in an ambush. We would use the same system as in the area closest to Katenga, where we had by now lifted all the ambushes because the number of Congolese had kept dwindling until only one or two were left. We left the ailing Azi behind with a couple of comrades and concentrated the rest together with ourselves. Despite our efforts, disease and dispersal at the various fronts left few men available, so that it was 13 who set off with Mbili for Kalonda-Kibuye. Ishirini was the second-in-command.

Ishirini was an ordinary soldier in Cuba. But his qualities were such that we decided to try him out on assignments of responsibility, as part of a plan of training leaders in case we built our army up into an operational group with enough Congolese soldiers. The comrades were scheduled to spend roughly 20 days at the ambush – not longer, because the rigours of the climate did not agree with the men, especially the Cubans. After that time had passed, another group would transfer the operation to a different region, so as not to saturate the same area with ambushes, while the first group rested and cleaned up. Mbili had already left to cross the Kimbi and begin operations when, with just a few hours' difference, an affecting little note arrived from Siki and another from Masengo. The one from Siki said:

Moja:

> *The guardsmen are advancing on Fizi, and there's nothing to stop them; nor do they want to stop them. We are going from Fizi to Lubondja. I'll try to knock out the bridges. Tell Tatu my trip was a failure.*
>
> *Siki 10-10-65*

The note from Masengo gave the news that Fizi had fallen and gave instructions that the whole of the Kalonda-Kibuye group should place itself under my orders.[15]

Meanwhile, some of the previous work was starting to bear fruit; a consignment of food and some medicine was brought up from the lake by a number of peasants, and we shared some of our things with them. It was not a lot, but we could give them some salt and sugar, and our men were able to have sweetened tea. A quite unnecessary letter arrived from Aly with the story of an ambush they had tried to set in the Kabimba area. Upon finding a packet of cigarettes on a trail, they turned back and finally reached the main path with their numbers much reduced; of the 60 Congolese soldiers, only 25 were left; they took prisoner some peasants who were passing down the road (they had been instructed to clear it), and who said that a lorry would be passing in a few hours from the cement factory in Kabimba. When the commander of the Congolese detachment heard this, he decided to lift the ambush an hour before the lorry passed,

---

15. This group was never incorporated in fact. A few isolated elements did come, under the orders of a political commissar who seemed a good type, but I couldn't do anything with that rabble. The rest had remained in the peasants' houses. I sent them all away, including the political commissar; I didn't want any more disorder there.

since guardsmen might be coming; that brought the week-long operation to an end. Shortly afterwards came the promotions – from captain to major or field commander, and so on; rewards were rained on them for the bravery of their action.

Siki arrived from Fizi, having travelled with forced marches because of the situation. He recounted the vicissitudes of the trip. The conversations with General Moulane passed through too many mouths (Siki speaks neither French nor Swahili, and the general no French) to have any guarantee of authenticity, but – to cut a long story short – Siki presented our ultimatum and argued that it was necessary to dig trenches immediately. The existing defences were a "barrier" consisting of three men, a bazooka man with his assistant and another with a *pepechá*,[16] plus the usual bit of wire in the middle of road to stop anyone passing; they had not dug a trench or done any reconnaissance. After I had spoken with Siki, General Moulane had his say and launched into an extremely sharp attack on Comrade Masengo, blaming him for everything because he had not asked for arms or ammunition and had not requested Cubans to come and fight. Under these conditions, he would not defend Fizi: he was not a corpse to be digging holes (fortunately he was still alive), and Masengo should take all the blame. Masengo did not even react. We don't know if this was due to his lack of character or to his being on enemy territory (which is how this area might be described) – anyway, he weathered the storm in silence. That night they no longer slept in Fizi.

Some comrades were of the view that the general could not be so stupid, that he must be colluding with the mercenaries. I have no evidence of this, and he did proudly remain in his Fizi area when we withdrew. I think that the time lag may explain this attitude of his, but in practice he played into the enemy's hands.

The fact is that internal dissensions were resulting in a number of extreme cases such as these. The 37 kilometres by road from Baraka to Fizi cross hills where there are many possibilities to lay an ambush, as

16. An old-model Soviet machine-gun, named after the letters PPCH indicating its factory of origin.

well as a river that forms a defensive barrier quite hard for vehicles to negotiate. The bridge there is already a semi-wreck and had only to be destroyed completely to create good defensive possibilities; at least this would have slowed down the enemy advance. But none of this was done.

On 12 October the enemy took Lubondja in a triumphal procession. Colonel Lambert had learnt of the capture of Fizi and set off there with 40 men, leaving some heavy weapons behind in Lubondja that were then lost in the scrub. He was not open to argument, and Masengo did not have the presence of mind to order him to stay and defend the last point preventing a link-up of the forces from Lulimba with those landing in Baraka: namely, the barrier in the mountains.

When Masengo arrived in our camp, I lost patience and told him that, with the men I had, I could not take responsibility for defending it from a two-pronged attack. Mbili had strengthened the eastern end by crossing with his 13 men on forced marches, but all we could count on were 13 Cubans on one flank and ten on the other; to go to extremes of defence would mean getting 23 men killed, since the rest were not willing to lift a finger. At the barrier they had an arsenal with 150 boxes of the most varied ammunition, especially for heavy weapons, mortars, artillery pieces and 12.7 machine-guns, and the previous night every means had been tried to get the people to save it. We had to threaten to throw water over them, to remove the blankets from on top of them, in short, to exert extreme physical pressure, while Masengo, who was spend-ing the night there, was powerless to force them to work and Lambert's deputies ran off with his followers.

Masengo's response was to send Lambert a letter ordering him to return and take charge of the defence with his men. I don't know if this letter reached its destination, but it certainly had no effect. Soon news arrived that the position, under threat from both the Lulimba and the Lubondja end, had fallen without a fight, and that the retreat had turned into a rout. The attitude of our men was bad, to say the least. They let the Congolese have weapons such as mortars for which they were responsible, and which were then lost; they showed no fighting spirit and, like the Congolese, thought only of saving themselves; and the retreat was so disorderly that we lost a man without knowing how, since his own comrades could not tell whether he had simply got lost or been wounded or killed by enemy soldiers who were firing on a hill over which they were retreating. We thought he might have headed towards the lake base or be somewhere else, until his failure to appear convinced us that he was either dead or a prisoner – in any case, we heard no more of him. At the end of the day, a huge number of weapons were lost. I gave instructions that any Congolese who unexpectedly turned up without being ordered for some reason to do so should be disarmed forthwith. The next day, I had a considerable war booty, as if we had laid the most productive of ambushes: the 75mm gun, with a good amount of ammunition; one anti-aircraft machine-gun intact, and remnants of another; mortar parts, five sub-machine-guns, ammunition, hand grenades and 100 or so rifles. The man responsible for the gun, Comrade Bahaza, had remained alone at the position, but when the guardsmen advanced and he received an alarmist report from another Cuban, he had pulled back and abandoned it. The mercenaries did not advance so quickly, and Moja gave orders in time for the gun to be saved, but I sharply criticized that comrade (a Party member), as well as a number of others.

I agreed with Masengo that all runaway soldiers should be disarmed and stripped of their rank; we would build a new force with those that remained, and I hoped in my heart of hearts there would be very few of them; I said I would accept only those who showed they were serious and had a fighting spirit.

A meeting was organized with the Congolese comrades, at which I told them very sharply what I thought of them. I explained that we were going to form a new army, that no one was obliged to come with us and anyone who wanted to leave could do so; but he must leave his weapons there, and the arsenal we had saved with so much effort would also remain with us. I asked those present to raise their hand if they wanted to leave; no one did. This seemed strange, as I had previously asked two or three Congolese (who had agreed to stay). Then, keeping an eye on one of those I had selected, I asked everyone who wanted to stay to take one step forward; two stepped forward, and immediately the whole column did the same – which meant that they would all remain part of the force. I was not convinced by the way this had worked out, so I asked them to think it over and discuss among themselves before we decided. The result of this was that some 15 men felt they would like to leave. But it did bring some gains; one commander decided to remain as a soldier (as I was not accepting former ranks), and the number of volunteers was larger than anticipated.

It was agreed that Masengo should return to the base together with Tembo, Siki and the doctor-translator, Kasulu. Paradoxically, the political situation could not have been better, since Tshombe had fallen and Kimba was making vain attempts to form a government. Things were ideal for us to mount further operations and take advantage of the disintegration in Leopoldville. The efficiently led enemy troops struck out on their own, however, far from events in the capital and with no serious opposition to face.

Comrade Rafael, who was in charge of our affairs in Dar es Salaam, came to do a tour and to have a talk with me. We found ourselves agreeing on the basic issues: the head of signals would be at the site of operations and would have a transmitter capable of reaching Havana; a weekly batch of food would be sent to the new army's base, which would be supplied as well as possible; and a comrade from Dar es Salaam would go to Kigoma to replace Changa, who did not speak Swahili and was having a number of difficulties; Changa would come over here and be in charge of the boats.

With regard to provisions, my previous attitude had proved wrong and I now changed it. I had come with the idea of forming an exemplary nucleus, of enduring all hardships alongside the Congolese and, with our spirit of self-sacrifice, displaying the true path of a revolutionary soldier. The result, however, had been that our men went hungry and had to make do with worn shoes and clothes, while the Congolese divided among themselves the shoes and clothes that reached them by another route; all we had achieved was that discontent became rife among the Cubans themselves. It was therefore decided to form the nucleus of an army that would be better equipped and better fed than the rest of the Congolese troops; it would come directly under my command; it would be the practical school converted into the nucleus of an army. To achieve this, it was absolutely necessary for us to be sent basic supplies regularly from Kigoma, with peasant carriers organized from the lake to take them to the front. For it was very difficult to get the Congolese soldiers to work, and if our men devoted themselves to that task we would not have any fighters.

We divided our force into two companies, led by Ziwa and Azima as second-in-command, since they would go into battle under orders from Mbili and Moja respectively, after a minimum period of training. The basic composition would be 15 Cubans and some 45 Congolese, with some others to be added as required; one company commander, three Cuban platoon commanders, and three Cuban squad commanders (with five men in each squad). Thus, there would be three squads to a platoon and three platoons to a company – with a total of nine squad commanders, three platoon commanders, the company commander with his second-in-command, and a small auxiliary squad, all Cubans.

We moved to the new camp, which was an hour by road from the previous one, in the first mountain foothills but still on the plain.

DISASTER

Tremendo Punto arrived and joined me during those days; his mission was to be a kind of high-level political commissar. Charles, who also accompanied me, would be a more practical, more ordinary commissar, working directly with the Kikembe-speaking people who made up the majority of our force. I considered Tremendo Punto's presence very important, because we were looking for people who could be developed as cadres. Our ambassador in Tanzania informed us of the very strong pressures of that country's government for a settlement with Gbenye. I didn't know what might happen, but I was prepared to keep up the struggle to the last moment; it suited me to have someone with me who would hold high the insurgent banner should we have any dealings with those people.

The new camp had better natural conditions than the previous one, but it was far from perfect. There was very little water – just a little spring that poured muddily forth, and we knew from experience the gastric upsets which that could produce. A hill that rose proudly between the main road and the camp prevented all-round visibility. It would have been much better to establish ourselves higher up, but all the hills looked as if they had no water and it would have been awkward to fetch it there for a group as large as ours. I gave orders for an ammunition dump to be created higher up, so that we would not have the burden of defending the 150 boxes of assorted ammunition that we had saved in Lubondja. I scoured the area for a suitable site and took some further precautions, such as keeping a platoon ready to defend the upper reaches in the event of a threatened attack.

With some peasants who had joined us, we already had the germ of a third company; I thought of continuing until we had four and then pausing to assess the situation, because I did not want to overdo the numbers until the men could be rigorously selected in combat. Local peasants came to join up in response to Comrade Masengo's appeal; he "read the rule book" to each one individually, translated by Charles into forceful language.

A note arrived from Machado at the lake, informing me that he could not cross because there was no boat available (in the end he left on a *motumbo* with an outboard motor). He was prepared to take Arobaini, the comrade wounded in a previous engagement, and try to save his finger; it was in a very bad state and could mean another reduction in our numbers. Machado said that he had spoken with the doctors who were planning to give up the struggle and tried to persuade them to stay another six months, until March. But when this did not work, he decided to leave them in the lurch. The procedure was a little hasty, but undeniably effective in achieving its aim – and I was totally in agreement with him.

We sent two scouts to inspect the ammunition dump from Lubondja and to make some attempt to put it in a safe place; it was bigger than the one we had saved at Lambert's barrier. They reported that the dump, though intact, was completely undefended there – but this was a mistake, because a group of men at a weak barrier had been mobilized from the lake to protect it.

Many scattered fighters from Lubondja, Kalonda-Kibuye and Makungo were wandering around the immediate area, taking shelter in villages and extorting things from their inhabitants. We decided to do something about this, and Charles was sent on a punitive trip to clear the soldiers out, demobilize them and take away their weapons. This was well received by peasants who had been bothered by the action of the vagabonds: something that felt much more outrageous than if it had been committed by a group displaying some elements of order.

We decided to start accelerated construction and training work to fill up all the spare time that both the Congolese and the Cubans had on their hands. We held two meetings to fix a plan of action: one with officers of the general staff, and one with Party members. The first of these established the method to be used for the military training; it defined the special features of each of the companies, drew up a list of forthcoming operations, and stipulated the means to achieve internal discipline and integration with the Congolese. The officers' spirits were not very high; they showed great scepticism about the tasks, although they performed them in an acceptable manner. A start was made on building the accommodation, the latrines and the hospital, on cleaning the well, and on digging defensive trenches in the most vulnerable areas. Everything went very slowly because the rain was by now more intense, and I did not have the resolve to make the men move the ammunition dump but waited for the upper-level construction work to be completed first – a weakness on my part that would prove fatal. At the same time, imbued with a false sense of security by the fact that the enemy was some kilometres away, we did not create outlying posts (as it would have been normal to do in such cases) but made do with quite close ones.

At the Party meeting I again stressed that they must support me in creating a disciplined army, an exemplary army. I asked which of those present believed in the possibility of victory, and the only ones who raised their hand were Moja and Mbili and the two recently arrived doctors, Fizi and Morogoro – which could be seen as the consequence either of real assurance or of greater affinity with me, a demonstration of loyalty, in fact. I warned that I would sometimes have to ask for sacrifices so great that they might have to put their lives at risk, and I asked if they were willing to do so. On this occasion, they all raised their hand.

We then proceeded to analyse weaknesses of various Party members, making criticisms that were accepted. When I came to the case of Bahaza, the comrade who had abandoned the gun, he was not in agreement. Bahaza had demonstrated extraordinary qualities, including an unshakable enthusiasm that was a model for both Cuban and Congolese comrades, but the moment of weakness had existed and the proof was that the gun had been saved after he abandoned it. I insisted again and again, until in the end he reproachfully replied: "Okay, I'm guilty." Of course, what I had been trying to achieve was not that but an analysis of our weaknesses, so

I asked several other comrades for their opinion and they agreed that the alleged failing had really existed.

By the time I closed the meeting, I could tell very few people shared my dream of an army that would carry the Congolese cause to victory, but I was reasonably sure that there were men willing to sacrifice themselves, even if they thought it futile.

The key task, however difficult, was to achieve unity between Congolese and Cubans. We had introduced communal kitchens to replace the anarchy of individual ones. But as the Congolese did not like our food and continually protested (the cooks were Cuban, because otherwise all the food disappeared), this led to a tense atmosphere.

Jean Ila, the commander at Kalonda-Kibuye, came to join us with 70 men. But I already had enough people and could not accept him; I therefore sent him back to his zone with the assurance that a group of Cubans would come and directly organize the ambush on the Lulimba to Katenga road, where we were still able to carry out effective actions. I took away his mortar, an antiquated machine-gun that had some parts missing, and a Soviet-model bazooka without any projectiles; he wanted to take the weapons back with him, but I ordered him to leave them there as I thought they would be more secure.

At Jean Ila's request, I spoke to his men before they left, warning them that we would have to work together and criticizing their way of behaving towards the peasants as if they had forgotten their own origins. This speech of mine, and another to our men in which I said that anyone who deserted would be shot, were not to the liking of the Congolese. People were deserting all the time and taking their rifles with them, and the only way to prevent this was to take more drastic measures while making it easier for those who did leave to do so without their rifle.

Nevertheless, our patrols kept searching adjacent areas for scattered weapons and we managed to find a machine-gun with some pieces missing; with this and one from Kalonda-Kibuye we were able to assemble one with all its parts. In response to my warning and to the offer I had made at the same time, some fighters began to discharge themselves.

Early on the 22nd of October, the constant sound of mortar fire from the direction of Lubondja made us think that the enemy was advancing there; we took some measures, and I sent a rather hurried letter to Masengo asking him to reinforce that position with men from the lake so that I would not be forced to wage a defensive battle just now. In passing, I also gave him several pieces of advice (so as not to lose the habit), such as that he should send some men to Fizi and Uvira to ascertain the disposition of our troops.

News arrived from Lubondja. They had put the ammunition dump out of danger by dividing it into two parts: we chose one location ourselves, while the Congolese comrades hid the rest in a place that they never felt willing to disclose to us. The Lubondja barrier needed Cubans, bazookas and containment weapons, but I did not want to grant any of the requests because it would have meant further splitting up our troops and their firepower.

We reached 24 October, a date that marked half a year since our arrival in the Congo. It was still raining a lot, and the straw huts get soaked when this happens. Some of the Congolese asked me for permission to go and look for some zinc sheets in the old camp, and I gave it to them. Maybe an hour passed and then we heard a volley of rifle shots and some grenade explosions; the Congolese had stumbled into an enemy offensive and come under attack. Fortunately for them, however, they were not at close range and they all managed to escape. Pandemonium swept the camp as the Congolese vanished and we were unable to organize ourselves; they had gone to the house of the *muganga* to get some *dawa*, and only then did they start to take up their positions. I began to organize the defence with Ziwa's company, which was supposed to occupy the front line, and we got ready to receive the soldiers in style. Soon a number of comrades told me that enemy units were approaching across the mountains; I could not see any and, when I asked how many there were, they said there were a lot; how many? it was hard to tell, but certainly a large number. We were in a difficult position; they might cut off our retreat and we would not be able to defend well if the ridge was in enemy hands; I sent a platoon under Rebocate to try to halt the soldiers as high as possible up there.

My dilemma was this: if we stayed put, we might find ourselves surrounded; but if we withdrew, we would lose the ammunition dump and all the equipment we had saved, such as two 60 mortars and a radio apparatus; we would not have time to take anything with us. I preferred to face up to the enemy, in the hope that we could resist until nightfall and then move out. While we were waiting like this, the enemy appeared by the logical way opposite the Lulimba road and we opened fire from there, but this lasted barely a minute. A comrade came running up – he seemed to have a serious wound, but it was only a blow he had received when firing the bazooka – and reported that the enemy had already broken through the front line. I had to give a hasty order to retreat; a machine-gun whose Congolese crew had fled was abandoned by its Cuban operator, who made no attempt to save it; I sent some men to tell those at the other end to retreat quickly to somewhere safe. Then we made off at full speed, leaving behind innumerable things such as books, documents, food, and even the two little monkeys that I kept as mascots.

One unit, which did not receive the order to retreat, faced the enemy and inflicted a number of casualties; Bahaza and Comrade Maganga did this and also managed to save the gun; then, after handing it over to the Congolese for safekeeping, they battled on together with Ziwa, Azima and some other comrades I do not remember. It was they who saved our honour at the end of the day. When they finally withdrew, they fired a bazooka round into the ammunition dump, but without effect.

We, as I said, were retreating along one flank, evading the circle that the soldiers were trying to draw around us from above. My own morale was terribly low; I felt I was to blame for the disaster because of my lack of foresight and my general feebleness. The group of men who followed me was quite large, but we sent some ahead to clear the way if there should be enemy soldiers trying to close the circle; I ordered them to wait for me on the side of a hill, but they kept on regardless and it was only a few days later that I met up again with the Cubans among them; the Congolese had begun deserting from the first moment on. As I rested on the hillside where they were supposed to wait for us, I reflected bitterly that there were 13 of us, one more than Fidel had had at a certain moment, but that

I was not the same leader. We were Moja, Mbili, Karim, Uta, Pombo, Tumaini, Danhusi, Mustafá, Duala, Sitini, Marembe, Tremendo Punto and myself; we did not know what had happened to the rest of the men. As night fell and the last shots of the soldiers who had overwhelmed our position died out, we came to a village abandoned by its inhabitants and grabbed some fat, well-fed hens, on the principle that everything there would be lost the next day as a result of the enemy action. We kept going in order to set a little more distance between us and the camp – which was only two or three kilometres behind us, since we had followed a very long bend on a bad road. One or one and a half kilometres further on, we found some peasants still there in another village. We took some more chickens and were going to pay for them, but the peasants said that we had all been defeated and were brothers in misfortune; they would not charge us anything for them.

We wanted someone to serve as our guide, but they were terribly frightened and merely told us that they knew the doctors and someone else were at another village a short distance away. We sent a man there, and in a while he came back with Fizi the doctor, Kimbi the nurse, and two other comrades; they had set out in the early morning on a trip round the villages and stopped there when they heard the noise of battle. Shortly afterwards, a good number of Congolese came fleeing through – including a wounded man who, after some treatment, continued on his way; everyone was heading in the direction of Lubichaco. They picked up news from the slightly wounded man they treated, and perhaps from another slightly wounded Congolese, and heard that Bahaza was in a serious state. A note reached Azima explaining where they were, and after a little sleep to gather our strength, we set off with a guide who had mastered his fear. At six o'clock in the morning, we reached the little village where Bahaza lay wounded; there was a good concentration of Cubans and Congolese there.

The causes and character of the disaster now became clearer. The men I had sent to stop the soldiers approaching on the nearby slopes did not find them; and later, when they saw the enemy enter the camp down below, they did not open fire because they assumed we would climb out through that area in the event of a retreat (which is not what happened, owing to reports that the enemy was in the mountains). Ziwa's later-confirmed statement that the soldiers in question were actually peasants who had fled through the sierra on seeing the real enemy's approach, and that in fact the enemy had never left the plain, made my distress all the more acute. For it meant that, owing to bad intelligence that disorganized our defence and to the unjustifiable collapse on one of our wings, we had wasted the chance to set a fine ambush and to wipe out a lot of enemy soldiers. Comrade Bahaza had been hit by a bullet at the time of the retreat and carried on his comrades' shoulders to this little village.

We took the sides of the hill, because we were still in a hollow while the treatment was being administered to Bahaza. The bullet had completely shattered his humerus and a rib and penetrated his lung. The wound reminded me of a comrade I had tended years before in Cuba, who had died within a few hours. Bahaza was more powerful, his stronger bones had slowed the bullet down, and it did not seem to have reached his mediastinum. But he was clearly in great pain. A splint was applied as well as possible, and we began a most tiring ascent through steep hills slippery from the rain. The very heavy load was carried by exhausted men, who did not receive the proper cooperation from the Congolese comrades.

We took six long hours to carry Bahaza, terrible hours in which the men could not keep him on their shoulders for more than ten or fifteen minutes at a time, and it became increasingly difficult to replace them, since the Congolese, as I said, did not offer to help and there were relatively few of us. At one point, it looked as if some soldiers were coming up to block our way and we would have to leave some comrades to protect the wounded man's retreat – but it turned out to be only some peasants on the move. From our vantage point we could see a large number of fires, since the soldiers were setting light to all the peasants' houses. They simply followed the path that joined the villages to one another and burnt each one to the ground. Their progress could be seen from the columns of smoke that rose into the air, and from the shapes of peasants fleeing toward the mountains.

We finally reached a little village, but there was practically nothing to eat there. It was full of refugees, all silently blaming the men who had come to take away their security, filled them with faith in eventual victory and then withdrawn to defend their own homes and fields. All this mute anger was expressed in one disconsolate and unconsoling phrase: "Now what do we eat?" For indeed, all their fields and little animals remained down below. They had fled with what they could carry in their own two hands, loaded down with children, as always, and unable to take food for more than one or two days. Other peasants explained to me how the soldiers had suddenly appeared and captured their women, adding in a rage that with a rifle they might have been able to defend themselves, but with a spear all they could do was run.

Bahaza seemed quite a lot better. He spoke and felt a little less pain (though he was still very agitated), and was able to eat some chicken broth. Reassured by his condition, I took a photo in which his large, habitually bulging eyes expressed an anxiety that we had not known how to forestall.

At dawn on 26 October, the nurse came to tell me that Bahaza had had a crisis, torn off his bandages and died – apparently of an acute haematothorax. Later that morning we carried out the sad and solemn ritual of digging a grave and burying Comrade Bahaza, the sixth man we had lost and the first whose corpse could be given the proper honours. It was a mute and virile accusation against my stupidity and lack of foresight, as had been his conduct from the moment he received the wound.

The defeated little band came together and I gave the farewell, almost a soliloquy loaded with reproaches against myself. I recognized my mistakes and declared – with perfect truth – that of all the deaths in the Congo the most painful for me was Bahaza's, because I had severely criticized him for his weakness and he had responded as a true Communist in what he did, whereas I had not been equal to my possibilities and was to blame for his death. I would do everything in my power to wipe out my failure, by working harder and more enthusiastically than ever. The situation was growing worse, and we would not be able to form our army unless the Congolese were integrated. I asked the Cubans to reflect that it was no longer only proletarian internationalism that should be impelling us to struggle, since the support of the base enabled us to have a point of contact with the outside; if that contact was lost, we would be cut off for nobody knew how long in the interior of the Congo. We would have to fight to keep that channel open.

Next I spoke to the Congolese, explaining the gravity of the situation and the fact that our defeat had been due to a fear of asking them to make an exceptional effort in their work. Appealing to their revolutionary consciousness, I said that there had to be more trust between us, and that we had to form a more unified army which would enable us to react more rapidly to any situation that might occur. With the mournful ceremony over, we moved on to Nabikumbe, quite a large village located on the banks of the river of the same name, in a pleasant and fertile valley. Two tendencies manifested themselves among the Congolese: a small one, headed by Tremendo Punto, which wanted at all costs to be closer to the base; and another, headed by Charles and comprising most of the men from the region, which wanted to remain close to where the guardsmen were operating and to defend the area against them.

I decided to stay. Constant retreat would add new defeats to the ones we had already suffered and increase the demoralization of the men who had almost completely lost faith. The Cubans would have liked to go to the base, because the lake had affected them too and they felt closer there to possible escape routes. But we stayed where we were and resumed the task of forming two companies with the men who had remained. We gathered together as many Congolese as we could, and called back all the Cubans who had stopped off somewhere else during the retreat.

I summed up the lessons of the disaster as follows.

From a military point of view, the first mistake I made was to choose the camp's location without making closer investigations or organizing more solid defences. There were no outposts sufficiently far removed to enter into action several kilometres from the camp. I was not able to impose the extra bit of work and effort required to establish the ammunition dump in the upper part of the site (which would have given us much greater flexibility in our actions) and to instal some weapons such as the mortar, which was lost in combat. On the other hand, the reports that soldiers were encircling us through the hills upset all our plans and made the defence not a coordinated operation, but a confused mass of people scattered around without rhyme or reason. Our own wing, which had quite a lot of Cubans, collapsed almost without a fight; this time we could not heap the blame on the fleeing Congolese; we were Cubans there and we retreated. When I was told that the soldiers were already on top of the little hill we were defending, my intention was to pick up an automatic rifle and go and fight there, but then I reasoned that that would be to risk everything on one throw and I preferred to beat a retreat. In reality, however, they were not on top of the hill; the report had been the product of momentary nerves, just as nervousness had made us see soldiers when there were only peasants or large numbers when there could not have been more than 15 men.

From the military point of view, we lost the whole dump and its 150 or so boxes of ammunition for artillery, mortar and machine-gun, as well as an 82 mortar and a machine-gun, two 60 mortars and two incomplete machine-guns, a Soviet bazooka without projectiles, a Chinese-model radio transmitter that I had finally acquired, and a lot of lesser equipment; the bazookas in the hands of the Congolese were lost, together with the bazooka men and the projectiles, and above all the embryonic organization we had managed to give our men up to that time.

The attitude of the Congolese had not been as bad as on the other occasions. It is true that at the first moment they all disappeared, but it was to get some *dawa* for themselves. They returned later, and there were some who gave a good account of themselves. We might have begun to select fighters among them, if the situation had not been so compromised by the defeat that it made them desert after a period of conducting themselves with dignity.

From a political point of view, all the credit we had gained through our fraternal, sympathetic and fair-minded attitude to the peasants foundered on the terrible fact that all their houses were burned. Expelled from an area where they had been able to eat, however poorly, they now had to go and live in mountains that had virtually no food for them and where there was a constant threat of an enemy advance.

The local chieftains paid us back with interest. All of them – Calixte, Jean Ila, Lambert and his commanders, a commissar called Bendera, and maybe a number of headmen – began to spread it around that the Cubans were a bunch of puppets who talked a lot but, at the hour of battle, retreated and left the peasants to take the consequences. They, instead, had wanted to remain in the mountains and defend the key points; now everything had been lost because of the charlatans.

This was the propaganda that the commanders conducted among their men and among the peasantry. Unfortunately, they had some objective basis for their insinuations; I had to fight long and hard to regain some of the confidence of their men, who, hardly knowing me, had placed their trust in me and our people, more than in the commissars and commanders whose arbitrary ways they had endured for so long.

THE WHIRLWIND

Our first concern was to fight for the peasants' loyalty. We had to do this because of the adverse forces that we faced. The constant withdrawals and defeats suffered by our army, the maltreatment or neglect endured by the inhabitants of the area, and now the ill-willed interpretations that various commanders were using to take their revenge: all this added to the difficulties of our situation. We gathered together the local *kapita* and leading figures from nearby villages, as well as the peasants living there, and spoke to them with the help of the invaluable Charles. We explained the present situation, the reason for our coming to the Congo, and the danger facing the revolution because we were fighting among ourselves and not focusing on the struggle against the enemy. We found the *kapita* receptive and willing to cooperate; he said to anyone who would listen that it was outrageous to compare us to the Belgians (which had already happened), since he had never seen a Belgian in these parts, still less a white man eating *bukali* with his soldiers from the same-sized bowl. The peasant's views did not fail to comfort us, but we had to do more than work at winning over individuals. To gain everyone's confidence, given the large number of villages in the area, I would have to spend days eating *bukali* from a bowl in each one – which made success rather unlikely.

We asked them to guarantee a supply of manioc and any other food they might obtain; to lend us a hand in building a hospital, at a nearby place away from the road that the guardsmen might use in any advance; to lend us their tools so that we could dig trenches and improve the site's defences; and to form a little group of scouts so that we could get to know the enemy better. They agreed at once, and it was not long before quite a large and comfortable hospital was in place, on a hill protected from aircraft, and where we had dug a number of ditches to keep the tools and to prevent everything falling into the enemy's hands, as had happened before.

An unfortunate incident helped to ensure the peasants' quick and enthusiastic response to our appeal. At the Lubondja barrier, a group of Congolese decided to rig up some grenade-traps for greenhorns but did so without informing their comrades; another group of Congolese passed by and fell into the trap designed for the enemy. Three slightly wounded men came in for treatment, plus a fourth with a more serious stomach perforation that they attributed to a mortar round fired by the advancing enemy. Those slightly wounded were soon healed, but the other man had to have a delicate intestinal operation in the open air, under very difficult conditions, with a constant threat from aircraft flying over the area. Despite everything, the operation was a success. It raised the esteem of Comrade Morogoro, the surgeon, and allowed us to insist on the rapid completion of the hospital, at a calm and peaceful spot where such tasks could be carried out in proper safety.

That same evening, another wounded man came in with a double perforation. What had happened? The whole group fled when they heard the explosion; the slightly wounded and the man with the stomach wound, who was able to help himself, also took to their heels and were later picked up by their comrades. But there was one who stayed behind – perhaps because his condition was too serious for him to move, or perhaps simply because he was terrified. With night approaching, it was clear that the guardsmen were not advancing and some of the Congolese resolved to go back closer and look for their weapons (which they had thrown away in their flight). It was then that they came across the wounded comrade and brought him into the hospital during the night. We had no lamps or proper lighting, nor adequate drugs, and so an even more difficult operation than the previous one had to be performed by the light from just a couple of torches, on a man in a truly terrible physical condition. At dawn, when the four perforations had finally been treated, the patient died. All these efforts, as well as our care for a woman wounded in a strange fight with a buffalo (which was eventually killed with spears), did a lot to lift the peasants' regard for us and to help us form a nucleus capable of withstanding the commanders' malign influence.

For the commanders were still spreading their insidious rumours. The incident with the grenades, for example, was reported by Radio Bemba in a way which suggested that the Cubans had laid the devices and that the Congolese had fallen into the trap. Such outrageous stories were the speciality of Commissar Feston Bendera, Commander Huseini and others of their ilk; Calixte and Jean Ila, as well as all of Lambert's people, never tired of heaping insults on me.

At the mixed barrier at Lubondja, they called together the Congolese soldiers under our command and poked fun at them for being forced to work at trench-digging, in contrast to their own soldiers, who stayed comfortably indoors and needed to have only three or four sentries posted. They also refused to show us the place where some of the ammunition was hidden. Our patience had to be infinite in enduring such deceit.

Commander Huseini called a meeting with all the Congolese, which we had someone monitoring for us. He complained that I rebuked him like a child, that we divided the food which was brought up from the lake only among our own companies, that we were taking away all their weapons and ammunition and eating up the maize and manioc; who could tell what would happen when the food ran out. The saddest thing about this was that they had asked for our presence there.

Contemptible though it was, this behaviour was mitigated by our really sharp treatment of the commanders, by their ignorance and superstition, their inferiority complex, the way we had offended their susceptibilities, and perhaps the pain these poor people felt that a white man should be rebuking them as in the bad old days.

Lambert's people did much the same thing and tried to clash directly with our men, accusing them of cowardice and of provoking the enemy army and then running away. This certainly stirred things up and did nothing to raise our men's flagging spirits. Several times Mbili proposed moving away a little from the commander, so as to avoid a clash with him or a total collapse of his men's morale. This situation was developing everywhere; Comrade Mafu wrote me the following note from Front de Force, which I swiftly forwarded to Masengo.

> This is to inform you of the present situation. I requested from the captain and the commander that we should go and cut the line, and they said they do not have bullets or food. The tinned provisions have all been eaten up.
>
> After receiving your message,[17] they said the same. On the day it arrived, the captain told us that the Congolese had laid an ambush for him, that they had pursued and disarmed them and brought their rifles here. The commander had been called to a meeting there, and he told me that the situation was very bad and that he could not go because the Congolese would kill him.[18] But they have two meetings a day, with lots of clapping and shouting. I thought they were preparing themselves for combat, but then I found out that the topic of the meetings was how to get out of the Congo. At first, they told me it would be next week, but at another meeting they decided to send some scouts to the lake to locate the boats and take them. They sent a captain and ten soldiers for that purpose. They also sent the commissar with another group to Kigoma, on a different mission but with the same objective.
>
> I should also tell you that the eight Congolese who came to a meeting were beaten, and only three of them are left here.
>
> The man who informed us did not say whether they spoke of us in the event of their leaving. He told me that if they caught him talking about this with us, they would shoot him. If I can find out anything more precise, I'll let you know.

Basing myself on this information, I ordered Mafu to go and strengthen the base, and Azi (who was at the Makungo front) to come and meet me.

17. This refers to a message urging them to carry out sabotage actions as soon as possible.
18. This was the meeting that Masengo presided over, to which we have referred before.

While all this was happening, I tried to regroup my men and sent scouts to look for all the weapons that had been scattered around in the flight and not fallen into the enemy's hands: Bahaza's gun, mortars, machine-guns, which had been left in the safekeeping of the Congolese, and which they had hidden so that they could flee more quickly. I sent a letter to Siki in which I repeated many of the things that had been reported to me. I shall quote just a couple of paragraphs to give some idea of how I assessed the situation.

The weakness of the men is terrible, and everyone wants to head for the lake; probably a lot are descending on you there; send them to me immediately, with plenty of ammunition. Only the really sick should stay behind. I have decided in principle to remain here at Nabikumbe, ten hours away from the lake (Upper Base), a day and a half from Kasima, and two hours from a feeble barrier that has been set up near Lubondja. If I were to go to the lake myself, it would be a huge political defeat, since all the peasants trusted us and would find themselves abandoned. Once we have reorganized, we will be able to offer effective assistance; this evening we begin shooting practice with a Soviet Mauser for which there are bullets here. We are lacking .30 ammunition (SKS) and are short on stuff for the FALs. If you've got it, send us 5,000 SKS and 3,000 FAL rounds. If you don't have it, please let me know; this lack of news is maddening.

Rumours have reached us that three boats arrived with ammunition, that Kabila crossed to Kabimba, and that there are 40 Cubans there. Try to take as few of them as possible and send them to me. After the (objective) situation there is known, it will be possible to make a decision.

The information about Kabila had come by word of mouth from a Congolese messenger, who assured me that he had seen the Cubans and that Kabila himself had landed in the area; the letter says Kabimba, but it should read Kibamba.

The comrades wrote to me at length, but the letters crossed and did not really answer each other. I will copy in full one of these from the last days of October.

Comrade Tatu

We deeply regret the death of Comrade Bahaza and sympathize with how you feel, given the circumstances surrounding his case. We are very glad that you and the other comrades are well.

We hope that, by the time you receive this letter, we will have made good in your eyes our apparent failure to send reports and materials. As you will see, the first messenger and the first letter were sent on the 21st, "two days after our arrival". Not much happened and another messenger was already leaving with our more extensive report, in which we told you of the men we have at our disposal at the present time.

We cannot understand how he could have so piously believed that Kabila arrived with four boats. (At best, he was meant to have brought four big boatloads.) In fact, he remains impassively in Kigoma. As for the arrival of the Cubans, the informants may possibly have confused their wishes with reality. The only Cuban to arrive has been Changa, who did two trips in the space of three or four days, after not coming for 19. He told us that he would like to go on making trips, since he is afraid they will embark us and that communication via the lake will be lost. This is a new problem, because I had already agreed to come, and it is due to the situation he senses both in Kigoma and here at the lake.

The messenger told us that there was a letter for Masengo but he did not come, although we think that any idea of dealing with him is pointless, since Masengo is at the moment a completely defeated man with no heart for anything; nor does he have the authority to give anyone orders, as he himself admitted in the talk we had with him yesterday. Masengo told us that not even Kabila, if he came, would have the authority to resolve anything, because everyone blames the two of them for the disaster. We can tell you that Masengo's attitude during our talk was enough to arouse pity. He said that he did not even have the authority to arrest those who had sent letters to fighters urging them to lay down their weapons. He attributed all this to tribal differences and things like that. He insisted a lot that we should help him find safe hideaways for weapons and ammunition, in case it is possible to relaunch the struggle in the future. If you put this together with what we have already told you about his preparations to go to Kigoma (which he did not want to tell us about, but which have been communicated to Njenje), you will have some idea of the state he is in.

As to the situation at the lake, at the base and at Aly's and Tom's front (Kasima), everything is as in the previous report. The only variation is that things have been getting worse every day. (But that is normal here.)

As to the check on things leaving here which you mention in your letter, a detailed account will be sent to you in each report. We still have some reserves here, except for clothing (which has not arrived) and shoes (which we have only in very small sizes). All we could give the ten Congolese you sent us were some trainers. Nor are there any weapons, for although Njenje is keeping a check on everything there, it started too late and there is nothing much to check. Fifteen FALs are left in our reserves at the base, but we are not sending them to you because we don't think you would want us to.

We think that our previous reports will give you a fuller picture of the general objective situation, and that this will help you to reach a decision, as you say in your letter.

The Cubans who have come here in the last two or three days are: Israel, Kasambala, Amia, Abdallah, Ami and Agano. We are sending them all back to you, minus Israel and Kasambala, whose feet are swollen from walking without shoes. Nor can we send you Baati at the moment, as he is still too ill. As for the bullets,

161

2,000 rounds of FAL and three boxes of 7.62 are on their way; we haven't got any for AKs.

We have been thinking that, given your situation, it might be a good idea for Tembo to come up and join you. We also think that either you should take a stroll down here or one of us should come up and exchange views with you about the general situation. We are maintaining contact with Kigoma and Dar es Salaam by radio.

In our opinion, everything that is happening both here and where you are is known to the enemy. That is Masengo's view too, since a lot of people – even high-ranking officers – have gone over to the enemy and we don't know the whereabouts of many more.

Something else that Masengo said to us (and we agree with him on this) is that he expects an attack on the base and the lake at any moment. The surprise attack they made on you confirms us in this opinion.

Siki considers that the position you have chosen is very bad, and that we could be cut off from each other at any moment. For the barrier is in the immediate vicinity of Kaela and, as you know from earlier reports, Kasima was captured several days ago and there are only four Cubans there together with Asmari and Tom. The Congolese cannot be relied on, as they run away.

To bring some order into our messages, we will wait for your reply before sending our next one. Then we'll be aware of what you know and what you need.

Remember that there's hardly anyone left here, that we have two comrades manning the lakeside mortars and two at an observation point around Ganya, and that we have to post a guard here to protect the stores (the Congolese are a light-fingered lot). They've already relieved us of half a sack of beans and a sack of salt on the way from the boat to the base.

> Yours,
> Siki
> Tembo

After receiving this letter, in answer to my one that I quoted before, I got another letter, dated 26 October, whose main paragraphs I will copy down here.

THE SITUATION AT THE LAKE AND THE BASE

The following agreements came out of Siki's meeting with Masengo. First, Njenje will be in charge of the lake base, with all the powers of the position and responsibility for defence. He is authorized to take all the measures he sees fit for his orders to be carried out, the only commanders above him being Masengo and Siki. Njenje and Kumi were also put in charge of everything reaching the lake by our own independent route. We attach sketches of the defence, with the location of all the fortifications and of the heavy weapons. As you see, the defence has been well organized with the means available to us, which include two lines of trenches. Siki (like myself) only trusts the weapons manned by Cubans, since with the rest there are the same problems as elsewhere. Hapana masasi, hapana chakula, hapana travaille; *and always the question is how best to retreat. The framework for all this is Masengo's evident lack of authority. It should be added that the lake has been turned into a refuge for all the runaways, with a consequent relaxation of discipline. At the meeting with Masengo, we put forward a chart for the organization of the general staff; it was agreed to use the military aspects of our proposal, as well as the civil aspects after some modifications on their part. A section on justice and finances was added, which will come under the military part. As we previously informed you, they are thinking of making you operational commander.*

We are able to report that we now have control of the provisions, and that the ammunition and other material are as Masengo left them with you. How long this happy state will last is another matter. We think problems will soon arise, because they request nothing for work or combat but are already asking for provisions, and there has been some friction both at the lake and at the base. But we are sticking firmly to our motto "everything for the front", and insisting that anyone who wants to have the benefit of the provisions must go off to the front. We also proposed solutions such as sending a third of the men to look for food in the nearby villages. Rather than solve the problem, however, they prefer to do nothing and stay hungry indoors. They certainly have nothing to eat.

SITUATION AT ALY'S FRONT: KABIMBA

In fact they are at Katala, a little closer to Kibamba, since the guardsmen took and burned Kabimba and then withdrew. The chief there did not allow Aly to put up any resistance, nor does he let Aly give him advice; he also stubbornly insists on hanging around at the lake, ignoring the danger that the guardsmen may capture the slopes. Siki sent orders to Aly that the Cubans should capture them on their own account, to avoid being encircled or caught unawares. Aly's situation is rather delicate, since the chief told him it would be best if the Cubans went off to the base (on the pretext of resting). A Congolese politico told Aly in private that the chief had called the soldiers together and said that it would be best if the Cubans went away from there. Siki discussed all this with Masengo, and he agreed to sort things out by personally talking with the chief of Kabimba. A few days ago, when they were travelling for three days to lay an ambush on the Albertville road, they picked up some civilians and detained them. The civilians stated that an enemy supply lorry was due to pass by soon, but the Congolese insisted on leaving without waiting for it. This will give you a picture of the state of morale at that front. We sent them some provisions. There are a total of eleven Cubans at that front.

SITUATION AT KASIMA

Kasima was captured by the guardsmen, as we reported before. They advanced by boat as far as Kaela, burned it and then withdrew. Everything was lost, including at least one anti-aircraft machine-gun. (It had not been used and was concealed by a Cuban who had been left alone by the Congolese and who, as he put it, had to retreat in the face of fire from aircraft.) We are telling you these things as they have been reported to us. Fifty Congolese were sent with a chief to the front to place themselves under Cuban orders and create a barrier. Later a commander who had been in Cuba arrived there with seven others, saying that he was going to Baraka. Tom, the politico, explained the situation to him and tried to make him give up the idea, but he stubbornly persisted and fell into an ambush in which he and three others were killed. Asmari asked Siki to go there with ten Congolese and first-aid supplies. At the present time, there are three ambushes between Kaela and here. Clearly, given all the difficulties of ambushes with Congolese who run away, it is necessary to pressure and threaten them; they get lost, etc. According to the politico Tom, he says he didn't start shooting them because he would have to shoot every one. In all there are six Cubans at that front.

COMMUNICATIONS

We make contact with Kigoma three times a day by R805 in code, at 8.00 a.m., 2.30 p.m. and 7.00 p.m. We are trying to get through to Dar es Salaam, although it is at the limits of our range. If contact is made, it will be twice a day in code. Kabila is using Kigoma's facilities to contact the base, so that now we are better led. It may be possible to instal a microwave on a launch so that we can communicate while crossing the lake (if you authorize it). We are reorganizing communications by telephone. Masengo agreed that two or three men should be sent to teach them how it works and how to repair it.

After the previous page was written, contact was made via the apparatus with Dar es Salaam. Reception and transmission was 100 per cent.

After the general report on the situation was completed, Njenje called us from the lake to say that Masengo was preparing to cross over to Kigoma. After a while, a second call from there informed us that all the "big guys" had had a meeting with Masengo; it had been attended by Njenje and Kumi. At the meeting, Masengo proposed that he should go to Kigoma, since he was the only leader inside the Congo. The "big guys" opposed this and Masengo agreed to remain. We were told, however, that preparations for his departure are continuing.

A third call informed us that they were continuing to meet; Masengo stated that he had received a message from Kasavubu offering him a ministry. The message said that a ship was waiting for him a little way from Kibamba, and that he had only to take a boat and board it. According to Masengo, he replied that his brother Mitoudidi had died in battle and that he was willing to die as well.

Njenje and Kumi were on the alert, with instructions to inform us of anything that happened. Masengo is deflecting all the problems they raise on to the Cubans, saying that it is they who will solve them. He even dodged Aly's problems with the chief at Kabimba (which he had been asked to solve personally), saying that Tembo would have to sort it out.

Tomorrow, Siki and I will go and talk with Masengo as if we knew nothing about these matters, in order to see what he says. Meanwhile, we remain in a state of alert.

We have informed Padilla of these events by radio in code, so that he can be on his guard, for we assume that if they have approached Masengo, they must also be "working" on Soumaliot and Kabila. The first time he made contact with us from Dar es Salaam, Padilla already requested a report on the latest events and the situation at the lake, and also – something that struck us as a little odd and may be starting to make sense – asked us to send our views of Kabila.

It will be appreciated that the points towards the end were highly alarming; they implied that Masengo was on the point of giving up the struggle. I wrote back as follows.

Tembo and Siki:

I will reply to your letter point by point, and then make an assessment of the situation here and of the remaining matters.

The international situation is not so bad, regardless of any betrayal by Kabila and Masengo. Soumaliot's declarations are good and we have a leader here; I spoke to Tremendo Punto so that he will take charge if Masengo goes off and organize out-and-out resistance. As regards Kabila's plans, there is no problem so long as he does everything over the radio; if there is a conflict, we'll criticize him and see what happens. By no means must we now leave the base. You should ask Dar es Salaam about the results of the interview with the Tanzanian government.

As to the lake and the base, the defence sketch indicates that they are very vulnerable to attack from the side. The machine-guns should be pointing landwards to defend the flanks, and trenches should also be dug there. Attempts should be made to ensure that the heavy weapons are manned by staunch Cubans *(which is not the same as plain Cubans, as I know from my own painful experience here). The slopes giving access to the base should be reconnoitred and defences set up there. Be as firm as you possibly can about the supplies.*

Concerning Aly, I sent a note for him to join in the defence; with them and Mafu's men, we have enough there and you can deploy them in such a way that we have some reserves in hand. Don't forget the bare hill overlooking the base; it is one of the keys to the defence (where the mortars and anti-aircraft machine-guns are located).

Concerning Kasima, I have already told you of the reconnaissance that I ordered to be done. I think that unless the guardsmen get a move on, we can give them a fright there as soon as I reorganize my outfit a little.

Concerning the communications, that is great news, but it strikes me as excessive to contact the other side three times a day and Dar es Salaam twice a day. You won't have anything to say to each other before long; the petrol will run out and the codes can always be discovered, not to speak of the base being spotted from the air. Leaving aside the technical conditions, which have to be analysed on the spot, I would recommend one normal daily communication with Kigoma and the allocation of a fixed hour for exceptional contact, plus once every two or three days with Dar es Salaam. This will allow us to save on petrol. The hours of contact should be at night, and the apparatus should be protected against attack from the air. I think the microwave is a good idea, with simple codes that are changed frequently.

When I received the preceding report on Masengo's attitude, I spoke with Tremendo Punto (as I said I would in my letter). He broke down and said that he was not the right man to take over the leadership; he had little personality and was too highly strung; he was willing to die there in the line of duty, with resignation, almost like a Christian martyr, but he was not capable of taking things further; that was something his brother Mujumba could do. It was then decided to write to Mujumba, but the situation could not be explained in a letter because of the danger that it might fall into enemy hands, so he was asked to come and discuss some important matters. The letter went off with two messengers but we never found out if it reached its destination, because we neither received a reply nor heard any more of the bearers.

I should place it on record that all these reports about Masengo seem to me exaggerated. The way he continued to behave with me makes me think that the reports from Siki and Tembo (which were not first-hand but came via others) had been blown up out of proportion through nervous anxiety, mistrust, lack of real direct communication across the language barrier, and so on. I am also reminded that on 27 October, a day after the letter from Tembo and Siki, Masengo himself sent me a long letter in which he listed all the precautions taken throughout the front, the peasants who had been asked for and the defensive measures that had been adopted. And he added a phrase: "Whatever happens, let us always be optimistic." Of course, it is no more than a phrase, but it does indicate a state of mind very different from the one attributed to him in our comrades' report and much closer to his real attitude, unless he is faking it in a masterly way (which seems out of character). I had decided to have nothing to do with Tembo's and Siki's appeals when, on the night of the 30th, a peremptory letter dated 29 October arrived from them. I give here some extracts from it.

Luluabut Base, 29 October '65, 6.00 p.m.
Tatu:

We are sending you this urgent message because, since 12.00 today, seven aircraft have been constantly bombing us and dropping large objects that look like petrol tanks in the direction of Kabimba and the Jungo area near the lake. This is the usual procedure before an advance or a landing, and so we are warning you now before it is too late. The bombing forced the machine-gunners to retreat, and one of them has not appeared again. Njenje will investigate and inform us immediately.

As we have said in all our previous reports to you, we have no confidence at all in the "Congos" who are defending the lake, especially as their demoralization is growing all the time. The number of Cubans at the lake and the base, many of them sick, is not enough to put up a serious defence of our sole and vital base for communications with the outside.

In our previous reports we tried to draw you the most objective possible picture of the prevailing demoralization, so we don't think it necessary to dwell on this again, but you should be aware that things are really alarming in this respect. Every shameless element at the fronts has taken refuge at the lake, joining the shameless ones already there. There are a large number of prisoners, despite the fact that, as we wrote yesterday, there is an even greater number of criminals and traitors that no one is capable of arresting. Masengo (who has not left yet) sends frequent daily messages asking Kabila to report on the loyalty of certain officers. Another often-made accusation is that some officers are urging the "revolutionaries" to lay down their weapons and spreading the rumour that Soumaliot is very friendly to Kasavubu.

As we said in our last report, we don't like at all the position you are in; we know that the guardsmen may seize roads away from the lake and leave us isolated. We think that the best solution would be to have a barrier where you are and to transfer the bulk of the Cubans here.

In our view, we are writing to you enough and filling you in on both the international situation and the situation here. We almost seem like two old gossips. Please do the same with us, as we are always anxious for news. Like that, we will be three old gossips.

Siki and Tembo S.A.

We decided to set off on our way to the base. Mbili would remain as commander of this area, basing himself at the first barrier. Rebocate would form a second line of defence at the place where we had our camp, with a good number of Congolese under training. This training is very basic, of course – shooting lessons, because the poor guys can't hit a cow at five metres, and a bit of basic drill. We talked with the peasants, who perfectly understood our decision; they felt secure with the men who were remaining, and with the doctors staying on at the hospital to look after the Congolese wounded and some sick Cubans. We said farewell in a very friendly way.

Another month, October, had passed, and this is what I wrote in my diary.

A month of unmitigated disaster. The shameful fall of Baraka, Fizi, Lubondja and Lambert's front was compounded by the surprise they gave me at Kilonwe and the loss of two comrades, Maurino (missing) and Bahaza (dead). All this would have been nothing if the Congolese had not completely lost heart. Nearly all their officers have run away, and Masengo seems prepared to weigh anchor. The Cubans are not much better, from Tembo and Siki to the ordinary soldiers. Everyone justifies his own guilt by shifting it onto the shoulders of the Congolese. But on top of my own mistakes, the Cuban fighters have shown some grave weaknesses in combat. It has also been very difficult to achieve cordial relations between them and to get the Cubans to shake off their scornful elder-brother attitude towards the Congolese, with special rights regarding provisions and burdens. In short, we are entering what may be the final month, when we will have to do our last bit.

My remark about relations between the Cubans and Congolese arose from the fact that the cooks, being Cuban, gave special helpings to their comrades, while the Congolese tended to be the ones who carried certain heavy loads. We have not established entirely fraternal relations, and we feel a little bit like superior people who have to give advice.

We did the journey to the base in two days. On the second day, when we were passing through Nganja, we learnt that planes had machine-gunned there the previous day, killing some 30 cows whose corpses were scattered around the immediate area. As we were profiting from this to eat a good chunk of meat, Mundandi arrived and we had a serious talk. I told him that his idea of going away now was crazy, that Rwanda's fate was bound up with that of the Congo, and that he would not have anywhere to continue the struggle – unless he was thinking of giving it up altogether. He admitted that it was crazy; some others had proposed it to him, but he had dissuaded them and had come precisely to discuss a sabotage operation against the power line to Front de Force, thereby focusing the enemy's attention on that point.

I reached the base and found a climate of defeatism and open hostility to the Congolese. This gave rise to some serious discussions with the comrades; they had a long list of all the officers who had fled to Kigoma, which was not exact but did reflect quite well the reality of the situation: that is, the cowardice of the officers, their disdainful attitude to combat, and their treachery. But the list also unjustly included the names of some who remained right up to the last moment. The following two notes give some idea of the mentality prevailing at that time: one is a letter from Tembo to a comrade that allows one to guess the recipient's state of mind and the letter he must have written (which I do not have and never read).

The "base", Thursday, 28 October 1965, 13.00 hrs

I have received your note. Although it is not dated, I assume it has crossed with one that I sent you via Comrade Chei.

You were writing after the painful loss of a comrade who – I won't conceal it – deserved a death no less glorious but more useful.

Your lines reflect the state of mind produced by recent events and the picture of desolation and liquidation presented by the so-called "Congolese revolution". This worries me. I want to tell you quite frankly what I think and ask you once more to have confidence in me, although I cannot assure you that this confidence won't suddenly end in a new embarkation.

I know that you are not a squeamish kid. On the contrary, I think you are a revolutionary who will do your duty whatever the circumstances. So I won't appeal to your resoluteness of character – which would be pointless and absurd – but I would like to remind you of the old saying that "Caesar's wife must not only be honourable but also look honourable". You mustn't allow anyone to think that your views about the situation, or about the particular measures taken to address the situation, imply that you feel defeated and have no heart for the struggle. You must keep yourself at a peak of combat-readiness, and your attitude should conspicuously serve as an example and a stimulus for other comrades in the difficult circumstances through which we are passing.

It is possible that there are some things you do not understand, or that measures are being taken which strike you as misguided, but you should not conclude that Tatu and the other comrades in charge are not aware of the real situation that is so objectively visible. Don't forget that, at difficult moments, it is necessary to take extreme measures to preserve the men's morale and to avert a debacle.

Siki and I have sent an extensive report to Tatu (which he is probably reading right now), telling him in great detail of how things stand. It is possible that, after reading it, he will decide to come and speak to us. If not, I will go to speak to him personally by next Thursday at the latest. Meanwhile, we must keep our spirits high and set an example of calmness, confidence and courage. You can rest assured that everything possible will be done to solve the problem in the most revolutionary and convincing manner, as befits Marxist-Leninist leaders.

I have more confidence than ever in Tatu, and you should feel the same.

I don't categorically deny that he can make mistakes. But if he makes a mistake, our duty – after discussing it – is to follow his directives, whatever they are. I'm not joking when I say that it is a thousand times preferable to die in battle, even if we think it is for a useless cause, than to produce a spectacle of defeat by refusing to fight. Cuban revolutionaries can die, but they cannot take fright.

I expect . . . I am sure that you will do your revolutionary duty as a soldier, a Cuban and a man; and that you will do this not only by fulfilling your personal duty but – as is the responsibility of a leader – by setting an example to others.

Venceremos.

The other note, dated the first of the month, is addressed to Tembo.

Comrade:

I am writing you these lines of greeting from a trench three kilometres from the Askaris. I also want to inform you of the situation here: the Congolese are trying to pick a quarrel with us and speaking ill of Tatu; they blame him for the burning of the peasants' homes, for the loss of weapons, the lack of food and the wandering life of the peasants.

On our side the disenchantment is total. I have learnt that a majority of the Cubans who arrived with Tatu will request a meeting with you and propose leaving here. This is the attitude of 17 men here, plus 7 in the group that has arrived. Emilio, this attitude has become almost universal among the comrades; we struggle to convince them that now is the time for maximum firmness, but there is great disenchantment, great mistrust, and a huge desire to leave the Congo. They base themselves on the attitude they see among the Congolese, for whom the struggle seems to be over. The comrades suggest that things have come to this pass because of Tatu, and they see little desire in him or his attitude to find a way out.

This is what I want to tell you, so that you can help as effectively as possible.

Politico

As this letter shows, there was an almost complete disintegration of the troops; some Party members even proposed to hold a meeting to ask me to pull out. I was extremely sharp in my replies, warning that I would not accept any such demand or any meeting of that kind and would treat it as treachery, and that I would brand as cowardice even any act of allowing such proposals to circulate. I still had a remnant of authority, which kept some degree of cohesion among the Cubans; that was all. But much worse things were happening on the Congolese side. I received a letter written during these days by Jerôme Makambila, a "provincial deputy and people's representative on the CNL", in which he accused Masengo of murdering women and, having presented the case at length, invited me to meet him at Fizi to analyse the situation in that area. At a time when communications with abroad were in greater peril and we had a central point and a general staff to defend, this gentleman was firing off letters all over the place (I received several from him) to organize the meeting. This paragraph will give some idea of the limbo in which the revolution was then sailing.

I will take the liberty of reproducing for you the aspirations, wishes and proposals of the whole population in the Fizi region.

1. The people demand that the military power of our revolution should be entrusted to the friendly forces who are coming to help us, until the country is stabilized.

2. The people request intensive aid from friendly countries, consisting of:

a military operations, personnel, weapons, equipment, money, etc.;

b technical assistance, engineers, various kinds of technicians, doctors, etc.;

c social assistance, teachers, traders, industrialists, etc.

The idea of handing all the military power over to Cubans was nothing other than an attempt to sow sedition with our support and had no other roots than tribal differences between these people and the Kabila-Masengo group – unless the enemy's hand was involved in it.

The only news that cut through this absurd and gloomy picture was a report from Aly that he had had two battles and inflicted a number of casualties on the enemy. All this was in spite of continual rows with the military commander of the region and the fact that, in practice, he and his group of comrades had had to carry out operations against the army alone. In one of these, they captured documents outlining the enemy's plans and a number of maps, as well as a radio, two mortars, a bazooka, four FALs, a Super-FAL, ammunition and reserves. It was a fine attack, a harsh blow for the enemy, but it was not enough to alter the situation. Among the captured papers was the following.

Secret

ORDER OPS No. 2

Ops South Map scale 1/200,000 No. 1 Bendera

Map scale 1/100,000 Katenga

1. Situation.

a) Enemy forces:

1) Enemy bttln. (± 360 men) under command of Captain Busindi, mostly composed of Babembe and a group of Tutsi (Rwandan) at Katale.

2) One pltn. (± 40 men) dressed as ANC:

Weapons: Chinese-made sub-machine-guns; they picked up 6 navvies in the week of 27 September '65 at 7 kms from Kabimba and obliged them to carry sacks to their position (camp) along the Mama-Kasanga-Kalenga road.[19]

b) Friendly forces:

– The 5th Col. has occupied Baraka and will maintain the Baraka-Fizi-Lulimba line.

– The 9th Command has occupied Lulimba.

– The 5th Inf. Bttln. has occupied Bendera.

– Detachment of (± volunteers) 5th Cd. + 1 police pltn. (ffl 30 men) is occupying Kabimba.

– The 14th Inf. Bttln. (-) holds the rail and occupies Kabega-Maji-Muhala.

– 1st Cpy. 14th Bttln. + one cpy. 12th Bttln. occupy Albertville.

– Air force:

The air force (WIGMO) is supporting operations with:

4 T-28s and 1 helicopter.

2 B-26s provisionally stationed at Albertville.

Extra air support may be obtained from the WIGMO squadron (4 T-28s stationed at Goma) if absolutely necessary.

1 DC3 FATAL, an air supply section, is at Albertville.

19. This refers to the failed attempt at an ambush recounted above.

Navy:

4 PT boats + Ermens-Luka (will prevent rebel elements crossing the lake throughout the operation).

c) Mission:

2nd Para-Bttln. (-) will execute movement from Albertville to Kabimba and take up final position.

2 – Phase 2:

2nd Para-Bttln. (-), with help from Chief Mama Kasanga's warriors, will reconnoitre north and north-east of Kabimba to locate enemy positions.

3 – Phase 3:

2nd Para-Bttln. will carry out a raid to wipe out rebels north of Kabimba, including the rebel base at Katale.

Intelligence about the enemy

1) Katsheka: ± 300 Tutsi assisted by ± Cubans. The store is to the north of the River Katsheka, under the command of Joseph Mundandi (Rwandan).

Weapons: 2 × 81 mortars

2 × recoilless 75 guns

2 × .50 anti-aircraft guns

2 × .30 machine-guns

30 sub-machine-guns + bazookas

Stock: 200 boxes ammunition + 100 mines

2) Makungo: Position on the side of the hill. ffl Babembe assisted by Cubans from Katsheka under command of Calexte (Mubembe). Arms comparable with Katsheka.

Stocks: ditto.

3) Katenga: Bivouac position in the forest. ± men (Babembe and others).

4) Kibamba: Enemy base by side of lake, bordering villages: port of arrival for supplies coming from Kigoma. EM rebel general (Javua).

Training centre for new recruits.

Connection: telephone network from the hillside to the lake/ to Balabala.

5) Katalo: North Kabimba; ± 300 men, former inhabitants of Albertville assisted by 12 Cubans. Commanded by Captain Businda (from Albertville).

Arms: 2 × 75 SR guns

2 × 81mm mortars

12 × .30 machine-guns

150 × AFN rifles

3 anti-aircraft guns

6) Lobunzo: ± 600 men, commanded by Colonel Pedro (Mubembe).

Important store in the house of Chief Kilindi.

7) Kabanga: store and port (ships entering the Luvu estuary).

8) Kalonda-Kibuye: occupied by rebels.

9) Fizi: administrative centre.

10) Simbi: supply and instruction centre.

11) Stores and port.

Their aim was to occupy the whole littoral and destroy our installations close to Kigoma. It can be seen that, apart from some mistakes, they had a very precise idea of our weaponry and human reserves, as well as of the number of Cubans here. The enemy intelligence service worked perfectly, or almost perfectly, whereas we did not know what was happening in its ranks.

The picture that presented itself when I arrived at the base was not at all promising. We knew what the enemy wanted, but we had not needed to capture those documents to find this out; it was already clear. And the spectacle of disintegration was terrible.

MEAN BLOWS

We took the first precautions to turn the base into an impregnable redoubt, or at least into one that could be taken only at the price of heavy enemy losses. The most sensitive areas were protected with a line of freshly dug trenches. Scouts went out to reconnoitre all the slopes in the direction of Rwandasi, and to make up a route to connect it with the road to its south that goes directly from Nganja to the lake. We ordered the construction of a series of protected wells in hidden places; Cuban comrades worked on these, and the idea was that all the impedimenta could be concealed there if we were forced to evacuate.

When I arrived, I reviewed the organization of the radio equipment; it consists of an apparatus with quite a long range that is not very practical under present circumstances, with twelve-volt accumulators charged by a small generator; this makes it necessary to have quite a large reserve of petrol. The apparatus reached Dar es Salaam, though not with much power, and got through perfectly to Kigoma. The three comrades responsible for transmissions – Lieutenant Tuma, the telegraph operator and the mechanic – performed their task in a thorough way. During the period from 22 October (the day it began to function) to 20 November (the night we left the lake), they transmitted 110 messages in code and received 60. The total dedication and efficiency of these comrades contrasted with the climate of dereliction and spinelessness prevalent in our force. It is a fact that experienced men with a love for their work (though, it is only fair to say, on the margins of the daily tussle with the Congolese soldiers) were able to achieve magnificent results. And with the qualification just noted,

I would venture to say that if all the cadres had been of the same quality, our performance – if not the final result – would have been different.

I spoke by telephone with Masengo as soon as I arrived, and he seemed in good spirits. The first proposal he made was to attack Kasima; it was his "pet idea". I replied that we would discuss it the next day. I went down to see him and we had another conversation about the subject. I had been informed by the scouts, Nane and Kahama, that there were no guardsmen in that village, and I told him as much. But he had different news; Captain Salumu's men were close by and were reporting directly back to him; he insisted that there were guardsmen there. We did not reach agreement about an attack and postponed the matter until fresh reconnaissance had been able to establish the exact situation.

Commander Mundandi showed himself willing to meet my demands for better protection of the base. These were that a sabotage operation should be mounted to cut the power line; that I should be sent one of the guns in their possession; and that he should concern himself with the defence of Nganja so that some men could be released to go towards Kasima. In return he asked for some uniforms, shoes and food, and requested some Cuban technicians to carry out the sabotage, to handle the gun and to help the Rwandans in their tasks. I promised to send him six men. Tom (the politico) and Aja would be responsible for burning down the electricity poles; Comrade Angalia would fire the gun simultaneously at Front de Force as a diversion and try to hit the water pipe; and Anchali would lead the group.

We received a cable reporting that some important messages had arrived for me, so I decided to wait at the lake. I took the opportunity to have a good number of talks with the cadres still remaining there. One of these was with Colonel Ansuruni, chief of staff of the Second Brigade (General Moulane's brigade), who had always been at loggerheads with Lambert and the people at Kibamba base, even with Masengo who was very distrustful of him. I criticized him sharply and urged him to change his attitude. I referred to the loss of Baraka without a fight (he had been present there), pointed out the result of all the intrigues and disorder, and recalled that he had frequently offered to train men in heavy weapons at the lake but had not once given the order for this to be done. He took note of my recommendations – among others, to send some men quickly to recover the gun from the Karamba barrier and take it to Kibamba as part of a battery of heavy weapons; he had been pestering me with stories about how it had been saved from our disaster; now, after many adventures, it showed up with 13 shells. At dawn Changa arrived, his entrance having long been heralded by tracer bullets in the sky from a veritable naval battle that had broken out when he was surprised by patrol boats. He was carrying a man who had been wounded in the hand by a machine-gun bullet, and Changa himself had a face wound from the recoil of a bazooka that his comrades had fired. The Congolese crew were very scared when they arrived, and it was difficult to get them to return in the days that followed.

A messenger came from Rafael just to deliver this note.

Comrade Tatu:

This morning Pablo was summoned by the government to be told that, in view of the meeting of African heads of state concerning non-intervention in the internal affairs of other countries, both they and other governments that have hitherto been giving aid to the Congolese Liberation Movement will have to change the nature of their aid. Consequently, they have asked us to withdraw what we have here, as our contribution to this policy. They recognized that we had given more than many African states. They stated that nothing would now be given to the Congolese Liberation Movement until such time as we have withdrawn, and that the president himself will therefore call its leaders and inform them of the decision taken by the African states. A report about this has been sent to Havana. We wait to hear your views.

Greetings,

Rafael

It was the *coup de grâce* for a moribund revolution. Because of the character of the information, I said nothing to the Congolese comrades. I waited to see what would happen over the coming days, but in conversation I hinted at the possibility of a Tanzanian change of policy by referring to such things as the blocking of supplies in Kigoma. On the 4th, a telegram was received from Dar es Salaam.

> *Letter from Fidel is being sent with messenger. Its main points are:*
> *1. We should do everything except what is absurd.*
> *2. If, in Tatu's opinion, our presence is becoming pointless and unjustifiable, we should think of withdrawing.*
> *We should act in accordance with the objective situation and our men's spirits.*
> *3. If it is thought you should stay, we will try to send whatever human and material resources you consider necessary.*
> *4. We are worried that your fears may be mistaken, or that your attitude may be viewed as defeatist or pessimistic.*
> *5. If it is decided to stay, Tatu can maintain the status quo while returning here or remaining at another location.*
> *6. Whatever the decision, we will support it.*
> *7. Avoid any annihilation.*

But then another telegram arrived.

> *To Tatu*
> *From Rafael*
> *Message received on the 4th. Whatever the new situation, Tshombe's white mercenaries will remain in the country, attacking Congolese people and committing all kinds of crimes and villainy. It would thus be treason to withdraw our support from Congolese revolutionaries unless they demand it or decide to abandon the struggle.*

The comrades who received these two cables were not yet *au fait* with the contents of Rafael's letter and felt there was a certain contradiction between them; the first summarized a letter from Havana in reply to the one I had sent on 5 October; the second was in response to the report from Dar es Salaam on the new attitude of the Tanzanian government. We drafted a reply to Fidel, which was transmitted by radio from Dar es Salaam.

Report to be sent by radio to Fidel:

Rafael:

During the days of your visit, Julio Cabrera Jiménez disappeared.[20] We thought he had made off in haste because of the nature of our retreat, which did not seem to present a major danger despite the fact that it had the disorderly features which have tinged our actions of late.

He has not reappeared, however, and we must give him up as killed or captured – the former being inherently much more likely.

Immediately after the retreat, I gave Rafael Pérez Castillo a severe warning for having abandoned the 75mm SR gun, which was saved by the Congolese. Conditions were very bad at the new camp, but I relied on the guardsmen's apparent immobility, and the work on establishing a dump with all the recovered ammunition was very slow. On the 24th, as if to celebrate our sixth month in these lands, the guardsmen advanced with the aim of burning down houses, as we can now clearly see. We learnt of their presence because they clashed with some Congolese who had gone out of the camp. I ordered on-the-spot resistance, so that we might hold out until nightfall and save the ammunition, but then I was informed that a large number of guardsmen were outflanking us through the hills, where I had not posted any defences because I had not thought they would come from there. This disorganized the defence; we had to change our lines in great haste and send a squad to engage with the guardsmen on the slope. In reality, however, they had been advancing along a road to our

20. Maurino.

front and – as we discovered later – the supposed guardsmen had been peasants fleeing across the hill. The defences were strong enough to stop them, but our people retreated and I was told that the guardsmen were already inside the camp (which was not true); the retreat was a scandal, and I even lost the supply of tobacco. Only one unit did honour to our army and resisted for another hour, although by then its numerical and positional inferiority was quite blatant; one of these men was Rafael Pérez Castillo (Bahaza), who extracted his gun from the danger zone and remained fighting with an FAL. He was seriously wounded, and we had to carry him along infernal roads, longer and worse than those in the Cuban sierra. At dawn on the 26th, when he seemed to be over the worst, he died. In the setback, we lost a 12.7 machine-gun (abandoned by a Cuban who had been left without his Congolese assistants) and all the ammunition; we also lost the trust of the peasants and the rudiments of organization that we had been acquiring.

During these days the guardsmen began to advance on all sides, giving the impression that they were preparing a final assault on our base. But this has not happened and the defences are quite solid, at least in terms of weapons, although we lack ammunition and the Congolese recruits cannot be trusted.

We hold a quadrilateral area in the mountains; it is framed by the following points (which you may be able to locate on a map and are in enemy hands with our own forces close by): Baraka, Fizi, Lubondja, Lulimba, Force-Bendera and Kabimba. The enemy has outposts this side of Baraka and Kabimba. Aly attacked them on three occasions at the Kabimba front, and the second time he captured their general orders for an offensive designed to take our base and clear an area 25 kilometres around it, while four PTs (Hermes Luckas) guarded the lake to prevent supplies reaching us. Their aviation consisted of eight T-28s, two B-26s and one DC-3 for reconnaissance and back-up, and a helicopter for liaison. This little air force is sowing terror among the Congolese comrades.

From a military point of view, the situation is difficult in that our troops are collections of armed men without the slightest discipline and without any fighting spirit; but the terrain could hardly be better for defensive purposes.

Today I have just been appointed area commander of operations, with full authority to instruct the troops and to command our artillery (a battery of 82-type mortars, three SR 75mm guns, and ten AA 12.7 machine-guns). The Congolese officers' fighting spirit has improved with the succession of defeats, and they are convinced that they have to take things seriously.[21] I have prepared them for the news from Tanzania, as if I were speculating on the basis of the Accra Conference and the fact that the Tanzanians are not handing over the weapons in store there. Some people here say they are prepared to risk their lives and keep up the revolution at all costs. But we don't know the views of Kabila, who has been saying that he will come here soon. I have received Fidel's recent cables; one seems to be a reply to my letters, the other to the last communication from Tanzania. With regard to my letter, I think people have been exaggerating again; I tried to be objective but I was not completely pessimistic. There was a moment when all the Congolese officers were said to be on the point of leaving en masse; I had decided that in such an eventuality I would remain here with 20 carefully selected men (that's all the milk that can be squeezed out), send the rest to the other side, and keep on fighting until things developed or all the possibilities had been exhausted – in which case I would go by land to another front, or avail myself of the sacred right of asylum on the neighbouring shores. Faced with the latest news from Tanzania, my reaction was the same as Fidel's; we cannot go away from here. Indeed, not a single Cuban should leave on the proposed conditions. There should be a serious discussion to settle matters with the leaders of Tanzania.

21. This optimism of mine was without foundation.

These are my proposals. Either a high-level Cuban delegation should visit Tanzania or Tembo should go from here, or there should be a combination of the two. Their case should be more or less as follows: that Cuba offered aid subject to Tanzania's approval, that Tanzania accepted and the aid has been effective. It was unconditional and unlimited in time. We understand Tanzania's present difficulties, but we do not agree with what is being proposed. Cuba will not go back on its promises, nor can it accept a shameful withdrawal that would leave its brothers in misfortune at the mercy of the mercenaries. We would abandon the struggle only if, for well-founded reasons or from force majeure, the Congolese asked us to do so, but we shall fight for this not to happen. It might be pointed out to the Tanzanian government that the accord which has been reached is like the Munich agreement; it gives a free hand to neo-colonialism. In the struggle against imperialism, there can be no retreat and no deferment; force is the only language. If the Congo were to stabilize under the present government, Tanzania would be in the dangerous position of being surrounded by countries more or less hostile to it; the revolution here might persist without Tanzania, but only at the cost of great sacrifices; we would not be responsible if it were destroyed for lack of aid, and so on and so forth.

The Tanzanian government might be asked to maintain telegraphic communications; to allow ships to depart with provisions once or twice a week; to permit us to bring over two speedboats; to give us some of the accumulated weapons for a one-off shipment; and to let mail through once a fortnight.

I raise the boat question because it has become desperately urgent: the little Soviet ferries are very slow and the enemy has speedboats; we have to shoot our way through, and last time Changa arrived hurt and one of our men was wounded in the hand; the boats have to cross in twos, because they frequently grind to a halt and one has to take the other in tow. Tanzania will certainly not accept such a situation (of daily combat), and so it will be necessary to keep the boats on our side of the lake, bring them out to pick things up and return the same night. One of the boats must be transportable over steep mountains, in case we temporarily lose control of the lakeside. We should insist on retaining our present ability to have a place in Tanzania known to very few people, where we can arrive at night and leave before daybreak, with good boats capable of the kind of smuggling operations normal on these shores. But we can play fair; that is our method, and we need to keep out of trouble so that we can devote ourselves to the important things. It is also advisable to give the Soviets and the Chinese a copy of the final text, to forestall any manoeuvre to discredit us.

Don't have any fears about us. We will do honour to Cuba and we won't be annihilated, but I will certainly free us of a few slackers as soon as our position becomes clearer. Warm greetings to all from all.

Tatu

P. S. I think you should talk to Karume to see if an air base can be obtained, either in Zanzibar with a stop-off in Tanzania, or just in Zanzibar. The type of aircraft will have to depend on what is achieved. One idea that might be acceptable to Tanzania is to have doctors at Kigoma Hospital, so that they can move around with some degree of freedom. They should speak English, be efficient doctors and good revolutionaries – or come close to this prototype. That's all.

Being worried about the inefficient command structure, I put forward a plan for a small, flexible general staff that would actually be of some use, but in the discussion we had with all the people in charge Masengo argued that it was impossible to change things so quickly, since a few days earlier a structure had been devised in which Siki would participate and which was still awaiting Kabila's approval. It was as if my operational idea had been for a general staff like that of the Soviet Army on the eve of the capture of Berlin, but the only thing to do was give way. I asked to be given responsibility for training and for the attempt to create a practically oriented school, but instead I was appointed head of operations (theoretically the second post in the army command) and given responsibility for the organization of artillery and instruction. The command post was to be taken with a large pinch of salt, but I did try to do what was humanly feasible to halt the collapse.

Azima's company, which had fallen apart after the disaster on the 24th and the flight of most of the Congolese, was brought back up to its complement. But now we did not have weapons; while we had been making fruitless efforts to organize a nucleus of fighting men, a huge quantity of weapons and equipment in Kigoma had been haphazardly distributed without any prior agreement, so that the supplies and stores at the base were at rock bottom. All our ills were thus now compounded by a lack of firepower. There were some reserves of 12.7 bullets and mortar shells, but nothing for the artillery and, most important, no ammunition for our most widely used rifle, the SKS or *point trente* in our jargon.

Doing the best we could, however, we organized the ammunition stores and took steps to hand out the weapons and form an artillery unit. Mafu, who had arrived from Mundandi's zone, was sent to Kisosi (between Kasima and Kibamba) to try to give the defence a little cohesion.

Before leaving, I had a hair-raising experience. One night two Congolese emissaries arrived in the camp from Calixte's nearby base. As it was already late, the comrades invited them to stay and sleep there, but they explained that Mundandi had asked them to spend the night in his hut and they left to go there. The next day they failed to appear. When Mundandi was asked about them, he said he had sent them away because they had tried to trick him into thinking they were political commissars, whereas they had been ordinary soldiers. Shortly afterwards, two Rwandans who had not been seen before in the camp appeared wearing those comrades' blue jackets and helmets (which the Rwandans do not normally use). Calixte then sent someone to find out where his men were, since they had not returned to their base. All this suggests that they were murdered by Mundandi's people for some motive that is unclear – whether simply for the sake of robbery, or because that is the extreme which differences between these groups have reached. I told Masengo of my suspicions, but nothing was done because of the sudden rash of misfortunes.

A letter arrived from Mbili at the Lubondja front, in which he said that the Congolese were exerting huge pressure on his men and he did not think he could hold out much longer; the demoralization was very great. He warned me of a plot to ask me to allow some Cubans to withdraw from the struggle. The politico Karim wrote me a deeply felt letter explaining that, if he had sent Tembo the previously mentioned note, it had been to warn us about the situation and that he himself would make every effort to fulfil his duty; he attached a list of comrades who were proposing to pull out of the struggle – a majority of those with Mbili. Subsequently, some of the men with the best record of conduct up to then personally made the same request to Mbili, but he managed to persuade them to withdraw it. Mbili himself wrote a note defending the politico from what I had implied when I said that I would treat as cowardice any toleration of open defeatism, for Karim was helping him a lot in a difficult and thankless task.

At the same time, Aly arrived from Kabimba to explain his quarrels with the officers in that area. After a talk with Masengo and Tremendo Punto, we decided that the latter should go with Aly to ascertain what was happening and, if necessary, to put another Cuban in his position of command or to withdraw all the troops. I wrote to Mbili authorizing him to put some distance between himself and the men at the Lubondja barrier. Meanwhile, we kept making improvements to the defences at the base, preparing gun emplacements and trenches, and waiting for the moment when the guardsmen appeared in force and we could deal them a heavy blow. The men who were to go and work with Mundandi were warned to stay all six together and split up into four and two only at the moment of an engagement; they were told to risk their lives only to the extent that the Rwandans did, for the acts of deceit to which we were accustomed had made me wary of some duplicity.

A telegram from Kigoma informed us that Vice-President Kawawa was there; he had spoken with Kabila and, according to the latter, had promised support, asked what else was needed, and given assurances that the lake would be opened. If Kabila's statements were true, what we had heard about the attitude of Tanzania was not correct.

News came that there were 150 guardsmen at Kasima, together with a proposal for an attack signed by the political commissar of the Congolese forces there.

In another communication, Mbili informed us that some men he sent on reconnaissance had not noticed any movement; they cautiously moved forward until they realized that the guardsmen had already abandoned Lubondja and left behind only some appeals to the population to lay down their weapons. I quickly gave the order for more reconnaissance, noting that there was no one at the former emplacement at Lambert's barrier, nor had any enemy forces been seen on the road to Fizi; shortly before, large-scale movement of vehicles had been observed in the area. With the field now open, Lambert showed up with heroic tales of attacks, enemy losses and captured weapons, announced that he had Fizi and Baraka surrounded with some 900 men, and that he wanted to collect the gun, the mortars and the anti-aircraft weapons to launch an attack. He was told that the mortars had been lost in the retreat and that the gun had been sent to defend the base. In his explanatory letter Mbili said: "I'd have liked to tell them everything that deserved to be said, but I considered that it was not a good moment because of the character of the situation. Once more we had to play the role of simpletons with these people."

We had an anti-aircraft machine-gun at the barrier, and this was quickly sent to the base so that Lambert could not lay claim to it. Given all the new information, Mbili was ordered to go to reinforce the base and to leave only one group of men under Rebocate at the training field located two hours away from the original barrier. It remained to be seen what would be the next step taken by Lambert's men, since they would obviously not give up the prize so easily.

In another report, Mbili told of a meeting that Lambert had with his men.

According to an observer of ours who had managed to slip in, Lambert explained to them that he and 23 fighters had stopped the guardsmen in their tracks, that he had then left 150 men there with the Cubans but they had not been able to do anything and had even lost all the heavy weapons. He also announced that the enemy was offering 500 francs[22] and the possibility of work to each soldier who gave himself up; he asked the fighters what they thought of this, and they said they did not agree with it. Lambert then warned them not to fall into the trap and, according to the informant, used quite a good line of argument; the attitude of the men seemed firm on this point. He made some criticisms of me for retreating to the base and advised the officer in charge to collect all his men and weapons, because they would be needed. This, too, was a direct attack on us which, despite his firm stance and his readiness to continue fighting, was designed to sow discord.

I had another talk with Comrade Masengo. Again I did not tell him about the new dispositions of the Tanzanian government, but mainly reported the idea of an attack at Kasima and, in this connection, repeated my view that more reconnaissance was needed before such a decision was taken. I was not keen on the proposed attack, fearing that it would turn into a rout and cause morale to fall still further. First I wanted to be sure that there would be some heavy weapons to keep the enemy under fire and prevent a counter-attack.

On 10 November, Hukumu suddenly showed up and reported that, after carrying out a mission to Lubondja, he had been joined in Nganja by some Rwandans who said that Front de Force had fallen into enemy hands. Shortly afterwards, the Cubans who had been with Mundandi arrived and informed me that, while they had been preparing to go down and carry out a sabotage operation, the Rwandan guards had reported the appearance of the enemy's first assault troops, perfectly guided in three groups by peasants from the region. Mundandi decided not to mount a defence because of the difficulties of the position, but he was

22. A little more than a dollar at that time.

able to save nearly all his weapons and ammunition and took refuge in Nganja. He asked our comrades to stay on, but Anchali misinterpreted my orders and immediately returned to the base. Having spoken with them and explained that, now more than ever, we needed them to support the Rwandans, I sent them off again under the command of Tom, the politico. The next day, news arrived that Makungo (the camp) had fallen to the same technique, and Calixte, the commander of that sector, joined us with his men.

For us it was important to hold the Nganja area, not only because it gave access to the base, but because we needed the cattle there now that the lake was more and more cut off and food was running short. We still had three animals that Comrade Nane had brought, but if that road became closed to us, we would be in quite a fix without any reserves at all. Meanwhile, we were hastily preparing our little artillery unit under Comrade Azi, which had three mortars and quite a lot of shells, a gun with 13 shells, and two 12.7 machine-guns (one without a tripod) and plenty of ammunition. With all this, we thought we could resist the final attack on the area and try to inflict quite a few losses on the enemy.

I sent Comrade Moja to take a look at Kisosi and all the adjoining areas, and the first thing he reported was that some planes had passed overheard strafing them and that all the Congolese comrades had abandoned him. He also said that there were three enemy boats in a threatening posture – no more than threatening.

The supply ship was not crossing the lake, and Changa informed me that this was because it did not have anything to bring. This produced a series of fiery telegrams from us to Kigoma and Dar es Salaam. I also signed a telegram for the attention of Cuba, which read:

> *Enemy pressure increasing and attempt to block lake continuing.*
> *Substantial Congolese funds urgently required to prevent isolation.*
> *Offensive continuing and advancing. Necessary to move fast. We*
> *are preparing to defend base.*

This was dated 10 November. The following telegram went at the same time to Dar es Salaam and Kigoma.

If as result of offensive we have to retreat and lose contact with you, do not fail to call us daily at twelve-thirty and at five p.m. until contact is reestablished.

We heard from Kigoma that Kabila would not be coming because his boat was not working properly. This was supposed to explain why he had not arrived on the 9th, as he had said he would do without fail – one of Kabila's long list of unkept promises. At the same time, he had sent a note to Kiwe telling him to prepare to go with him to the Tricontinental Conference in Havana. Make of it what you will.

Our defensive disposition at that time was the following.

Mbili, with a group of Rwandans under his command, controlled the road leading straight from Nganja to the lake, while the one that passed by the base was defended by Azima and the Congolese.

Moja was responsible for defending the lake from Kasima, and Aly in Kabimba. We had what seemed to me reasonable chances of resisting the enemy, when the following note arrived from Comrade Mundandi:

Comrade Tatu:

With regard to the very serious nature of the situation, I must tell you that I am unable to maintain the position and ensure its defence. The local population has already sold out and given cows to the enemy soldiers, and is now beginning to work with them, so that the enemy is better guided and has better intelligence about our position than we have ourselves. Please understand me: I have decided to call a retreat; I am not abandoning the Cuban comrades, but I must assume my responsibility towards the Rwandan people. I cannot expose all the Rwandan comrades to annihilation. If I did, I would not be a good revolutionary commander, for a good revolutionary (a Marxist, moreover) must analyse the

193

situation and avoid a war of attrition. It would be my fault if all the comrades were wiped out. I have tried to help this revolution so that it will be possible to make another one in our country. If the Congolese will not fight, I prefer to die on soil intended for the Rwandan people. If we die on the way, that is all right too.

With revolutionary greetings,

Mundandi

Mundandi, then, was preparing to give up the struggle. This worried us because it was the flank (the Nganja area) where we could reasonably expect the enemy to attack, and where we would be left more weakened by desertion. Just when we thought we had stabilized our defences, a new turn of events shook everything up again.

THE EASTERN FRONT SINKS
INTO A COMA

It was already 12 November when I received the following letter from Masengo.

Comrade:

Following yesterday's telephone conversation with you, I see nothing wrong with Comrade Moja's proposal. In fact, I think it is a good idea.[23]

I still insist, however, that my own proposal should be discussed; namely:

First, that some artillerymen should be made available to me, their number to be communicated later.

Second, that I should be loaned 50 FAL rifles to give to trusted people: 20 rifles to the 20 unarmed fighters stationed in Ruandasi; 10 rifles to the Kibamba school; 20 rifles to the Kavumbwe barrier; 20 rifles to fighters that you would have to bring down from the base.

My main objective, despite the present difficulties, is to launch an attack on Kasima. I am willing to take on this responsibility.

In the present circumstances, I think that the Cuban comrades should mainly concern themselves with the defence of the lakeside base and of Nganja. I think that you will agree with me about everything that follows from this.

23. To defend the base from the north.

There were a number of problems with this letter. Apart from the arithmetical mistake of requesting 50 rifles and handing out 70, it was based on Congolese wishful thinking about our FAL reserves that was contradicted by what we had already said to Masengo himself. We had distributed as many as 15 rifles to the Congolese comrades, and at that moment there were only one or two left in reserve. We had distributed the others with considerable misgivings, since they had belonged to comrades in charge of handling heavy weapons who would now be left unarmed if we lost those pieces or if we were forced to retreat and leave them in a safe place. Not believing us, Masengo insisted on the figure of 50 or 70. And after assuring us that he would take responsibility for the attack, he advised us to concentrate on defending the lake and Nganja. This was just a few days after I had been given wide powers as head of operations in the region – which implied that I should concern myself with the whole defence of the front. The lack of trust persisted.

In addition to these aspects of "disloyalty", there were a couple of other problems with the letter: the order to lay anti-personnel mines on some of the access roads, against my express request to delay the action until it could be properly coordinated in a way that avoided accidental injury to our patrols; and Masengo's refusal to accept that Aly should concentrate his forces in Kibamba to defend the southern end of the base from attack.

I spoke with the chief of staff again, and on this occasion too I did not mention the semi-official attitude of the Tanzanian government. I stressed that we had to have a strategy of making ourselves independent of the lake, and insisted that my position as head of operations was purely theoretical. We talked about the attack on Kasima, for which he accepted responsibility as chief of staff (although I thought it was not the right time to attack there, especially as the very poor reconnaissance work of both Congolese and Cubans meant that we had no precise knowledge of the enemy positions). But I could not accept being relegated to the defence of one sector, because – as one can easily appreciate – defence has to be coordinated harmoniously, with a reserve that can be moved to the points of greatest danger in a fast-moving sequence of events. Finally,

I recommended several times that no weapons or ammunition should be given out to phantom units that would simply lose them. I said that most of the reports about major actions at Fizi and elsewhere were a pack of lies.

Comrade Masengo complained about our attitude at Kasima, where things were tense following an attempt to make the Congolese forces withdraw. In fact, I had ordered Moja to concentrate all the Cubans in Kisosi as a reserve force and he had interpreted this to include the Congolese as well; they refused to obey and in the process caused some parts of a mortar to vanish, so that it was left incomplete in the hands of its Cuban operator.

Masengo undertook to call Salumu in for an interview with Moja and agreed that he should lead the mooted attack in accordance with a simple plan: an advance at one or two points, with ambushes at others where reinforcements might come or the soldiers might try to flee. He would try to ensure that the attack would cost as little as possible should there be a sudden disorderly retreat. He also consented to allow Aly to come, and agreed not to give out ammunition without a precise idea of why it was needed.

In the course of our conversation, I showed him the letter from Mundandi. Furiously, he said that he would go there in person the next day to disarm him; since I knew what the Rwandan comrades were like, I immediately wrote to Mbili so that he could prepare things there, ask them for the heavy weapons still in their possession, and say that I guaranteed they could cross to Kigoma if they handed over all their arms. Wanting to avoid a pointless spilling of blood in these tense days, I thought I could influence Masengo to allow their smooth passage. It did not come to blood, because Masengo could not go there himself and promised to send a political commissar. In the end, no one went to disarm Mundandi.

We also had a talk in which Masengo assured me that Kabila would be coming in the next few days. My reply was categorical: Kabila would not cross over, because he saw that things were coming to an end and had no interest in coming under such conditions. Our conversation on this sensitive point was awkward, since other comrades were present, but I made my views clear about the arrival of the commander-in-chief.

The undermining activity of the people in Fizi continued throughout all this, as if it had been an election period in a war-free country. Two or three further communications arrived, one suggesting that I attend a meeting on the 15th and asking me to acknowledge receipt. In reply, I explained that I thought the meeting a waste of time, that it would be impossible for me to attend as I had to defend the base at all costs, and that I considered these events as a revolt against the revolutionary power; my government had not sent me to take part in such activities. Things went to such an extreme that, in one of their letters accusing Masengo of murder, they nevertheless guaranteed to respect his life during the days he was in Fizi. Members of the army guaranteeing to respect their commander's life – no less. That was now the state of things.

The public health minister, Comrade Mutchungo, also showed that he had taken leave of reality when he sent some letters that brought forth violent replies on my part, and then came to explain things away.

In one of these letters, he said that Lambert had written to him denouncing our removal of the heavy weapons and asked to be given them back so that they could carry out some actions; I had to entangle myself in a lengthy discussion of Lambert's attitude in this whole business. A second letter referred to a meeting of peasants in that area, at Jungo, and informed me of the outcome of the meeting. I was not invited and had no reason to go to such meetings, which did not fit in with my work, but the list of requests reached such absurd proportions that I must have provoked a reaction on Comrade Mutchungo's part. Just to give a flavour of things, point three said:

Request to our friends:
Head of friendly country should send me 12,000 volunteers. These are revolutionary countries. Tshombe is fighting us with the help of foreigners.

Assuming that the number of friendly countries was two or three, this would have meant 24,000 or 36,000 men. This could be considered a children's game, in the context of a meeting of peasants at a low level of development who were in despair at the situation they faced. But I must have provoked some reaction in Comrade Mutchungo, given his position as public health minister and a high representative of the Supreme Council of the Revolution.

After pointing out the childish nature of the proposal, I asked him if he was aware of the Fizi comrades' undermining attitude. He replied that he had heard something, but what he did know was that 300 men were marching from Fizi to reinforce and save Kibamba; these statements made it impossible to continue discussing such topics. Moving on to more personal matters, he complained of Masengo's attitude and said that he was refusing to evacuate his wife and six children – which was creating a very difficult situation for him. I spoke about this with Masengo, and it was decided that all the fighters' wives and children would be evacuated to Kigoma at the first available opportunity.

Changa crossed the lake at dawn on the 14th, this time without incident. He brought abundant provisions and a message for me from Rafael explaining that the situation remained the same with regard to the Tanzanian government, which was awaiting a reply from us; it had given no sign of trying to speed things up or of changing its attitude. Rafael asked whether I thought that, given the Tanzanian government's attitude, it might be wise to start establishing a clandestine base. I answered at once that this should indeed be done.

That same day Masengo, who was still unaware of Tanzania's explicit decision, sent the following telegram. It illustrates the general situation, and his own state of mind in particular.

Kabila:

Military situation very grave. Mundandi front invaded by enemy, who are advancing on Nganja in direction of base. Mundandi, Calixte and Mbili have taken up position in Nganja. We have enemy infiltration on many roads in direction of base. I am notifying you of food shortage. Send urgently beans, rice, salt. We insist on immediate dispatch of weapons and .30, Mauser,

*"pepechá" and mortar ammunition, artillery, bazooka and anti-
tank shells, and mine fuses. Favourable possibility for encirclement
of enemy offensive at Mukundi. Lack of immediate supplies threat-
ens our force with annihilation. I request energetic intervention
with Tanzanian authorities. We consider crushing of Congolese
revolution negligence by African countries. Consider this final
appeal. To prevent starvation, send financial aid.*

Masengo

Apart from the optimistic statement about the possibility of an offensive at
Mukundi's front, for which there was a lack of relevant information,
Masengo's telegram summed up the situation. Some of our own telegrams
almost gave a sense of panic, partly to stir the comrades, partly as a result
of the actual situation. When our man in Kigoma consulted me about
Kabila's request to go to Dar es Salaam, I answered:

*Indispensable that they (i.e. the boats) come today, we are starving
and encircled, Kabila can go.*

The SOSes circulated with the utmost pathos. Among the impedimenta
brought by Changa were 40 Congolese who had been studying in the
Soviet Union. Full of themselves, they asked at once for a fortnight's leave,
complaining that they had nowhere to put their suitcases and that there
were no weapons laid out for them; if it had not been so sad, it would have
been rather comical to see the cast of mind of these kids in whom the
revolution had placed its faith.

Masengo subsequently put these elements under my orders, and for me
the only satisfaction was "to read them the rule book" with perfect clarity,
now that we were able to speak French. There was certainly not an atom
of revolutionary spirit in them. I got the officers to come to the Upper Base
and put things to them very sharply; I told them that they would be
examined in shooting and that those who passed the test would go straight
to the front; if they were happy with this, I would accept them – otherwise

they should pull out because I didn't want to waste any time (I didn't have any to waste). The chief one among them, who was quite reasonable, accepted the conditions, and over the next few days they went up to the base to strengthen our defences or, more accurately, to take the weapons of some who fled (for they went there unarmed).

Mbili sent the latest intelligence: scouts had seen the guardsmen near the Jungo road, and so he had sent some comrades to lay mines at the entrance to the road. This minelaying put our men in danger, since Mbili was doing it on one side of the road and I had sent scouts out on the other side in the same direction. It was only by chance that a mine did not go off under the feet of our men: the mechanism had no pilot; each part moved under its own momentum.

From the Nganja-Karianga area it was possible to leave for the lake by four different roads; we did not know along which one the enemy would make his push, or if he would do it along all of them. They had the advantage over us even in knowledge of the terrain; they had the better guides, in the shape of local peasants who lived among them and supplied them with food. This time the soldiers had learned some lessons in anti-guerrilla warfare, and they seemed to be treating the peasants with the greatest deference, whilst our mistaken attitude in the past meant that we had to bear the consequences of their present lack of loyalty.

Following his custom of sending us all groups of men who appeared around there, Masengo treated me to seven "suicides" whose longing for destruction was directed towards the sinking of a transport ship that linked Albertville and Kigoma. I explained to them that the operation was relatively easy and could be carried out at any moment, since the ships did not go in convoy, but I thought it very untimely to do it at a time when relations with Tanzania were so cool and it could be used as a pretext for further restrictions. But I had other work for them: to cross with some Cubans behind enemy lines, to carry out actions and capture weapons – only they had to be subject to strict discipline. They said they would think about it and I never heard from them again.

Changa had difficulties crossing the lake. Each time there were more boats keeping watch, and his Congolese crew were not inclined to face the dangers of the crossing. Some annoying situations developed, because the order had been given to evacuate the women and children, but among these were some big shots aged 20 to 25 who shoved everyone else aside and dominated things. As the ship made two or three attempts to leave, situations of this type occurred night after night and gave rise to friction among those of our men who were responsible for the ship's security, as well as causing a sense of dejection among our men themselves.

A message arrived from Kabila saying:

> *Masengo,*
>
> *I am passing your message on to the Tanzanians. I leave today for Tabora and will come back with weapons and ammunition. I am sending you all the remaining Congolese money. The crushing of our struggle is a plot between the authorities and the imperialists. There is no money.*
>
> *Kabila*

Kabila announced here that he was going to Tabora, but to us he had said he was going to Dar es Salaam – and that is what he did. He went to discuss with the authorities, but at the moment of the disaster he was not at Kigoma but at Dar es Salaam.

On 16 November, Comrade Siki received the following letter from Azima.

> *Comrade Siki:*
>
> *These lines are to explain that I have only 16 Congolese and nine Cubans; it is very difficult to retreat, and the position we have is completely open; there is no way of withdrawing to hide ourselves from the aircraft. The Congolese are planning to leave; they won't fight, I hold them here with a gun; as soon as the soldiers start advancing, they will be off. I am telling you this because the situation is very difficult; forgive the expression, but I think I have*

*lost my nerve. We are forcing men who don't want to fight, and
I don't think that makes sense; I honestly don't think it is right
to force them. I don't have any great knowledge, but it seems very
bad to me. There is no food, there is a meat crisis, there's nothing
to give them to eat. And it rains every day; it starts pouring in
the morning and there's nowhere to take shelter. Well, forgive
any spelling mistakes I may have made.*

Azima

I thought this was a very worrying letter and I ordered Siki to go and
investigate. His view was that it was due to a sudden attack, of the kind
that Comrade Azima often had. My doubts made me send Kiswa up
there, Aly's second-in-command who had arrived with Aly and his men
from Kibamba, in order to take charge of the defence in case Azima was in
a very bad way.

Tremendo Punto arrived at the same time as Aly, having travelled with
him. He sent me a letter explaining that the tense situation in Kabimba
was due to Aly's character and recounted a number of incidents he had
had there. He said that he had done everything possible to create unity,
that relations with the other Cubans were friendly, but that Aly and the
major did not see eye to eye. Then he repeated these statements in person
and added some anecdotes, but Aly reacted violently to the claims and
recalled, among other things, a funny episode arising from Tremendo
Punto's lack of caution; he insisted on going on the lake by day, against
Aly's advice, and they had hardly left the shore when an aircraft appeared
on the horizon. Quick as a flash, Comrade Tremendo Punto dived into the
water with such force that he overturned the boat, but the worst of it was
that Aly did not know how to swim and nearly drowned. His resentment
against Tremendo Punto, expressed in frequent interruptions to his story
that caused him to stammer with indignation, was a very funny aspect of
those tragic moments.

Mbili sent me fresh reports about what he had done at the Jungo
junction; there had been an enemy advance, and neither the Congolese

nor the Rwandans had occupied their positions. There were eight Cubans on each of the two defensive wings, and it was not possible to rely on many more. Commanders Calixte and Huseini stayed at the rear, despite being urged to accompany their men. Mbili trusted only the Cubans – and not even them completely – to defend the position. He estimated there to be 400 guardsmen facing them, and it looked as if some reinforcements had been brought up.

Such was the situation on 16 November when various telegrams were sent off. One of these, signed by myself, said:

> *Rafael,*
> *We urgently need SKS bullets, 75mm Chinese bazooka shells; if possible, 200 rifles and ammunition. The former is very important. They are blocking things in Kigoma. If they're not going to let them go, they should say so straight out. Insist on clear language. Changa cannot leave here. There are enemy ships. We need things to move fast.*

Masengo sent another:

> *Impossible for me to carry out offensive. So planned evacuation enemy siege impossible. I stress gravity of situation. Request urgent information about possibility of provisions, weapons and ammunition.*
> *Masengo*

The situation was growing more difficult all the time and there were no favourable signs anywhere. We simply had to wait and see how large the enemy forces would be, and how determined they were to push things to a conclusion.

THE COLLAPSE

Siki reported from another inspection trip that it had gone quite well; the defensive positions were good; it was possible to fight while carrying out a gradual retreat, since it did not make sense to organize a fixed defence with men in such a low state of morale. He said that the Congolese could not be trusted, but the Rwandans had reacted quite well and would support Mbili; the only thing they could do was not mix with the others; they had given all kinds of assurances of loyalty. Azima sent a personal message swearing to defend that place as if it were a little corner of Cuba; it was not necessary to replace him.

Siki had left early in the morning. He had not delivered his entire report or rested from the tiring journey when a messenger arrived with the following letter from Mbili; the first part bore the time 9.00 a.m.

Tatu:

The Congolese who have remained refuse to dig trenches, and the one I think of as their leader plans to go off and attack the guardsmen; he says it's better than digging trenches. We sent Charles to explain to him that it was better to dig trenches; there was a sharp discussion between Charles and the leader of the Congolese; they threw a few punches at each other and the Congolese leader picked up his rifle to kill Charles; we took it away from him. He said to Charles that he belonged with the Cubans, that the Cubans were bad and Charles was too, and that when the guardsmen came they were going to retreat and shoot at us. This is because one of the officers here is the one who told me at the ambush that the Cubans were bad.[24] *I think he has continued making the point here; the attitude of the Congolese is one of open hostility and shows itself in not doing anything.*

Important: 11.15 a.m.

Tatu: All the Rwandans have gone. I was told the news at ten o'clock. I sent Akika off to check and it was true, they were gone. We agreed a plan yesterday, and today they've gone off without saying a word to me. I think they're heading for their country, since that is what they have talked of doing previously. When the news came, Mundandi's adjutant was with me and I told him. He was stunned, went away and didn't come back. As I see it, they have gone off with the weapons and said nothing. Yesterday they agreed to give me ten extra men and a machine-gun on a trolley. Since the Congolese were gone and no one came, I sent someone to find out from Calixtc what was happening. But no one has seen him, and no one can tell me where he is.

This may be a case of treachery. I propose that we pull back a little as planned, split into two groups, take up new positions and mine the road. We urgently need reinforcements. I'll take some precautionary measures in case we have been betrayed. The comrade bearing your reply should come by the new road. Patria o Muerte.

N.B. The Congolese here already know the news and are leaving.

After a few hours, some planes strafed the positions previously occupied by Mbili, but he had withdrawn. This may be a coincidence or it may mean we have simply been betrayed. We began to look for men to reinforce us; we disarmed some who came fleeing towards the base and gave their weapons to others. This exchange did not promise a lot, but it was all we could do.

---

24. At the time of the Katenga ambush, this officer had canvassed his men with the same arguments.

At each of the ambushes we had eight Cubans and roughly ten Congolese.

The new recruits, the students who had arrived from the Soviet Union, were told that they had to go to the front line. They declared that they could not go in dribs and drabs but must all go together. After the appropriate rebukes and warnings, however (either you go or you can clear off from here), a few were prepared to occupy the front line.

Tremendo Punto arrived in the evening with a comrade whose name I unfortunately do not remember and have not written down; he seemed intelligent and willing to do something, except that he did not have any experience. We talked about a lot of things, but mainly about my argument that, being faced with total collapse, we could either put up an elastic defence, give ground and retreat to another place, or mount a fixed defence and fight to the limits of our strength. What we could not do was wait with our arms folded for the guardsmen to advance and take a new position from us without a fight; that would lead to the desertion of more men; such a tactic (or lack of a tactic) would result in our losing everything and remaining completely disorganized. Comrade Tremendo Punto asked to speak and said that, if there were two possibilities, he would immediately opt for a fixed defence. The Cubans with me looked as if they could kill him or eat him alive; it was very awkward for me. The location and the circumstances recommended a fixed defence, but a fixed defence with whom? The Congolese and the Rwandans were gone. Could I ask the Cubans to die in their trenches to defend this piece of nothing? More important: if they did this, would it produce any result? The fact was that I had raised the fixed defence as a pedagogic alternative; the only thing to be done was to "leave a mark".

Despite the bad weather, Tremendo Punto went down that same night to talk with Masengo, and I did the same the next day. Those who took part in the discussion were: Tremendo Punto, the comrade whose name I do not remember, Comrade Kent from Kenya (who had joined the Liberation Army), Charles Bemba (who had gone to report his worries), and one other. There was some deliberation on the military options. A fixed defence was excluded, because I eventually admitted that there were too few people (only ours) and I could not totally rely on them; a retreat to Fizi was also excluded because of the conditions prevailing there. That left two possible places of refuge: one was Uvira, which had to be reached via the lake on foot along a dangerous road, first crossing enemy lines and then passing through Fizi territory on a very long and difficult march; the second area was to the south, where a few villages such as Bondo offered the possibility of organizing a defence. It was decided that Aly and Moja would go to have a quick look around Bondo and make the decision on the same day. Aly attributed this to more unreliability on Tremendo Punto's part, since in his view it was a bad position. I had a little altercation with Aly, who growled about how great it was to run around the hills without the cooperation of those people; I replied cuttingly that we would organize the evacuation from Bondo and that he could leave with the group that gave up the struggle. He shot back that he would stay with me to the end, but so as not to lose the argument, he added: "rushing around the hills for 20 years".

I thought the time had come to inform Comrade Masengo of the decision taken by Tanzania, because I did not think it proper to keep it secret any longer. That government's attitude was not honest; one might accept that it behaved correctly with us, but there was a revolutionary way of doing things that they did not respect. I told Masengo that a few days earlier I had received a cable communicating the government's decision, but I had tried to stop it leaking out, even to Cubans, because of the current situation; I was now telling him alone so that he could draw his conclusions. He seems to have immediately discussed it with the comrades, for Tremendo Punto showed up as night was falling and informed me that Masengo had come to me to propose the abandonment of the struggle but that, when I spoke to him of evacuating to a different place and of a whole series of tasks that we had before us, he had made up his mind not to go ahead; all the comrades in charge were agreed to end the struggle now.

I answered that it was a very serious decision. There were men still organized at the front at Fizi and Mukundi, as well as the ones at Uvira, and there was also Mulele's front. As soon as we left, enemy troops would be free to attack those groups; our flight would hasten their dispersion, because we knew that they were not strong enough to resist. I asked him to give me a letter in which Masengo set out that decision. Tremendo Punto looked taken aback and a little aggrieved, but I pressed the point by saying that there was a thing called history, which is composed of many fragments and which can be distorted. In short, I wanted to have that letter in my possession in case our actions were ever misinterpreted, and in support of my argument I reminded him of recent calumnies against us. He replied that it was a tough thing to demand and he did not know whether Masengo would accept. It was clear to me that if Masengo did not agree to give me the letter, he must think he was doing something wrong and the responsibility for the retreat could never be ours. I said as much to him.

The conversation remained incomplete because Tremendo Punto went to confer with his comrades. At that point, a telephone call came through from the Upper Base; the guardsmen had advanced and Azima had retreated without a fight; there had been many of them and they had come in three columns. They were attacked during the retreat without suffering any losses, but the observer seems to have taken refuge from the air attack that preceded the advance and not to have seen the guardsmen coming; they had little hope for his safety; Suleiman was his name. The other man who was on guard with him, a Congolese, also disappeared.

Straight away, I went to inform Masengo and proposed the organization of an immediate retreat; this was accepted. Tremendo Punto spoke up to say that they had talked things over and that we should retreat for good. The chief of the military police was there listening to the conversation. Five minutes later, all the telephone operators and all the military policemen had fled; chaos reigned supreme at the base.

I suggested to Masengo that he should grapple with his men and that I should organize the retreat at every point where the Cubans were present. This was done. I gave orders that all the equipment, including the transmitter, should be kept under guard in the places prepared in advance, that everything remaining should be set on fire that very night, and that the ammunition and heavy weapons should be hidden; I would wait for them down below. It was necessary to carry the portable transmitter with which we had already made contact with Kigoma from the Upper Base; at least we received and got through well, despite the fact that the equipment was designed for 20 kilometres rather than the 70 or so to the Tanzanian port.

In the meantime, a number of telegrams explaining the situation had been sent by radio; this one went on the 18th:

Rafael:

Things are falling apart; whole units and peasants are going over to the enemy. None of the Congolese troops can be relied on. From today we may not be able to go on the air with the main apparatus. We will maintain contact with Kigoma by auxiliary apparatus. Changa here because of mechanical difficulties. Crew and boats in good condition urgently needed.

In the end, it was possible to get Changa across, with a huge load of women and children, which caused a row with the Kigoma commissioner; he said that we were only bringing him idlers and parasites, and that we should take them back to where they came from – which we did not do, of course.

On the same day, Rafael sent me the following telegram.

Tatu:

Second conversation with Kabila; we forcefully presented the situation to him and asked for immediate supply of materials; he promised to resolve this before leaving for Korea. We saw on the road to Kigoma a lorry with very few things for there. We spoke with Cambona yesterday; he promised to look into it and give us reply today from conversation with president. It was a direct and definitive discussion that made them responsible for consequences. We spoke with Soviets and Chinese and informed them of absurd situation with delivery of material they have sent. We propose telling ambassadors of UAR, Ghana and Mali that, under Accra agreement, Tanzania is not delivering material to nationalists resisting white mercenaries, that responsibility for annihilation will lie with African leaders and Tanzanian government. Kabila in coordination with ourselves met government figures and made the same points, also to Chinese and Soviets.

I sent him the following reply.

Rafael:

We want to know result of last report to Cuba about commission to discuss with Tanzanian government. On discussions with governments of Ghana, Mali and UAR, put it in form of question: what was actual agreement, and was it to leave us in present plight? We think measures you are taking will come too late. That will take around a month. We are thinking of evacuating here and then evacuating most Cubans in second stage. A small group of us will remain as symbol of Cuba's prestige. Inform Cuba.

I was intending to send back the sick, the frail and everyone "weak in the legs" and to fight on with a small group of men. With this in mind, I carried out a little "decisive test" among the comrades that yielded discouraging results; if it was up to them, almost no one was disposed to keep on fighting.

One of the problems of an evacuation was that Mafu had sent a couple of his men to reconnoitre Kasima and they had not returned. It was decided that another comrade would go to find them and come back as soon as possible. They should leave the heavy weapons that they could not transport and move off with the rest; some comrades such as Mbili and his group would have to complete a very long march if we wanted to abandon the lower base at dawn. Basing my reasoning on the character of the enemy attacks, I calculated that they would leave us a day's respite before trying other manoeuvres; this would allow us to leave quite easily, but we had to take steps to avoid contact and to save most of the things.

Our three sick men, together with Njenje, the man in charge of the base, left by boat for a little village called Mukungo where we thought of organizing resistance; they took with them some of the heavy weapons from Azi's unit – some but not all, because the Congolese element of our own forces had also been affected by dissolution and a lot of things had been scattered around. The Congolese were now making for the Fizi area. At first I planned to attack them but, thinking better of it, ordered anyone who wanted to leave to be allowed to do so, for if it came to an evacuation we would not be able to take everyone with us.

At dawn we set fire to the house that had served as our accommodation for nearly seven months; there was a lot of paper, many documents that could be consigned to oblivion and that it was best to destroy all at once. Shortly afterwards, when it was already daylight, they began to burn the ammunition dumps without consultation; neither Masengo nor I had given any such orders, and in fact I had tried to persuade the Congolese that it was important to take the material with them, if not to the new base then at least to the nearby mountain. Instead, someone put a light to quite a lot of material. As the valuable store burned and exploded, I watched the fireworks from the first hill on the way to Jungo and waited for the many stragglers to catch up. They came with an age-old weariness, an alarming lack of vitality, dropping parts of heavy weapons to lighten their load without a thought for what the weapon might mean in a battle. Virtually no Congolese remained in the units and the Cubans carried everything; I stressed the need to look after those weapons, which would be vital to us if we had to sustain a final attack, and the men set off dragging their feet and making frequent stops, bearing one gun and one machine-gun; they had already left two along the way.

I was waiting for the communications unit; at six o'clock we were supposed to attempt the first contact and I watched the head of the team, Tuma, coming down the hill opposite me from the Upper Base to the lake. It was infuriating; the comrades were spending three hours on a hill that should normally take ten minutes to climb down, and then they had to take a break before continuing on their way. I ordered them to leave anything superfluous and try to walk faster; but among the superfluous things, the telegraph operator forgot the code and someone had to be sent back for it. I had a serious word with the operators, trying to make them see their importance for communications and urging them to make another effort to reach the rendezvous point. We tried to make contact as usual at ten o'clock and failed. We kept moving at the slow pace dictated by the three comrades, who were completely unused to hill walking and marched only with their mind. We had made rather little progress; someone walking normally should take three or four hours from Kibamba (where our base was located) to Jungo. But at three in the afternoon, when we were scheduled to make our second contact with Kigoma, we were still quite a long way from the rendezvous point. At that time we managed to send the following message, which was successfully received.

Changa:
We have lost the base, we are proceeding with emergency equipment, reply urgently whether you can come tonight.

Then a second message.

Changa:
Today the enemy is not at the lakeside, our position is Jungo, some ten kilometres south of Kibamba. Masengo decided to abandon the struggle and the best thing is for us to leave as soon as possible.

When the comrades present heard the "understood" from the lake, all their faces changed as if a magic wand had touched them.

Our last message was to ask whether Changa had arrived. The messages were coded and it was necessary to decode them and to encode the reply. The response seemed to be: "No one has arrived here." Then they said they were having difficulties with the apparatus and went off the air.

The precoded message meant that the expected crew had not arrived, but it corresponded to our question. Apparently Changa had had difficulties on the lake (enemy aircraft were flying over it that day) which would imply that the boats had been lost and we could not get away; the faces again clouded over with the weariness and anxiety. At seven o'clock we made another attempt at contact and failed; conditions at the lake meant that our little apparatus could only transmit well at three in the afternoon.

We reached Jungo in time for bed; things were chaotic there, and no food had been prepared for us. When we counted up the men, four were missing: the look-out who had been lost during the guardsmen's advance; the two who had been reconnoitring at Kasima; and a fourth who had come in one of the units from Upper Base and inexplicably disappeared. A comrade had been sent to look for the men at Kasima, but he had returned without locating them. Desperate not to be left behind, he had had a quick look around and come back – as a calculation of the number of hours indicated to me. But I said nothing to him, because there was nothing to be done about it. We organized a unit under Rebocate's command to take the road coming through the mountains from Nganja, so that we would have a commanding view of the two points from which the guardsmen might appear: the heights and the lakeside. As the men were heading for their objective, we heard an explosion at the top of the hill over which the road passed. Since the ground was mined, we thought it was the guardsmen advancing and that we would have no time to organize a defence on the heights. We occupied some slopes, putting together a limited defence, and continued on our way towards Sele, a village quite close to Jungo.

The attempts to make contact at six o'clock and ten o'clock on 20 November were also unsuccessful. The telegraphists walked so slowly that we only reached Sele at midday, whereas that stretch was supposed to have been done in no more than an hour. Most of the men were gathered at Sele and we had something to ease our hunger. Dusk saw the arrival of Banhir, the man who had been left behind on the march. He had sprained his ankle and asked a comrade to let the others know so that they would go and find his rucksack. While waiting, he stayed where he was – but the other man did not do what he had been asked, or did it badly, and in the morning he was still at the place where he had suffered the accident, completely alone. He was at the base until 9.00 a.m. on the 20th, and then he left it believing that he had lost contact with us. The guardsmen had not entered the base; all the roads were deserted, all the houses abandoned.

At 2.30 p.m. we made contact with Kigoma. Our message read:

Changa:
   Total men to evacuate less than 200, will be more difficult each day that passes. We are at Sele, 10 or 15 kilometres south of Kibamba.

And I received the longed-for reply.

Tatu:
   The crossing is set for tonight. Yesterday the commissioner did not let us cross.

The men were euphoric. I spoke with Masengo and suggested leaving from that very point at night. As there were a lot of Congolese, the general staff held a meeting at which it was decided that Jean Paulis would remain in the Congo with his men and we and the various leaders would evacuate; the troops who were originally from that area would remain there; they would not be told of our intention to withdraw but would be sent on various pretexts to the nearby village. One of the little boats we still had to ply between various points on the lake arrived and took a large number of the Congolese, but those who were part of our force smelt a rat and wanted to stay. I ordered a selection to be made of those who had conducted themselves best up to that point, so that they would be taken across as Cubans. Masengo gave his authorization for it to be done as I saw fit.

For me it was a critical situation. Two men who had comprehensively

25. They were rescued a month later by a group of volunteers consisting of Ishirini, Anchali, Aja, Alasiri and Adabu, on Siki's responsibility and with the cooperation of Changa and the group of marines who had arrived at the last hour.

fulfilled their mission would now be left behind unless they made their way back within a few hours.[25] The full weight of calumnies – both inside and outside the Congo – would fall upon us as soon as we left. My troops were a mixed bunch, and my investigations suggested that I could extract up to 20 to follow me, this time with knitted brows. And then what would I do? All the leaders were pulling out, the peasants were displaying ever greater hostility towards us. But I was deeply pained at the thought of simply departing as we had come, leaving behind defenceless peasants and armed men whose poor battle sense left them effectively defenceless, defeated and with a feeling of betrayal,

For me, to stay in the Congo was not a sacrifice – not for a year, or even for the five years with which I had scared my men. It was part of a concept of struggle that had fully taken shape in my brain. I could reasonably expect six or eight men to accompany me without furrowed brows. But the rest would do it as a duty, either towards me personally, or as a moral duty to the revolution; I would be sacrificing people who could not muster any enthusiasm to fight. Not long before, I had been able to sense this right here, when I broke into a conversation and they turned to me and in a jocular vein asked about some of the Congolese leaders. I replied sharply that they should first ask themselves what our own attitude had been, whether we could say with hand on heart that it had been of the best; I did not think so. Silence fell, awkward and hostile.

In reality, the thought of remaining in the Congo continued to haunt me long into the night, and perhaps I did not so much take the decision as become one fugitive more.

The way in which the Congolese comrades would view the evacuation seemed to me degrading; our withdrawal was a mere flight, or worse, we were accomplices in the deception with which people had been left on the land. Moreover, who was I now? I had the feeling that, after my farewell letter to Fidel, the comrades began to see me as a man from other climes rather distant from Cuba's specific problems, and I could not bring myself to demand the final sacrifice of remaining behind. I spent the final hours like this, alone and perplexed, until the boats eventually put in at two o'clock in the morning, with a Cuban crew who arrived and set off immediately that very night. There were too many people for the boats at that late hour. I set three o'clock as the last possible hour for departure, since it would be daylight at 5.30 and we would be in the middle of the lake. Work got under way on organizing the evacuation. The sick went aboard, then the whole of Masengo's general staff – some 40 men chosen by himself – and finally all the Cubans. It was a plaintive, inglorious spectacle; I had to chase away men who kept imploring us to take them too; there was no element of grandeur in this retreat, no gesture of defiance. The machine-guns were in position, and I kept the men at the ready, as usual, in case they tried to intimidate us by attacking from the land. But nothing like that happened. There was just a lot of grumbling, while the leader of the would-be escapees cursed in time with the beating of the loose moorings.

I would like to record here the names of the comrades on whom I always felt I could depend, by virtue of their personal qualities, their belief in the revolution, and their determination to do their duty come what may. Some of them flagged at the last minute, but we will pass over that final minute, because it was a weakening of their belief not of their readiness to sacrifice themselves. There were certainly more comrades in this category, but I was not on close terms with them and I cannot vouch for it in their case. It is an incomplete, personal list, much influenced by subjective factors – may those who are not on it please forgive me and consider that they belong to the same category: Moja, Mbili, Pombo, Azi, Mafu, Tumaini, Ishirini, Tiza, Alau, Waziri, Agano, Hukumu, Ami, Amia, Singida, Alasiri, Ananane, Angalia, Bodala, Anara, Mustafá, the doctors Kumi, Fizi, Morogoro and Kusulu, and the ineffable Admiral Changa, master of the lake. Siki and Tembo deserve a special mention. I often disagreed with them, sometimes violently, about our assessment of the situation, but they always offered me their guileless devotion. And a final word for Aly, a fine soldier and bad politician.

We crossed the lake without any problems, despite the slowness of the boats, and reached Kigoma in daylight in the company of the cargo ship that was making the crossing from Albertville to this port.

A mooring rope seemed to have broken, and the excitement of the Cubans and Congolese rose like boiling liquid over the little container of the boats, affecting but not infecting me. During those last hours of our time in the Congo, I felt more alone than I had done even in Cuba or on any of my wanderings around the globe. I might say: "Never have I found myself so alone again as I do today after all my travels!"

EPILOGUE

It only remains, by way of an epilogue, to draw some conclusions about the setting of the war, about the way in which the various factors operated, and about my views on the future of the Congolese revolution.

I will dwell especially on the area of the eastern front, which is the one I know personally, and not generalize from my experience in a country with such varied features as those of the Congo.

The geographical setting in which we came to live is characterized by the great depression that takes in Lake Tanganyika, some 35,000 square kilometres with an average width of approximately 50 kilometres. It is this which separates Tanzania and Burundi from the territory of the Congo. There is a range of mountains at either end of the depression: one belongs to Tanzania-Burundi, the other to the Congo. The second of these, at an average height of some 1,500 metres above sea level (the lake is at 700 metres), stretches from the environs of Albertville in the south, through the whole setting of the war to the region beyond Bukavu in the north, where it falls in hills into the tropical forest. The width of the system varies, but we may estimate it to be an average of roughly 20 to 30 kilometres. There are also two higher chains, steep and wooded, one to the east and the other to the west, with an undulating altiplano between them that is suitable for agriculture in its valleys and for livestock husbandry. (The latter is mainly practised by herdsmen from the Rwandan tribes, who have traditionally specialized in cattle-rearing.) To the west, the mountains fall sharply down to a plain some 700 metres above sea level, which forms part of the basin of the River Congo, a savannah plain presenting tropical trees, grasses and some natural pastures that break the woodland continuity. Nor is the woodland close to the mountains completely compact; but as it moves westward to the Kabambare region, it takes on fully tropical characteristics. The mountains emerge from the lake and give the terrain a very uneven aspect. There are little plains where invading troops can land and stay, but they are very difficult to defend if the adjoining heights are not also taken. The land route to the south ends at Kabimba, where we had one of our positions; the road to the west skirts the mountains on its way from Albertville to Lulimba-Fizi, and from there one branch continues to Bukavu via Muenga, while the other passes along the shores of the lake to Baraka and, finally, Uvira. After Lulimba, the road enters the mountains; this is a convenient setting for ambush warfare, and so too – though to a lesser degree – is the part that crosses the plain of the Congo Basin.

Rain is a frequent, daily occurrence from October to May and almost non-existent from June to September, although some isolated showers begin towards the end of the latter month. It rains all the time in the mountains, but less often in the dry months. The plain abounds with game animals of the deer type; in the mountains one can hunt buffalo (not very plentiful) and elephants or monkeys (the last of these very common). Monkey flesh is edible and has a fairly pleasant taste; elephant meat is tough and rubbery, but goes down easily enough when seasoned by hunger. The basic food crops are manioc and maize, while oil is extracted from palm trees. There are a lot of goats, bees are kept on small farms, and pigs are scattered here and there. With some difficulty, guerrillas who do not have an operational base can feed themselves in the region.

There is a wider variety of crops to the north of Baraka-Fizi, and a sugar mill a little north of Uvira. A lot of rice and groundnuts are grown in the Kabambare-Kasengo area. Cotton also used to have a presence, but by the time we were there it had virtually disappeared; I don't know how this plant would be managed in an agricultural context, but it used to be exploited on a capitalist basis, with modern clearances introduced at strategic centres by foreign corporations.

The lake is rich in fish, but there has been little fishing there of late, because of aircraft by day and boat raids by the dictatorship at night. For an analysis of revolutionary forces, we may divide the human geography into three groups: peasants, leaders and soldiers.

The peasants belong to different tribes, of which there are very many in the area. If we look at the enemy army's report on its general plan of attack, we notice that it always specifies the tribe to which people belong; this is an important piece of information for political work. Relations between the tribes are usually cordial but never truly fraternal, and there is serious rivalry between some of the tribal groups. This phenomenon may be seen between the Rwandans and the rest of the Congolese tribes, but it is also clearly visible between tribes belonging to the North Katanga ethnic area (who occupied the southern part of our guerrilla territory) and tribes belonging to the ethnic area of Kivu province (who occupied the northern part of our territory); these were most conspicuously represented by Kabila on one side and Soumaliot on the other.

The peasants pose for us one of the most difficult and absorbing problems of a people's war. In all wars of liberation of this type, a basic element is the hunger for land, involving the great poverty of a peasantry exploited by latifundists, feudal lords and, in some cases, capitalist-type companies. In the Congo, however, this was not the case – at least not in our region, and probably not in most of the country. It has only 14 million inhabitants spread over more than two million square kilometres (that is, a very low population density), with land that is often highly fertile. On the eastern front, there is no significant land hunger or even individual enclosures; mere convention ensures that the crop belongs to those who grow it. Nor, in practice, is property defended against intruders; only where there are some gardens is there a little protection against goats and other animals that might cause damage. The concept of land ownership hardly exists in any of the areas we visited, and the huge expanses of the Congo Basin permit anyone who wishes to acquire land simply to go and work there. As far as I can gather, in the area around Bukavu to the north, feudalism is much more developed and there are real feudal lords and serfs, but in the mountainous region where we lived the peasants are completely independent.

How should one describe the level of development of these tribes? It would be necessary to conduct a much deeper study than we have had the opportunity to make, with much more data and with a proper geographical breakdown, for it is clear that the development of each sub-region depends a lot on its particular historical and social conditions. I think there are features of primitive communism among the nomadic groups, and some traces of slavery in the way women are treated, though none could be observed in relation to men. Women are a commodity, an object to be bought and sold, and there is no law or convention restricting the number that may be owned; economic clout is the only limiting factor. Once a woman is bought, she becomes the absolute property of her lord and husband, who in general does not work at all, or only very little, in the house or fields. At most he does things such as hunting, but always accompanied by women, who actively participate. It is women's responsibility to till the land, to transport crops, to prepare food, and to look after the children; she is truly a domestic animal. Feudalism, as I said before, may be seen in northern parts of the region, but not here, where there is no landed property. Capitalism does not dominate the picture but operates in superficial forms, through small traders who establish themselves on the periphery, and through what we might call (following the North Americans) the demonstration effect of certain items used by the peasantry. Aluminium pots are fast replacing earthenware ones, for example, and industrially made spears are taking over from ones made at home or at the local forge; modern clothing is worn by some peasants, and radios can be seen in better-off houses. It is by trading the products of agriculture or hunting that they are able to acquire industrial goods.

At some time in the past, the peasants worked as paid labourers, or simply through middlemen, in the extraction of gold from the rivers that flow down from the mountains to the Congo Basin. The trenches dug for this purpose can still be seen, but the workings have been abandoned. Some crops, such as cotton, are processed and packed on a capitalist basis with the help of modern machinery. Textile factories are not present in the region, although some are to be found in Albertville; there are no industrial workers (except those at the power station, whose status is unknown to me), nor did I see any signs of wage labour. The peasants gave their labour to the army and, for the rest of the time, used it to support themselves through hunting, fishing or agriculture; any surplus was sold for money. The Congolese currency is accepted as a measure of value, but it does not penetrate deeply into the relations of production.

Imperialism gives only sporadic signs of life in the region; its interest in the Congo is mostly based on the strategic mineral resources of Katanga (where there is an industrial proletariat), on the diamond resources of Katanga and Kasai, and on tin deposits located close to our region, though not actually within it. Cotton and groundnuts are cultivated, and to some extent palm trees for the extraction of oil, but in these cases, too, the harvesting and trade are carried out on the basis of primitive relations.

What could the Liberation Army offer these peasants? That is the question which always bothered us. We could not speak here of dividing up the land in an agrarian reform, because everyone could see that it was already divided; nor could we speak of credits for the purchase of farm tools, because the peasants ate what they tilled with their primitive instruments and the physical characteristics of the region did not lend themselves to credit-fuelled expansion. Ways would have to be found of fostering the need to acquire industrial goods (which the peasants were obviously willing to accept and pay for) and therefore a need for more widespread trade. In the conditions of the war, however, we could not give any real thought to this.

We should make a priority of clarifying the type of exploitation to which the peasants are subjected. The visible appearance of this is the mistreatment of the population: it can be shown that, in the enemy-occupied areas, there are increasing numbers of rapes of women and killings of men, women and children; they are compelled by force to supply food and other services. The key feature is the negation of people as individuals – which may go as far as physical elimination. For the modern army, with its organized logistics, anticipates a shortage of supplies or hostility on the part of the population.

On the other hand, what had we to offer? We did not give much protection, as our story has shown. Nor did we offer any education, which might have been a great vehicle of communication. Medical services were provided only by the few Cubans there, with inadequate medicines, a fairly primitive system of administration, and no sanitary organization. I think that some deep thought and research needs to be devoted to the problem of revolutionary tactics where the relations of production do not give rise to land hunger among the peasantry. For the peasantry is the main social layer in this region; there is no industrial proletariat and the petty bourgeoisie of middlemen is not very developed.

What kind of leaders has the revolution had? We may divide them descriptively into national and local leaders. The national leaders I got to know were first and foremost Kabila and Masengo. Kabila is certainly the only one of them who, in addition to a clear head and a developed capacity for reasoning, has the personality of a leader: he asserts himself by his very presence; he is capable of creating bonds of loyalty, or at least of submission; and he is skilful in direct dealings with the population (though these are very rare). In short, he is a leader capable of mobilizing the masses. Masengo is an individual with very little character, no knowledge of the art of war and no talent for organization; he was totally overwhelmed by events. His one distinctive feature was an extraordinary loyalty to Kabila, and he showed a wish to continue the fight beyond what had been planned, even against the views of a large number of his followers. It would be unjust to ask more of him; he did what he was capable of doing.

Of all the section heads on the general staff and the so-called brigade leaders, not one can be mentioned who had all the qualities of a national leader. The only one who might develop in the future is Comrade Mujumba, but he is still in the Congo and we do not know what his situation is. He is a serious young man, who seemed intelligent and resolute insofar as we were able to observe him, but that is all we can say about him.

Of the national leaders in the Congo, Mulele remains the big mystery, almost a ghostly figure. He was never seen at meetings, nor did he ever leave his zone after the struggle began. There are many signs that he is a man of superior qualities, but his envoys – or those said to be his envoys – presented all the negative features of their counterparts in the various commissions and sectors of the Liberation Movement who roam the world swindling the revolution.

Of the men who have gained some prestige in recent times, we have already related what others say of General Olenga's history. Without judging whether they are true or not, we can say that these stories indicate his incapacity for any sacrifice during the months, which will turn into years, of living off the myth of the revolution as a general in exile. Others do this as political leaders, but he is a general who conducts his operations by telepathy from Cairo or another such capital city.

Another is Soumaliot, whom I consider useful as a middle-grade leader of the revolution. With the right guidance and supervision, he might have rendered some service as president of the Supreme Council of the Revolution; the main things he does are travelling, living well and giving sensational press conferences – that is all. He lacks any ability for organization. His tussles with Kabila, in which both employed a multitude of ruses, contributed as much as anything to the temporary defeat of the insurrection.

It is not worth speaking of Gbenye; he is simply an agent of the counter-revolution.

It may be that some young people have emerged with the qualities of genuinely revolutionary leaders, but I have not met any or they have not demonstrated those qualities up to now.

The local leaders fall into two categories: those in charge of military formations, and peasant leaders. The military leaders were appointed by the most arbitrary methods, with no theoretical, intellectual, military or organizational training of any kind. Their only merit is that they exercise some influence over the tribes in the region where they live, but a line could be drawn through their names without any loss to the revolution.

The local peasant leaders are the *kapitas* and chairmen, appointed by the old Lumumba administration or its successors, who would like to be the germ of a civil power. But, faced with tribal realities, the easy way was chosen of making traditional chiefs the chairmen and *kapitas*. For they are nothing other than the old chiefs in disguise, some better or more progressive than others, some more conscious of the meaning of the revolution, but none has reached even a middling level of political development. Being in control of a group of peasants, they are responsible for the provision of food to soldiers passing through the area or of load-bearers to take something from one place to another, for organization of supplies to some unit installed nearby, for help with the construction of housing, and so on. They were useful intermediaries in the solving of such problems, but did not do anything faintly resembling political work.

The men had their political commissar – a title copied from the socialist versions of a liberation army or from people's armies. Anyone who had read about the work of commissars in the various liberation wars, or who knows of the heroism and self-sacrifice of such comrades from stories about them, would not be able to recognize them in the Congo. There the political commissar is selected from men with a certain degree of education – nearly always with a knowledge of French – who come from urban petty-bourgeois families. Their activity was like that of sporadic loudspeakers; the men would assemble at a certain moment to hear the commissar "sound off" on specific problems, and were then left to their own devices to follow his verbal recommendations. Neither the commissars nor the officers, with a few honourable exceptions, participated directly in combat; they looked after their own skin, had better food and clothing than the rest of the troops, and enjoyed frequent breaks when they could go and get drunk on the notorious *pombe* in nearby villages. The political commissar, as this task is discharged in the Congo, is a veritable sponger off the revolution and could also be eliminated without any harm to it – although the right way to proceed would be to develop genuine revolutionaries for this task, which is so crucially important in a people's army.

The soldiers are of peasant stock and completely raw, for whom the main attraction is to have a rifle and a uniform, sometimes even shoes and a certain authority in the area. Corrupted by inactivity and the habit of ordering the peasants around, saturated with fetishistic notions about death and the enemy, devoid of any coherent political education, they consequently lack revolutionary awareness or any forward-looking perspective beyond the traditional horizon of their tribal territory. Lazy and undisciplined, they are without any spirit of combat or self-sacrifice; they do not trust their leaders (who show a lead only in getting hold of women, *pombe* or food, and making an easy life for themselves); they lack the constant experience of battle which would enable them to develop, if only as killers of men; indeed they lack training of any kind, since drilling exercises were the only ones we ever saw them do during our stay there. All these traits make the soldier of the Congolese revolution the poorest example of a fighter that I have ever come across up to now.

If the leaders had given their full support, it would still have been a gigantic task to make revolutionary soldiers out of such individuals. But given the incompetence of the high command and the obstruction by the local chiefs, this became the most thankless of all our functions and one that ended in signal failure.

The political commissar or special weapons instructor was often someone who had returned from a six-month course of study in one of the socialist countries. The largest number of these graduates came from Bulgaria, the Soviet Union and China. You could not perform miracles with such men; the prior selection was very bad, and it was a lottery whether it would include genuine revolutionaries or at least people tested in struggle. They brought back with them a great sense of their own importance, a highly developed conception of the duty to protect the cadre (meaning themselves), and a well-formed idea, clearly expressed in their actions and demands, that the revolution owed them a lot for their period of study abroad and should somehow reward them now that they were sacrificing themselves to be with their comrades. Almost never did they take part in any fighting; they were usually instructors – a task for which they were not qualified, with a few exceptions – or formed parallel political organizations that called themselves Marxist-Leninist but actually served to deepen divisions. In my view, most of these evils were due to flaws in the prior selection. Good education can do an extraordinary amount for someone with an awakening consciousness. But for this kind of pliable and domesticated revolutionary, all that developed during his months in a socialist country was the ambition to get a leadership position on the basis of his colossal knowledge – and also, at the front, a nostalgia for the good times spent abroad.

We need to ask what remains after our defeat. From a military point of view, the situation is not so terrible. The small villages controlled by our army did fall, but all around the troops are still there, with less ammunition and some lost weapons but generally intact. The enemy soldiers occupy only the territory through which they pass – that is an important truth. Nevertheless, from a political point of view, all that are left are scattered groups still undergoing decomposition, from which one or several nuclei should be extracted as the basis for a future guerrilla army. As things stand today, forces are present in the Fizi-Baraka area but do not occupy any locality or have permanent control over any territory; others remain relatively well organized at Uvira, controlling a good stretch of the main road from Baraka to Bukavu; and at Mukundi, Mujumba has what might be the germ of an organization with a political understanding of the struggle. There are also some troops at Kabimba who used to be quite well armed, and there must still be some nuclei in the hills at Kabambare and Kasengo, although we had not been in touch with them for some time.

It is important to note that all these groups have very little to do with one another: they rarely obey any orders from above, and their vision hardly extends beyond their own particular enclave. For all these reasons, they are not the embryo of a new army, but the remnants of the old. There may be somewhere between four to five thousand weapons in the area, dispersed without rhyme or reason among individual peasants, and it will not be easy to recover them. Some heavy weapons have also escaped loss, but today I cannot say precisely how many. If a single leader with the right characteristics were to emerge at just one place, the eastern front would soon have the same territorial gains that it had achieved at the moment of the defeat. Recently, a rival to Soumaliot and Kabila has appeared in the person of Mbagira, the minister for foreign relations in the Supreme

Council of the Revolution, who has been based in Uvira, but we cannot make any detailed judgement about him. Only events will tell whether he really is a leader with the capacities demanded by the struggle in the Congo.

What are the characteristics of the enemy? First, it should be said by way of explanation that the old Congolese army which remained as a legacy from the Belgian colonial period, badly instructed and without a leadership cadre or a spirit of struggle, was swept away by the revolutionary wave; it was so badly demoralized that towns could be taken without a fight. (It seems quite certain that the *simbas* would telephone in advance their intention to capture a certain town and the government troops would promptly withdraw.) Subsequently, it came under North American and Belgian instructors, who turned it into a force with the characteristics of a regular army capable of fighting without assistance – although in the final stage of the war it received help from white mercenaries. It is well trained and disciplined, with proper cadres. The white mercenaries fight efficiently – as long as they do not have to take a pounding – and the blacks fight alongside them. Their weapons do not currently add up to much: the most telling have been their PT boats, which have made it difficult to cross the lake; but their aircraft, to which I have referred before, are antiquated and not very effective; their infantry weapons only began to be replenished in the closing moments.

In general, the Liberation Army has better infantry weapons than Tshombe's army – hard to imagine but true. This was one of the reasons why the patriotic forces did not bother to capture the weapons of those who fell in battle, maintaining complete indifference to that source of supply.

The enemy's tactics were the usual ones in this type of war: air cover for attacks on columns or populated centres; protective aircraft patrols along the main roads; and in the final phase, when the demoralization of our army was already evident, a direct attack on mountain strongholds by columns advancing against and capturing our positions, though naturally without a fight. This is an army which one has to hit hard if one is to undermine its morale – and given the geographical conditions, this can easily be achieved by adopting the correct tactics.

An analysis should now be made of our own contingent. The great majority of the men were blacks. This could have added a sympathetic note of unity with the Congolese, but things did not work out like that. We did not see that it made much difference to our relations whether we were black or white; the Congolese knew how to identify each man's personal traits, and only in my own case did I sometimes suspect that my being white influenced matters. What is true is that our own comrades had a very poor cultural basis, as well as a relatively low level of political development. As often happens in such cases, they arrived brimming with optimism and good intentions, thinking that they would march triumphantly through the Congo. At one meeting before hostilities commenced, some men remarked that Tatu was too remote from military matters, that his timid concern for the relationship of forces would not stop them breaking in at one end and coming out at the other; then the country would be liberated and they could go back to Havana.

I always warned that the war would last three to five years, but no one believed it. They were all inclined to dream of a triumphal march, a departure with big speeches and great honours, then medals and Havana. The reality came as a shock: food was short, often consisting of plain manioc without even salt, or *bukali*, which is the same; there was not enough medicine, nor sometimes clothing or shoes; my dream of a fusion between our experienced men with army discipline and the Congolese never came true.

There was never the necessary integration, and it cannot be blamed on the colour of people's skin. Some Cubans were so black that they could not be told apart from the Congolese comrades; yet I heard one of them say: "Send me two of those blacks over there" – two Congolese, that is.

Our men were foreigners, superior beings, and they made it felt rather too frequently. The Congolese, ultra-sensitive because of past insults at the hands of the settlers, felt it in the core of their being when a Cuban displayed gestures of disdain towards them. I could never manage to obtain totally fair distribution of the food, and although it must be said that Cubans more often than not carried the heaviest burdens, they would rather insensitively load up a Congolese whenever the opportunity presented itself. It is not easy to explain this contradiction, which involved various subjective interpretations and subtle nuances, but one simple fact may throw some light on the subject: namely, my inability to get the Cubans to use the term "Congolese". Instead, they referred to "the Congos" – apparently simpler and more intimate, but carrying a hefty dose of venom. Language was another real barrier, as it was difficult for a force such as ours – submerged in the mass of Congolese – to work without having their language. Some of those who from the start lived amicably alongside the Congolese very soon learnt to rattle things off in basic Swahili, a halfway language, but they were not many and they always ran the risk of a misunderstanding that might sour relations or lead us into error.

I have tried to paint the collapse of our force in the way in which it happened. It was a gradual but not steadily incremental process, which gathered explosive material and then burst out on occasions of defeat. Culminating moments were: the fiasco at Front de Force; the series of Congolese desertions at the Katenga ambushes, where the men suffered a lot from illness; my personal disaster in the procession carrying the wounded man, when we got very little help from the Congolese; and the desertion of our allies in the final stages. Each of these moments signalled a sharpening of the demoralization and loss of heart among our force.

By the end it had suffered contagion from the spirit of the lake. The men dreamt of returning home and, generally speaking, showed themselves incapable of laying down their lives so that the group would be safe, or so that the revolution as a whole could march on. All wanted to reach safety on the other shore. To such an extent did discipline break down that a number of really grotesque episodes took place, which would merit very severe penalties against some of the fighters.

If we made what we might call an impartial analysis, we would find that the Cubans had considerable justification for the collapse of morale, but that many comrades maintained until the end, if not their spirit, then their discipline and sense of responsibility. If I have dwelt more on the weaknesses, it is because I think that the most important aspect of our

231

experience is an analysis of the collapse. This occurred under the impact of a concatenation of adverse events. The problem lies in the fact that the difficulties we had to face will be hard to avoid early on in the next phases of the struggle in Africa, for they are characteristic of countries with a very low degree of development. One of our comrades said in festive tones that all the preconditions for revolution are present in the Congo; this caricature has some truth in it if one looks through the lens of a mature, crystallized revolution, but the magma from which the craftsman must draw out the revolutionary spirit had basic features very similar to those of the Sierra Maestra peasantry in the early stages of the Cuban revolution.

It is important for us to discover what are the demands we can place on a militant, so that he can overcome the violent traumas of a reality with which he must do battle. I think that candidates should first pass through a very rigorous process of selection, as well as being subjected to prior warnings. As I have said before, no one believed the admonition that the revolution would require three to five years to achieve success; when the reality confirmed this, they suffered an internal collapse, the collapse of a dream. Revolutionary militants who go off to take part in a similar experience must begin without dreams, abandoning everything that used to constitute their lives and exertions. The only ones who should do it are those with a revolutionary strength of mind much greater than the average (even the average in a revolutionary country), with practical experience gained in struggle, with a high level of political development, and with solid discipline. The incorporation process should be gradual and built around a small but tempered group, so that the selection of new combatants can proceed directly and anyone who does not meet the requirements can be removed. In other words, a cadre policy should be pursued. This will allow a steady increase in numbers without weakening the nucleus, and even a formation of new cadres from the donor country in the insurrectional zone of the host country. For we are not simply schoolmasters; we also study in new schools of the revolution.

Another difficulty we endured – to which very special attention should be paid in the future – is that of the support base. Quite large sums of money vanished into its insatiable jaws, while minute quantities of food and equipment reached the troops in the field. The first requirement is for a command with undisputed and absolute authority in the zone of operations, able to exert rigorous control over the support base and to disregard the natural checks made by the higher centres of the revolution. The selection of men to carry out this task should have been seriously implemented a long time in advance. It has to be seen what a packet of cigarettes means for someone doing nothing at an ambush for 24 hours, and it has to be seen how little the hundred packets of cigarettes that might be smoked each day really cost in comparison with things that are either unnecessary or uselessly squandered in the course of the operation.

The time has come for me to make the most difficult analysis of all, the one that concerns my own role. Taking self-criticism as far as I was capable of doing, I came to the following conclusions. From the point of view of relations with the revolutionary command, I found myself impeded by the slightly abnormal way in which I entered the Congo, and I was not able to overcome this disadvantage. I tended to lose control in the way I reacted to things; for much of the time my attitude might have been described as complacent, but sometimes I displayed very bitter and wounding outbursts, perhaps as a result of a trait of character; the only group with which I maintained unfailingly correct relations was the peasantry, because I am more accustomed to political language, direct explanation and the force of example, and I think that I was successful in this field. I did not learn Swahili quickly or well enough – a defect mainly attributable to my knowledge of French, which allowed me to communicate with the leaders but alienated me from the rank-and-file. I lacked the will-power to make the necessary effort.

As to my contacts with the men, I think I sacrificed myself sufficiently that no one can hold anything against me personally or physically, but my two basic weaknesses were satisfied in the Congo: tobacco, which was rarely lacking, and reading, which was always possible in plenty. The inconvenience of having a pair of worn-out shoes or a dirty change of clothing, or of eating the same meagre fare as the men and living in the same conditions, was not a sacrifice for me. But my withdrawal to read, thereby escaping everyday problems, did tend to distance me from the men – not to speak of certain character traits which make it difficult for me to get close to people. I was hard, but I don't think I was excessively so. Nor was I unjust: I used methods that are not current in a regular army, such as making someone go without eating, which is the only effective way I know in times of guerrilla warfare. At first I tried to apply moral coercion, but this failed. I tried to ensure that my men had the same view of the situation as myself, but I failed. They were not prepared to look optimistically at a future that had to be glimpsed through such a dark fog in the present times.

When the decisive moment came, I could not bring myself to demand the highest sacrifice; it was an inner, psychological obstacle. For me it was very easy to remain in the Congo. From the point of view of a combatant's vanity, it was the fitting thing to do; from the point of view of my future activity, it may not have been the most appropriate course, but there was no reason not to follow it at that time. When I weighed up the decision, I was swayed by the realization that it would be so easy to make the decisive sacrifice. I think I should have overcome this useless burden of self-criticism and demanded the final gesture from a number of the men; only a few, but we should have remained. Furthermore, I did not have the valour or the vision to break our ties to the lake and – together with all the Cuban troops, or a pared-down selection – press on to places where we would not have been constantly tempted by the lake and its hopes of a return in the event of failure.

Lastly, my farewell letter to Fidel played a role in my relations with the men in the final days; I could feel this, although the letter was completely objective. It meant that – just as they did many years ago, when I was starting out in the Sierra – the comrades saw me as a foreigner in contact with Cubans; before it had been at the moment of arrival, now it was at the moment of departure. There were certain things that we did not have in common, certain longings that I had tacitly or explicitly renounced but which each individual holds most sacred: family, land, immediate surroundings. The letter that aroused so much favourable commentary in Cuba and abroad caused a distance to develop between myself and the combatants.

These psychological considerations may appear out of place in the analysis of a struggle that is almost continental in scale. I remain faithful to my concept of a nucleus; I was at the head of a group of Cubans, no more than one company strong, and my function was to be their real leader who carried them to the victory that would hasten the development of a genuine people's army. My peculiar situation, however, made of me a soldier representing a foreign power, an instructor of Cubans and Congolese, a strategist and high-flying politician in an unfamiliar setting, and a tiresomely repetitive Cato the Censor in my relations with the leaders of the revolution. By pulling on all these threads, I formed the Gordian knot that I did not have the resolve to cut. Had I been a more authentic soldier, I might have had more influence in the other spheres of my complicated relationships. I have described how I reached the point of safeguarding the cadre (my own precious person) at particularly disastrous moments in which I found myself, and how I allowed subjective qualities to gain the upper hand in the closing moments.

I learnt certain things in the Congo. Some mistakes I will never make again, others perhaps I will – and there will be new ones that I shall commit. I set off with more faith than ever in the guerrilla struggle, yet we failed. My responsibility is great; I shall not forget the defeat, nor its most precious lessons.

What does the future hold in store for us in the Congo? It certainly holds victory, but a distant one.

The liberation struggle against new-style colonial powers inevitably presents extreme difficulties in Africa. In fact, there is not a single case that allows us to show its various phases all the way to victory: so-called Portuguese Guinea is an incomplete example of a well-conducted people's war, but it has been fought against colonialism; nor can Algeria be considered a useful model for us, because France developed neo-colonial forms there which we might call typical within its colonial oppression.

The Congo is the setting for the most cruel and bitter liberation struggle, and so a study of this experience will give us some useful ideas for the future.

Unlike Latin America, where the process of neo-colonization took place amid violent class struggles and where the national bourgeoisie participated in the anti-imperialist struggle before its eventual capitulation, Africa presents a picture of a process planned by imperialism. Very few countries there have obtained their independence through armed struggle; on the whole, everything has happened with the smoothness of a well-oiled machine.

Practically speaking, it is only the southern cone of Africa which remains officially colonized, and a general outcry against that system is likely to bring about its rapid extinction, at least in the Portuguese colonies. The Union of South Africa presents different problems.

In the African liberation struggle, the advanced stages of the process have an affinity with current models of people's war. The problem is how to root it more deeply, and this is where questions arise that I am not able to answer. I would simply like to set out a few points of view resulting from my weak and fragmentary experience. If the liberation struggle is to be successful in the present conditions in Africa, it is essential to bring some of the Marxist analytic schemas up to date.

What is the primary contradiction of the epoch? If it is between the socialist and the imperialist countries, or between the latter and their working classes, the role of the so-called Third World is much reduced. But there are ever more serious reasons to believe that the primary contradiction is between the exploiting and exploited nations. I cannot begin here an attempt to demonstrate this point, and to show that it is not opposed to the characterization of the epoch as one of transition to socialism. It would take us on to difficult sideroads and require an abundance of data and arguments. I will leave it as a hypothesis that has been thrown up by practice.

If this is so, Africa will play an active and commanding role in the primary contradiction. If, however, we take the Third World as a whole to be an actor in this contradiction, at the present moment of history, then we can see that there are gradations between countries and continents.

236

In sum, Latin America as a whole has reached a point at which the class struggle is intensifying and the national bourgeoisie has totally capitulated to the power of imperialism, so that its short-term historical future will be one of liberation struggle crowned by a revolution of a socialist type.

Asia is witnessing the same process, although the framework is much more complicated. It includes colonized imperialist countries such as Japan, as well as important socialist countries such as China, and puppets of imperialism as large and dangerous (because of elements of a former prestige) as India. But in what we might call the typical countries where a war of liberation might be victorious, the national bourgeoisies have not exhausted their role as opponents of imperialism, although it is important to realize that they are rapidly moving in that direction. These are countries which have just achieved liberation, or which do not have the fictitious liberty that Latin America has enjoyed for more than 100 years, and so it will take some time for the inevitability of revolution to become apparent there.

In Africa, especially in the part called Black Africa because of the colour of people's skin, you can follow a long chain from primitive communism to dots on the map where there are a proletariat and a developing bourgeoisie. In keeping with the new imperialist plan of action, there is no opposition of any kind between the national bourgeoisies and the neo-colonial powers. Each individual country, when drawing up its plan for the liberation struggle, must start by treating as its enemies not only the imperialists and the layers on which their strength is based (such as the surviving colonial armies and, more dangerous still, the colonial mentality of their officers), but all the *nouveaux riches*, importers and emergent industrialists who are closely linked to monopoly capital in the form of bureaucratic capitalism.

In these conditions, the class that wages the struggle against foreign powers is the petty bourgeoisie. But what is the petty bourgeoisie in the African countries? It is a layer which, having served imperialism or neo-colonialism, has become aware of certain limitations imposed on its own development or human dignity. This class sends its children to study in the more intelligent colonial countries (the ones that offer most facilities) or, in this new period, to the socialist countries. Of course, as the leading stratum of a people's war, it is extremely weak. In the Congo, as I pointed out before, the peasants are divided into an infinite variety of major or minor tribal groups, whose bonds become stronger as their territorial compass becomes smaller: the variety ranges from certain large groups (I knew the Katanga and the Kivu) which are bound together with ties akin to "nationality", through more compact territorial groups, right down to small tribal groups at village level.

The solidarity among villages of the same group is very great, and the solidarity among members of the same village is even greater – though within the limited framework of the natural life I have described, at least for our zone. In other regions, they are obliged to gather products of the marvellous Congolese nature to serve the capitalists: for example, resin, elephant tusks in a previous period, or palm nuts for oil. This gives rise to relations of a different type, which I have not closely examined. At the other extreme, there are nuclei of a developed proletariat in areas where the Union Minière felt the need to run some of its processing operations in the Congo. At first, these workers were brought in by force, since their natural environment did not require them to change the way they lived after all. Now it seems that, despite being paid starvation wages (in European terms), this proletariat is not a rebellious element. Perhaps it still has a nostalgia for the free life, but it has been won over by the little comforts that civilization provides. Once again I must apologize for the superficiality of the analysis, which is based on fragmentary practical experience and poor general knowledge of the social question in the Congo.

In any event, what strategy should be pursued? Evidently there are points of conflict in the towns: major inflation, recolonization with a marked discrimination not only by whites against blacks but now also by rich blacks against poor blacks, and a certain return to the villages by many people who had drawn close to the city lights. These sources of discontent may give rise to isolated revolts, but the only force capable of deciding things is the colonial army, which has all the good jobs and intervenes only to protect them or to develop them further.

Poverty was absolute among the peasantry. But it is a poverty for which the balance-sheet is no more negative today than it was ten years ago. Except in the war zones, the peasant does not feel inclined to pick up a gun because objectively declining conditions of life make it a vital necessity. And it should be said here that, in order to evaluate the objective conditions properly, it is much less important to consider one people's level in comparison with that of other peoples, than it is to consider it in comparison with itself. The poverty of our peasantry in South America is genuine with respect to itself; exploitation is increasing, as are hunger and poverty. In many parts of the Congo, however, this is presumably not the case. All this gives some idea of how difficult it is to raise the country to revolt around slogans with a strongly economic character. I have already referred to the main demand of this kind in a people's war and the one that immediately comes to mind: namely, the demand for land. Tribal relations are one lever that is widely used, but you can't get very far with that in a war of liberation. I cannot say whether it is useful or necessary to have recourse to it in an early stage, but obviously there can be no advance unless it leads towards destruction of the tribal concept. As long as this remains in place amid attempted advances, the evolving tribal group will tend to clash not with the army of the oppressors, but with the neighbouring tribe. In the development of the struggle, it will be necessary for tribes to unite in pursuit of a common objective – which is why it is so important to find that objective, and the party or the man who symbolizes it.

A very important factor in the development of the struggle is the universality that the concepts in play have been acquiring. Evidently imperialism scores a victory when there is a retreat in popular struggles anywhere in the world; and just as evidently, it suffers a defeat when a genuinely progressive government comes to power anywhere in the world. We should not think of countries as self-enclosed areas for the purposes of social analysis. Indeed, we may say today that Latin America as a whole is a neocolonized continent where capitalist relations of production prevail, despite the numerous examples of feudal relations, and where a struggle that has a clearly popular, anti-imperialist (that is, anti-capitalist) significance is, at the end of the day, a socialist struggle. Similarly, in the Congo or any other country of Africa, we must accept the possibility that new ideas about the world will develop that afford a glimpse of something entirely new, beyond the little local preserve for the hunting of game or the growing of crops for immediate consumption. The impact of socialist ideas must reach the broad masses of the African countries, not as a transplant, but as an adaptation to new conditions. And it must offer a down-to-earth image of major changes that can be, if not actually felt, then clearly imagined by the population.

For all this, the ideal goal would be to organize a party with a really national basis and real prestige among the masses, a party with solid and well-developed cadres. Such a party does not exist in the Congo. All the Lumumbist movements are vertical structures, with leaders of a certain intellectual level totally surrounded by vacillating and accommodating petty-bourgeois cadres.

In the conditions of the Congo, a new party based on the teachings of Marxism and adapted to the new conditions should, at least initially, base itself on prestigious figures who are recognized as honest, genuinely representative of the new Congolese nationality, self-sacrificing and capable of commanding and binding people together. These men of our imagination will issue from the struggle.

Today Comrade Mulele is still there, doing underground work the details of which we have no knowledge. It may also be that work is continuing in the eastern zone where the basis of the guerrilla army was first laid in man's revolt against oppression, in the experience with firearms and an inner conviction of the possibilities which they afford. This, however, is a people without faith in its leaders, and without a party to lead it. The fundamental task at the present moment is therefore the development of a party to lead the revolution at national level, with slogans linked to the people and with cadres it respects – a task which itself requires a capable, heroic and far-sighted team of leaders. The link with the workers will be achieved in later stages. This is not to say that we deny the so-called worker-peasant alliance, which will actually arise early on in an alliance of the highly backward peasantry with the ideology of the proletariat. Later, the industrial workers – who, under present conditions in the Congo, are privileged in their exploitation – will close ranks with the guerrilla movement, as a result of the catalysing effect of armed activity. The propaganda of arms, in the Vietnamese sense of the term, should be the fundamental task in the development of the whole process.

It is essential to stress again that the people's guerrilla war is a mass struggle. We cannot accept the contraposition that is sometimes made between mass struggle and guerrilla warfare (that is, selected nuclei of armed combatants); such an idea is equally false when it is espoused by dogmatic followers of a general strategy based on the predominance of the working class, and when guerrilla warfare is put forward as a mere instrument of struggle by the groups most determined to wrest power from the exploiters. The main function of guerrilla warfare is to educate the masses in their possibilities of victory, by showing them, at the same time, the possibility of a new future and the necessity of changes to achieve that future in the process of the armed struggle of all of the people.

Inevitably it will be a long war. But what is important for us is not the process that will ensue once the war has taken root in rural areas and spread to new areas, thereby causing fresh enemy defeats; what concerns us is to know how it can develop today. For we are at a moment of regression and defeat, but the basic conditions for armed struggle are present in this part of the Congo: a peasantry which has tasted revolt; which has been defeated, abused and harassed but has tasted revolt; which has experience of armed struggle and has weapons; which has lived through war.

Today it is divided into autonomous groups with local leaders, without a vision of a unified Congo, or even a vision of the Congo as a nation. For them, the nation takes in the surrounding tribes. That is why it is so important to organize the best fighters into a nucleus (even a single one, made of steel), for there is no need to increase the guerrilla force by one man unless he brings some qualitative contribution. A start can be made on this basis, with military leaders present on the territory where the guerrilla campaign is to be conducted. It will then grow by educating a people which, in the revolutionary struggle, has to cross the different stages of history at breakneck speed. From the earliest level (which, in some cases, is close at hand today), through primitive communism, slavery and feudalism, it is necessary to move on to the most advanced conceptions. This people must gradually arm itself, essentially through its own resources. Its own effort is what enables it to be educated. Let every weapon be a reward to the guerrilla fighter; let him receive it if and only if he carries out the necessary tasks for the maintenance of the people's army; let the weapon be confirmation of his state of grace as a people's fighter. For this huge and patient task it is clear that we will have to begin by sweeping aside the present cadres; we should simply disregard them, and begin with a nucleus as small as necessary, as large as possible. In this way new leadership cadres will emerge, acquiring polish through sacrifice and combat as they undergo death's rigorous selection on the battlefield.

Given these conditions, it is indispensable that the most far-sighted leader should emerge, a self-sacrificing and prestigious leader who, operating inside the country, is an actor in the headlong development of the conditions of revolution. This great process of struggle will have to create simultaneously the soldier, the cadre and the leader; for, strictly speaking, we do not have any of these today. The struggle will have to move from the countryside to the villages to the towns, first of all in small groups that do not require a rigid defence of territory. These groups will have to improve their technique of rapid concentration and dispersal and undergo a methodical apprenticeship in modern military technique and guerrilla warfare, constantly sowing the revolutionary seed through example. This is the road to victory. It will come the sooner, the more rapidly capable and self-sacrificing leaders emerge who can in turn lead capable and self-sacrificing middle cadres, guiding the development of the people's army on the basis of a peasantry that is rebellious in its core.

The scale of the problems is enormous. We need to turn our attention to revolutionary theory and practice, to make a serious study of methods, to find the most appropriate ways of linking the peasantry to the people's army and turning all this into a single force. A long but irreversible stage of protracted warfare will then begin, through which other layers will be won over in remote regions and the proletariat of the industrial areas of the Congo will itself be incorporated. It is not possible to say how long this will take; it can be done – that is all. We have powerful assistance in the shape of the present conditions of humanity, the development of socialist ideas, and the cruelty of an enemy who always offers a negative counter-vision to the hopes placed in the people's army. After some years, victory will come.

I believe that Africa is important for North American imperialism, especially as a reserve. When people's war develops in all its magnitude in the regions of Latin America, it will become difficult to keep supplying on the same scale the great natural wealth and the markets that are the basis of the power of imperialism. But if Africa meanwhile calmly develops its system of neo-colonialism, with no great commotion, investments could be transferred there – it has already begun – as a way of ensuring survival. For that vast and immensely rich continent has hardly yet been tapped by imperialism.

In the framework of a struggle with global features, the strategy for Africa is to prevent the reserve bases of imperialism from remaining quiescent. Each of its peoples must impel to the maximum its struggle for genuine liberation, as part of its duty within the great struggle of the peoples of the world. And our obligation is to give consistent support to the movements that offer hopes of a real and serious mobilization for victory.

How shall we participate in all this? Perhaps we should send a nucleus of cadres chosen from among those who already have some experience of the Congo and have not undergone the collapse that I have described; perhaps we should send weapons, if the allies permit it; perhaps we should give financial aid and help in training cadres. But we must change one of the concepts that has guided our revolutionary strategy up till now; we have spoken of unconditional aid, and that is a mistake. The giving of aid implies the taking up of a position – and that position is taken on the basis of certain analyses of the trustworthiness and effectiveness of a revolutionary movement in the struggle against imperialism, in the struggle for the liberation of a country. In order to settle such analyses more securely, we have to know the movements in question, and to do this we have to intervene in them. Aid should be conditional, if we are not to risk its turning into the exact opposite of what we intended: into money that allows the lords of the revolution to take holidays worthy of a prince, and the freedom fighters to sacrifice and sell out their people and hold back the development of the revolution. If that happens, we turn ourselves into allies of imperialism. Nothing is cheaper for it than to drop a few thousand dollars on the table at a conference of liberation movements in Africa. (I have no doubt that, if it does not already do this, it will in future.) The distribution of the money then causes more disturbances, divisions and defeats than an army would inflict on the battlefield.

We should draw our conclusions from these visible objective facts and tie our aid to the revolutionary conduct of the movements and their leaders. To replace colonialism with neo-colonialism, or one group of neo-colonialists with another that does not look so bad, is not a correct revolutionary strategy.

Finally, if I were asked whether I think there is any figure in the Congo who could become a national leader, I would not be able to answer in the affirmative – leaving aside Mulele, whom I do not know. The only man who has genuine qualities of a mass leader is, in my view, Kabila. The purest of revolutionaries cannot lead a revolution unless he has certain qualities of a leader, but a man who has qualities of a leader cannot, simply for that reason, carry a revolution forward. It is essential to have revolutionary seriousness, an ideology that can guide action, a spirit of sacrifice that accompanies one's actions. Up to now, Kabila has not shown that he possesses any of these qualities. He is young and it is possible that he will change. But I will make so bold as to say, in this text that will see the light of day only after many years have passed, that I have very great doubts about his ability to overcome his defects in the environment in which he operates. The other well-known Congolese leaders will all be swept away by events. The new ones are probably today somewhere inside the country, beginning to write the real history of the liberation of the Congo.

January 1966